SEVEN
DAYS OF
INFAMY

SEVEN
DAYS OF
INFAMY

PEARL HARBOR
ACROSS THE WORLD

NICHOLAS BEST

THOMAS DUNNE BOOKS   ST. MARTIN'S PRESS   NEW YORK

THOMAS DUNNE BOOKS.
An imprint of St. Martin's Press.

SEVEN DAYS OF INFAMY. Copyright © 2016 by Nicholas Best. All rights reserved. Printed in the United States of America. For information, address St. Martin's Press, 175 Fifth Avenue, New York, N.Y. 10010.

www.thomasdunnebooks.com
www.stmartins.com

Library of Congress Cataloging-in-Publication Data

Names: Best, Nicholas, 1948– author.
Title: Seven days of infamy : Pearl Harbor across the world / Nicholas Best.
Other titles: Pearl Harbor across the world
Description: New York : Thomas Dunne Books, an imprint of St. Martin's Press, [2016]
Identifiers: LCCN 2016024093| ISBN 9781250078018 (hardcover) | ISBN 9781466890336 (e-book)
Subjects: LCSH: Pearl Harbor (Hawaii), Attack on, 1941. | Pearl Harbor (Hawaii), Attack on, 1941—Public opinion. | Pearl Harbor (Hawaii), Attack on, 1941—Influence. | World War, 1939–1945—Campaigns—Pacific Ocean.
Classification: LCC D810.P8 B48 2016 | DDC 940.54/26693—dc23
LC record available at https://lccn.loc.gov/2016024093

Our books may be purchased in bulk for promotional, educational, or business use. Please contact your local bookseller or the Macmillan Corporate and Premium Sales Department at 1-800-221-7945, extension 5442, or by e-mail at MacmillanSpecialMarkets@macmillan.com.

First Edition: November 2016

10 9 8 7 6 5 4 3 2 1

CONTENTS

INTRODUCTION

Another book about Pearl Harbor? Why?

Several reasons, chief of which is that only a bit of it is about Japan's attack on Hawaii. I have written a brisk account of the raid for newcomers to the subject, but that is not the purpose of the book. The real aim is to examine the three days leading up to the attack and then look at the extraordinary aftermath—the impact it had not only on the United States but also on a variety of widely different countries across the globe.

People everywhere were affected by Pearl Harbor. It was one of those very rare days in world history, like the Armistice of 1918 or the assassination of President Kennedy, when millions of ordinary folk across the planet remembered exactly where they were and what they were doing when they heard the news.

Their individual stories are fascinating. Marlene Dietrich, Clark Gable, and James Cagney were in Hollywood when they heard. Kurt Vonnegut was taking a bath at Cornell, Ernest Hemingway was on the road, and Dwight Eisenhower was having a well-deserved nap in Texas. Kirk Douglas was a waiter in New York, getting nowhere with Lauren Bacall. Jack Kennedy was playing touch football in Washington, while Ed Murrow was preparing for a round of golf before meeting President Roosevelt at the White House.

In Europe, Churchill and Hitler were both delighted when they were told about Pearl Harbor late in the evening. Anthony Eden was on his way to Russia, and Eamon de Valera was preparing for bed. Thousands of Jews were being herded to their deaths in Latvia and Poland. Menachem Begin was wandering through Soviet Central Asia, seeking an escape route to Palestine.

In the Far East, Lady Diana Cooper was fast asleep in Singapore. Jawaharlal Nehru had just been released from prison in India. Ho Chi Minh was in the jungle, and Mao Tse-tung was in his three-room cave at Communist Party headquarters in China.

Wherever they were in the world, millions of people stopped what they were doing to absorb the news and ponder the implications of Japan's sudden assault on the industrial might of the United States. For better or worse, the event had consequences for a vast swath of people. I have gathered some of the more interesting stories to give an account of Pearl Harbor as seen through the eyes of mostly famous characters not usually associated with the attack. I have done it in their own words wherever possible.

As for the attack itself, I have interviewed some survivors and have come up with several eyewitness accounts—three of them British—not hitherto seen in print. I hope my account is as accurate as anyone else's, but I won't go any further than that. Pearl Harbor was such a chaotic affair, with so many mildly contradictory stories, that it would be a very foolish author who claimed that his was the definitive version of events.

There are indeed several alternative realities to Pearl Harbor. Admiral Husband Kimmel remembered his words on being hit by a spent bullet differently every time he was asked. Lots of other people did the same, changing their stories slightly from one interview to the next. Many remained convinced that they were still under attack late in the morning of December 7, when historians who were nowhere near the action assured them that they weren't.

I have done my best to gather everything together into a reasonably coherent account. If any grumpy academics want to fall on some minor misapprehension and loudly trumpet their own superior knowledge, I will cheerfully put up my hands and utter those words that Americans so love to hear, especially in a British accent: "I surrender . . . just so long as you're absolutely sure that your version is correct."

The immediate aftermath of Pearl Harbor is every bit as gripping as the attack itself. The frenzied few days following the raid culminated on December 11 with the German and Italian declaration of war on the United States. I hope readers will agree with me that there have been very few weeks like it in the history of the world.

Warm thanks to Noel Cunningham-Reid and Joan Evans (née Fawcett) for their personal memories of the attack on Pearl Harbor; to Danielle Oser for providing her grandmother AraBelle Fuller's account; and to Senator Bob Dole for sending me his memories of listening to President Roosevelt's address to Congress on the radio.

Thanks also to Soozi Stokes and Fiona Cunningham-Reid for help with their parents' accounts, to the Earl of Halifax, Lady Holderness, and Chris Webb at the Borthwick Institute for Archives, University of York; and to Daphne Hughes and Lesley Parris for allowing me to use previously unpublished letters and photographs from HMS *Repulse*. The book is much richer for their help.

"You heard, did you?"

"What?"

"The Japs."

"What about them?"

"They've gone and bombed some bloody harbour in Hawaii. The Yanks are in!"

—LANCE-CORPORAL DIRK BOGARDE, *SNAKES AND LADDERS*

SEVEN
DAYS OF
INFAMY

ONE

WHERE ARE JAPAN'S AIRCRAFT CARRIERS?

The New Public Offices building lies just across the road from St James's Park, in the heart of central London. It is an unremarkable office block completed in 1916, one of many similar government buildings clustered around Downing Street and the Houses of Parliament. Nobody walking past it in the dark days of December 1941 ever gave it a thought as they passed the concrete blast wall erected against the bombing and continued on their way.

But appearances are deceptive. There was far more to the New Public Offices building than met the eye. For more than two years, ever since the last days of peace in August 1939, the anonymous gray building had been the nerve center of Britain's fight against Hitler and the Nazis. It was where Winston Churchill usually spent the night, rather than the prime minister's official residence at 10 Downing Street. It was also where his staff conducted the war, from the seventy or so windowless cubicles in the basement known collectively as the Cabinet War Rooms.

The basement had not been designed with war in mind. It wasn't even bombproof, although it was safer than anywhere else in the vicinity. As war approached and a conflict with the Germans became inevitable, the

British had set up their headquarters below ground level with all the pipes, wiring, and electronic equipment that they needed for a prolonged confrontation that would probably have to be fought all over the world. The lights in the Cabinet War Rooms had been switched on for the first time on August 27, 1939, four days before Germany invaded Poland. They had not been turned off since.

The rooms could only be entered from inside the building. A steel-helmeted marine with rifle and bayonet stood guard at the door. Nobody was admitted if their name wasn't on the list, or if they didn't know the password, which was changed every day. From the inside, the war rooms seemed more like a ship than anything else, with narrow, cramped corridors, humming machinery, ventilation pipes overhead, and seamanlike marines who said "Aye-aye, sir" when addressing an officer.

Most of the men who worked in the war rooms were servicemen. They were usually retired officers from the three fighting arms taking desk jobs that would free younger men for active duty. Most of the women were civilians—young typists, secretaries, and decoders who worked long hours in atrocious conditions and saw so little daylight that they were provided with sunlamps to make up for the vitamin deficiency. Those sleeping in the dank accommodation beneath the war rooms had to ask the sentry's permission to visit the bathroom on the first floor, flashing him a bare ankle as they hurried past in their nightclothes, clutching towels and soap.

Central to the war rooms, the single most important place in the whole complex, was the Map Room. It was here, next door to Churchill's emergency bedroom, that three senior officers, one each from the army, navy, and Royal Air Force, worked around the clock with a team of map plotters to collate the information that came in to them from all over the world.

Sitting at a bank of red, white, green, and black telephones, each with a different function, the Map Room staff labored tirelessly for twenty-four hours a day, seven days a week, updating the war and pinning the latest situation reports to the maps, charts, and bulletin boards that covered the walls. Only a handful of people were allowed into the Map Room. Those who had authorization could tell at a glance exactly how the war was progressing at any point across the globe.

On the British front, there was something of a lull on the morning of December 4, 1941. British convoys were still losing to the U-boats in the Battle of the Atlantic, but not so badly as before. Fewer ships were being sunk as the Royal Navy's tactics improved, and more were emerging from the shipyards to make up the lost tonnage. The map of the Atlantic on the wall was covered with tiny pinpricks as the progress of the various convoys and escort ships was charted across the sea.

The British weren't losing so badly in North Africa either. Troops from a variety of countries were holding the Germans at bay, preventing the Afrika Korps from sweeping across Egypt toward the oil fields of the Middle East. The Germans had the upper hand, but the British were still in contention, enjoying successes as well as defeats as the battle swung to and fro. They had everything to gain as the fighting continued.

The most interesting battleground that morning belonged to Britain's Soviet allies. The map of the Russian front (actually several maps pinned together) was so large that it had a whole wall to itself at the end of the room. It too was covered with pinpricks as the Map Room officials tracked the German army's movement across the Soviet Union.

Progress had been relentless since the invasion in June. Hitler's troops and tanks had pushed ever onward for the past five months and were poised now at the gates of Moscow. They were besieging Leningrad in the north and had long since taken Kiev in the south. Until recently, it had seemed that nothing could stop them as they thrust deeper and deeper into the heart of the Soviet Union.

The exact position of the front line was marked by a row of pushpins linked by a length of black wool yarn—a crude but effective way of seeing how far the Germans had gotten. Until the past few days, all the pinpricks on the map had been to the west of the yarn, following the Germans as they advanced from one forward position to the next.

But then something extraordinary had happened, something unprecedented in the history of the war: One or two of the pinpricks now lay to the east of the black yarn, marking places where the German army had fallen back instead of pressing on.

There was nothing unusual about falling back. It was a routine military procedure if the supply lines were overextended or the front needed straightening out, but it had never happened to the German army in Europe. Not since their first attack on Poland had the Germans ever given up ground that they had won. They had always gone forward, taking the capital cities of Warsaw, Oslo, Copenhagen, Brussels, Amsterdam, Paris, and Athens with consummate ease. No one had ever managed to stop them.

Until now. The Germans were still advancing steadily in Russia, but in the few places where they had fallen back it wasn't because they had supply problems or needed to straighten the line: It was because the Russians had prevented their advance and forced them to retreat.

Far too early to read anything into it. A few withdrawals were neither here nor there while the Germans still had the upper hand. All anyone could say in the Map Room that December morning was that the fighting was fierce on the Russian front and the casualties on both sides were enormous. It would be a long time yet, months at the very least, before anyone knew what the outcome would be.

The day shift came on at 9:00 a.m. The overnight report had already been written by then, a typed summary of all the information that had come in to the Map Room during the past twenty-four hours. Uniformed messengers stood ready to deliver copies to Winston Churchill, the chiefs of staff, and the king at Buckingham Palace.

There wasn't a great deal to report. The Germans were trying to take Moscow, but the capital was stubbornly resisting. The Afrika Korps was threatening Tobruk, in the Western Desert. The New Zealanders had taken a heavy pounding in holding them off. The RAF had crippled an Axis tanker in the Mediterranean; the Royal Navy had sunk it with gunfire.

And the Japanese were at sea. The British and Americans had been tracking them for days, sharing their reports across the Atlantic. The Japanese had been at war with China since 1937 and had just changed their naval call signs for the second time in a month. That almost certainly meant that they were about to launch an operation somewhere.

Nobody in the Map Room could say where. All they knew for sure was that Japan's aircraft carriers had recently gone missing, along with numerous other warships. They were at large somewhere in the Pacific.

The best guess that Thursday morning was that the Japanese might be about to attack Thailand, or the Burma Road, to cut off the flow of military supplies to China. Or they might be going for Malaya, whose tin and rubber they needed for their war effort. Or maybe the Philippines, to protect their flank. The only certainty was that wherever the Japanese were aiming for, the rest of the world would find out soon enough.

On the Russian front, the Germans had been so close to Moscow on the morning of December 2 that they thought they could see the towers of the Kremlin through their field glasses. Some of them were convinced that they had seen movement in the streets as well. But that had been earlier, before the weather closed in. The Germans could hardly see one another's faces now that the snow had begun to fall again.

The snow was still falling as Lieutenant Heinrich Haape and his two companions drove up to the front line from the railway town of Klin. According to the map in the Cabinet War Rooms, the front lay directly ahead of them, a neat length of black yarn crossing the road a few miles short of Moscow. The reality, in the murk and chaos, was rather harder to determine.

Haape was a medical officer attached to the Eighteenth Infantry Regiment. Together with Oberleutnant Kageneck and Fischer, their driver, he was bringing up a carload of cognac, chocolate, cigars, cigarettes, and medical supplies—gifts from the Luftwaffe, which still had access to such luxuries. Sitting beside Kageneck while Fischer followed the tracks of some other vehicle through the snow, Haape could hardly believe that they were almost in Moscow at last.

Already there were signs of an approaching city all around them: houses, side streets, billboards along the way plastered with enormous pictures of Lenin and Stalin. Now and then there was even a two-story building among all the wooden shacks. But no people. None that Haape could see. The whole place appeared to be deserted:

Not a soul was in sight. Many of the buildings were burnt-out shells, a heap of rubble bearing mute evidence of a bombing raid or concentrated artillery fire. Not a building was occupied—every man, woman, child and beast had fled. The snow had drifted up against the doors of the wooden hovels, and on the window-sills. An occasional Wehrmacht sign-board, in code, showed us that we were still on the right road.[1]

By Haape's calculation another fifteen minutes at the same speed would bring them to Moscow's city limits. He found it sobering, frightening even, to think that they could be in Red Square fifteen minutes after that, if the Russians didn't stop them first.

They drove on for some time before coming at length to a front-line post beside the road. Two officers emerged as they drew up. One asked where they were going.

"Moscow," Kageneck told him.

"That's where we're going too. Perhaps you'd better wait for us."[2]

The officer pointed with his leather glove. There were Russians to the right and left of them. The tram stop to Moscow lay just ahead, but the trams weren't running. The officer advised them to come back next week if they wanted to drive any farther into Moscow.

He told Haape that the men in his unit had taken 25 percent casualties from frostbite alone in the past few days. They were still waiting for their winter clothing to arrive. All any of them could think about was getting to Moscow before Christmas and finding somewhere warm and dry to spend the rest of the winter. The troops had convinced themselves that the fall of Moscow must surely mean the end of the war:

"One more jump and we'll be there," the officer said confidently. "It'll be over. Surely we can't be denied it now?"[3]

Haape wished he could be so certain. Like many in the German army, he was beginning to have his doubts about the wisdom of invading Russia.

He walked over to the tram stop. It was a stone shed with wooden seats. The tramlines were invisible under the snow, but a row of telegraph poles pointed the way to Moscow.

A bin on the wall was full of old tram tickets with Moskva stamped on them. On impulse Haape pocketed a few as a souvenir. Then he and the others returned to their car and drove back the way they had come. It was probably as near as any German got to Moscow that winter.

Some 130 miles to the south, General Heinz Guderian was acutely aware of the difficulties facing the troops as they struggled to fight a war in the bitter cold, with the temperature continuing to plummet. If he had his way, the men under his command would dig in for the winter, recoup their strength, and wait for spring before attempting to advance any further. But Hitler's orders were unequivocal. Guderian was to push on, regardless of the weather. There was nothing else he could do if he wanted to retain his command.

Guderian was one of the stars of the war so far. He had never needed any urging to push on in the past. His panzer tanks had led the way in Poland and France, moving forward so fast that his men had nicknamed him *"Der schnelle Heinz"* as they visited blitzkrieg on their enemies. It was only an order from above that had prevented him from annihilating the British at Dunkirk.

Guderian's panzers had led the way in Russia too. They had swept all before them as they aimed straight for Moscow. They might have taken the capital already if Hitler hadn't suddenly diverted them south to reinforce the Kiev front.

Guderian was in command now at Tula, covering the approaches to Moscow from the south. He had set up a temporary headquarters at Yasnaya Polyana, the country estate just outside Tula that was home to the Tolstoy family. Guderian had arrived on December 2, taking over one of the two big houses on the property for himself and his staff. The other was still occupied by the family.

It had not escaped the Germans' notice that Yasnaya was where Russia's most famous novelist had written his most famous novel. Leo Tolstoy had spent most of the 1860s writing *War and Peace*, a tribute to the courage of the Russian people during the Napoleonic campaign of 1812, in which his father had fought. The Germans knew all about *War and Peace*, even if they hadn't read it themselves. In particular, they all knew how it turned out in the end.

There was a Tolstoy museum at Yasnaya, whose contents the Russians had prudently removed before the Wehrmacht arrived. Guderian had given orders that the Tolstoy family's remaining furniture and books were to be locked away in two rooms for safekeeping. He had also ordered that the novelist's descendants were to be left undisturbed in their own house on the estate.

But *War and Peace* was not so easily locked away. The 1812 campaign was on everybody's minds as the Germans braced themselves for a struggle that was clearly going to be much harder than anticipated. Russian accounts of the 1812 campaign attributed Napoleon's defeat to the formidable fighting qualities of the Russian soldier; French ones blamed the weather. Both seemed eminently plausible to the Germans.

The resilience of the Russian army had been their first big surprise. It was poorly equipped and led after Stalin's purges of the 1930s. The Germans had expected to cut through it like a knife through butter, as they had with every other army over the past two years.

They had been wildly successful at first, driving the Russians back across one endless horizon after another. But their success had not led to a Russian surrender, as it had with everyone else. It had steeled the Russians' resolve, if anything. The fighting was just as determined as ever.

The real revelation, however, had been the weather. The Germans had never seen anything like it before. Winter had hardly begun and already they were knee-deep in snow. The temperature had dropped to unbelievable levels, –30° F as a matter of routine, –60° on occasion.

That meant that nothing worked as it was supposed to. The breechblocks on rifles froze, as did the oil in crankcases. Dynamos didn't function, engines wouldn't start, axles seized up, and cylinder blocks cracked open. Panzer crews had to light fires under their tanks for hours just to thaw out the machinery. And that was before winter had even hit its stride.

Human bodies couldn't function properly either in the extreme cold. The Germans had little winter clothing because Hitler had refused to accept that the campaign might last this long. Wounded men were freezing to death as a result. Frostbite was causing as many casualties as normal battle wounds, often resulting in amputation.

Without overcoats, men with dysentery staggered outside to relieve themselves and died from congelation of the anus as soon as they opened their bowels. Without gloves and fur-lined boots, healthier men could do little to help them. It was no way to fight a war.

All along the line German commanders were recognizing the inevitable and abandoning the advance for the time being. They were going over to the defensive, digging in for the duration of the winter and waiting for better times in the spring.

It was the sensible thing to do, but it was not popular with the high command back in East Prussia. Field Marshal Gerd von Rundstedt had just been sacked for ignoring Hitler's order to stand fast, and evacuating Rostov before his troops could be overwhelmed.

Guderian's relations with Hitler were equally strained. Surrounded by yes-men who only told him what he wanted to hear, the Führer did not take kindly to plain speaking from professional soldiers. Guderian never hesitated to query decisions of the Führer's when he didn't agree with them. As a result, his own position was far from secure that morning as he prepared to leave Yasnaya Polyana for a visit to the headquarters of the Thirty-First Infantry Division farther along the line.

Guderian was looking forward to the visit. His old infantry battalion was part of the division. He was going to see his old comrades after he had been to headquarters, chatting with the men and finding out for himself how much fight was left in ordinary soldiers.

His immediate military objective was to close the ring around Tula to prevent the Russians from reinforcing the city. It wouldn't be easy, after everything his troops had been through. As he set off for the Thirty-First Division, Guderian needed to satisfy himself that the men under his command still had the appetite for a fight before sending them into action again in the middle of a Russian winter.

Adolf Hitler was on his way back to East Prussia after a trip to Ukraine to see his generals and assess the military situation for himself. He wasn't a happy man as his aircraft touched down near Rastenburg. For one thing, the weather in Ukraine had been so awful that his return flight had been delayed and he had had to stay overnight at Poltava. For another, he had made a mess of sacking Rundstedt after the German retreat from Rostov.

Rundstedt had already evacuated the city when Hitler ordered him to hold his ground. The field marshal had offered to resign his command if the Führer no longer had confidence in him. Hitler had accepted the offer on December 1, only to be told by his pusillanimous generals when he arrived in Ukraine that Rundstedt had been quite right to withdraw. There was nothing else the Wehrmacht could have done.

Hitler was sick of them all as he returned to Rastenburg. He told Heinz Linge, his valet, that he was never going to visit his generals in the field again. "Linge," he confided, as they flew home, "I'm glad it's you sitting behind me, instead of one of those Obergruppenführers who could shoot me in the back with a pistol."[4]

He was relieved to get back to the Wolf's Lair, his military headquarters at Rastenburg. It lay in the forest close to the airfield, a giant network of steel and concrete bunkers, heavily camouflaged and protected from attack. Hitler had spent most of his time there since the invasion of Russia in June.

There were three security zones at the complex, spread out over two and a half square miles. The outer zone was ringed with mines and barbed wire, defended by elite troops in pillboxes and machine-gun emplacements. The middle zone housed the soldiers' barracks and accommodation for various Nazi officials.

The inner zone was for Hitler and his close wartime associates, men like Hermann Göring, Martin Bormann, Alfred Jodl, and Wilhelm Keitel. It comprised ten camouflaged bunkers with six feet of steel-reinforced concrete overhead. It was in the inner zone that Hitler oversaw his campaign to conquer the world.

The gates swung open to receive him. Hitler had a great deal on his mind as the car drew up and he returned to his bunker. The crisis on the Russian front was coming to a head as the German advance ran out of steam. His generals were urging tactical withdrawal to avert disaster, but withdrawal would mean a considerable loss of morale as well as much-needed equipment too frozen to move.

More than that, and far more seriously, it would also mean the loss of Hitler's reputation for invincibility. Hitler was the demigod who had descended from the clouds in *Triumph of the Will* (Leni Riefenstahl's film of the 1934 Nazi Party rally at Nuremburg). He could not afford to lose that reputation now. As he prepared for the six o'clock military briefing that evening, Adolf Hitler was surely aware that he would never regain his aura of divinity, if ever his generals lost it for him in the wastelands of Russia.

In his office at Prague's magnificent castle, high above the Vltava River, Reinhard Heydrich was preparing to meet a delegation of agricultural workers in one of the castle's tapestried halls. He had summoned them to the Czech capital for a pep talk about war production.

Heydrich was the Reich's newly appointed acting protector of Moravia and Bohemia. It was part of his job to court Czechoslovakia's farm and factory workers and keep them in line. They would clearly be needed for Germany's war effort, now that it was going to be a long war.

Half a million pigs had vanished from the Czech countryside immediately before Heydrich's arrival. So had 20 percent of the cereal crop. By inviting delegations of workingmen to visit him at Hradčany Castle, Heydrich was trying to show ordinary people that they had nothing to fear from the German occupation of their country. They could actually profit from the experience, if they were willing to increase war production.

But agriculture wasn't uppermost in Heydrich's mind as he worked on his speech for the meeting next day. He had other things to do beside boost war production. He had been given the much more important task of preparing Czechoslovakia and the other occupied countries for Germanization now that they had been conquered. That meant, in effect, the "ethnic cleansing" of large numbers of people who didn't fit into the plan.

Heydrich had been appointed to the task by Hermann Göring. In a letter of July 31, 1941, the Reichsmarschall had been quite explicit about

what he wanted: "I hereby charge you with making all necessary orga-
nizational, functional and material preparations for a complete solution of
the Jewish question in the German sphere of influence in Europe."[5]

Heydrich had been working on the details ever since. Dogged by
rumors that he himself was part Jewish, he hadn't dragged his feet. He was
almost ready to deliver his suggestions for a "final solution" to the question
at a specially convened conference in Berlin. The invitations had just been
sent out. All the right people had been invited, the gauleiters (Nazi district
leaders), party officials, and government ministers who would be most involved in implementing his proposals.

Heydrich intended to explain the plan to them at a breakfast meeting
beside the Wannsee, one of the most beautiful lakes in Berlin:

> *Given the extraordinary significance of the Jewish question, and to reach
> a consensus as to how a final solution may be achieved, I propose to hold
> a discussion. The matter is imperative because since October 15, 1941,
> Jews have been transported out of Reich territory, including the protec-
> torate of Bohemia and Moravia, and evacuated to the East.*
>
> *I invite you to a breakfast discussion to be held on December 9,
> 1941, in the offices of the International Criminal Police Commission,
> Berlin, am Kleinen Wannsee, Nr 16.*[6]

Wannsee, the following week. That was where the fate of the Jews in
the East was to be decided. The proposals that Heydrich was taking to the
meeting were radical in the extreme. If they were implemented, though,
they would certainly settle the Jewish problem once and for all.

At the American embassy in Berlin, U.S. diplomats were following the Wehr-
macht's progress on the eastern front every bit as closely as Heydrich in
Prague, Hitler in Rastenburg, and the British in London. A large map of
the Soviet Union hung on the wall of George F. Kennan's office in the old
Blücher Palace beside the Brandenburg Gate. Studying it every day as the
Germans pushed forward, Kennan had been struck repeatedly by the par-

allels between their advance and Napoleon's over the same ground. The two campaigns were often uncannily alike.

There was no ambassador at the U.S. Embassy. The last one had been withdrawn in 1938 in protest at Kristallnacht, the glass-smashing Nazi attack on Jewish life and property, and had never been replaced. U.S. interests in Germany were represented now by Leland Morris, the chargé d'affaires, his administrative head, George Kennan, and a tiny staff of beleaguered Americans. They were feeling increasingly isolated in hostile territory as their government edged ever closer toward supporting the British side in the war.

There were other neutral embassies in the capital, but few natural allies for the Americans. Spain was on Germany's side in all but name. Sweden was neutral with a German bias. The Swiss were on nobody's side but their own. The Americans only had one another to talk to as their relations with the Nazi regime grew steadily worse and the situation deteriorated by the day.

The Blücher Palace, next door but one to the Brandenburg Gate, had been a gift from the king of Prussia to the Prussian commander at Waterloo. Rebuilt in 1869, and again after a fire in the 1930s, it had served as the U.S. Embassy since 1939. It was a great warren of a place, grand rather than functional, occupying a corner of Pariser Platz in the very heart of Berlin.

The windows of the consular section looked out across Hermann-Göring-Strasse toward the Reichstag and the Tiergarten, the Berlin equivalent of New York's Central Park. The balcony of the embassy section overlooked Pariser Platz and the tree-lined avenue Unter den Linden. The Americans could not have been better placed to watch the comings and goings of the Nazis as they marched through the Brandenburg Gate or headed around the corner toward Hitler's Chancellery on Wilhelmstrasse.

The Americans were actually *too* well placed for comfort. They had lost no time spelling out USA in large letters on the roof after the war had broken out, in the hope that British bomb aimers would see it and drop their loads elsewhere. They followed the blackout regulations to the letter and always had their window shutters up by 2:00 p.m. in winter, as ordered. They had suffered some bomb damage nevertheless, but remained in business as an embassy, although for how much longer was anybody's guess as the situation continued to worsen.

They were also horribly overworked. As well as representing American interests in Germany, the embassy staff were looking after the affairs of Britain, France, and half a dozen other countries that no longer had diplomatic relations with the Nazis.

The consular staff were swamped with applicants for U.S. visas, almost invariably Jewish in the early days, all with terrible stories to tell. The applicants weren't allowed to take any money with them when they left Germany, so they were happy for the Americans to have it instead, if that would buy them a visa. They had to be discouraged from showering cash on the officials examining their applications.

The embassy itself was full of German spies, low-level typists, cleaners, and maintenance workers reporting back to their Nazi masters. The Germans took photographs, bugged rooms, tapped phone lines, and retrieved carbon copies of classified documents from wastebaskets. They never ceased to wonder at the way the Americans ignored their own rules and left top secret information on their desks during their lunch hour. The Americans didn't even bother to lock their office safes when they went out.

The Germans were also interfering with the embassy's mail, secretly opening diplomatic pouches in defiance of international convention. President Roosevelt had made no secret of where his sympathies lay in the European war. The Germans regarded the Americans as Britain's unofficial allies, rather than the neutrals they were striving to remain.

It couldn't go on much longer. George Kennan had already recognized the inevitable by sending his Norwegian wife, Annelise, and their two small daughters to safety in America. He had taken them to Italy and seen them off by ship from Genoa, hoping they would make it through the Strait of Gibraltar and across the battleground of the Atlantic. Kennan had wondered if he would ever see them again as he waved good-bye to the tearful faces peering at him through a porthole.

His wife and children had arrived safely, but Kennan was no closer to seeing them again. Following the Wehrmacht's progress on his map as the Germans struggled to take Moscow and Leningrad, he could not help thinking that events in Europe were slipping inexorably out of control. Not just Hitler's control, or Germany's, but everybody else's as well.

Where it would end, Kennan had no idea. All he knew for certain was that the situation couldn't continue indefinitely. The end must surely come soon, so far as American neutrality was concerned.

TWO

STILL A CHANCE TO CALL IT OFF

Across the Atlantic, President Franklin Roosevelt shared Kennan's view, although he was still doing his best to keep the United States out of the conflict. He had won reelection in 1940 on the promise that no American serviceman would lose his life in someone else's fight.

"Your boys are not going to be sent into any foreign wars," he had assured the electorate during the campaign, and he meant it.[1] American sailors were already dying in the Battle of the Atlantic, but Roosevelt remained determined to honor that promise to the best of his ability.

He was being kept fully informed about events on the Russian front and elsewhere, but his thoughts were not on Europe that morning, or even on the Atlantic. He was far more concerned about the Japanese in the Far East.

Their movements were hard to track, but it was clear from signal traffic and other sources that Japan's armed forces were poised for an attack somewhere in the Pacific, perhaps even several places at the same time. The problem for the United States was where they were likely to strike, and how to respond when they did.

In common with Winston Churchill, Roosevelt liked to begin his working day in bed. He ate breakfast from a tray in his bedroom at the White

House, reading dispatches in his pajamas and leafing through the newspapers until his staff came in to discuss his schedule for the day.

After the breakdown of peace negotiations with the Japanese, there was only one serious item on the agenda when he awoke that morning: the threat from Japan's armed forces and how to counter it when it came, preferably short of all-out war.

The quarrel was not of American making. The Japanese were short of the resources they needed for their war in China. The Americans had imposed an embargo on the export of oil, gas, metal, steel, and scrap iron to Japan in an attempt to stop the fighting.

Rather than remain dependent on the United States and other Western countries for the technology and raw materials that they needed to make war, the Japanese wished to become self-sufficient. They wanted to carve out an empire of their own in the resource-rich countries of Southeast Asia.

They had already forced the Vichy French (the puppet government collaborating with the Germans) to give them effective command of French Indochina. They wanted further territories controlled by the Dutch, British, and American governments. These would never be conceded voluntarily, so the Japanese intended to take them by force.

Looking at the map, Roosevelt knew that the Japanese could strike in any number of directions if they chose. As a noncombatant ally of Germany, they could seize the Russian port of Vladivostok, forcing the Russians to fight on two fronts at a time when Moscow and Leningrad lay in grave danger.

They could invade Thailand—then known as Siam—and from there threaten the Kra Isthmus at the top of Malaya, whose rubber and tin were essential for the British war effort. Or they could attack Java, Sumatra, or the Philippines. The possibilities were almost endless.

Roosevelt's fear was that the Japanese were trying to do it like Hitler, one country at a time. He had already made clear to them that the mistakes of Munich would not be repeated by his administration. If Japanese forces crossed the line, they could expect an armed response from the United States.

Yet where *was* the line? Unlike Poland, the oceans were open to all.

Would it be aggression if a Japanese fleet sailed below the southernmost tip of Indochina? Would the American people want to go to war if the Japanese invaded Thailand and nowhere else?

Roosevelt had a meeting with congressional leaders scheduled for later that day. He was going to explain the situation to them and try to find out what the mood of the two houses would be if push should come to shove and war became inevitable.

He was also going to make an appeal for peace to the Japanese emperor. Grasping at straws perhaps, but it was hoped in Washington that an appeal to Hirohito's honor over the heads of his generals might just persuade him to intervene. The appeal wouldn't be made until all other avenues had been exhausted, but the wording had already gone through several drafts and was almost ready for delivery.

The appeal was to begin with a reference to Commodore Matthew Perry's visit to Japan in 1853 to request diplomatic relations between the two countries:

> Almost a century ago the President of the United States addressed to the Emperor of Japan a message extending an offer of friendship of the people of the United States to the people of Japan. That offer was accepted, and in the long period of unbroken peace and friendship which has followed our respective nations, through the virtues of their peoples and the wisdom of their rulers, have prospered and have substantially helped humanity. . . .
>
> During the past few weeks it has become clear to the world that Japanese military, naval and air forces have been sent to southern Indo-China in such large numbers as to create a reasonable doubt on the part of other nations that this continuing concentration in Indo-China is defensive in its character. . . .
>
> It is only reasonable that the people of the Philippines, of the hundreds of islands of the East Indies, of Malaya and of Thailand itself are asking themselves whether these forces of Japan are preparing or intending to make attack in one or more of these many directions.[2]

That might do it, although Roosevelt had his reservations. Hirohito appeared to have little influence over his government. If the appeal did fall on deaf ears, Roosevelt was in no doubt that the United States would just have to contain the Japanese by force. They had no other option, if the Japanese refused to listen to reason.

The Americans were already prepared for the task, with aircraft and a mighty fleet at their disposal. The British were prepared too. Between them the two navies had more than enough battleships in the Pacific to keep the Japanese in check. But they couldn't fire first and risk an accusation of aggression. They had to leave it to the Japanese to strike the first blow.

At the MGM studios in Culver City, just outside Hollywood, the movie director William Wyler was grappling with a slew of problems on the set of his latest motion picture. *Mrs. Miniver* was supposed to be a tribute to the British in their fight against the Nazis, but the work wasn't going well. The script wasn't quite right, for one thing. The cast wasn't happy, for another. The film could easily slip out of control if Wyler didn't get a grip on it soon.

Part of the problem was Wyler himself. He was on loan from another studio, unfamiliar with MGM's way of doing things. A relentless perfectionist, Wyler was quite capable of making his stars repeat a take forty times until they had gotten it right.

His preferred method of direction was to watch silently and then tell the actors to do it again, but without saying where they were going wrong. He wanted the actors to follow their own instincts, but they found his lack of communication very difficult to work with.

Greer Garson found him as difficult as any. She was the star of the picture, a thirty-three-year-old actress playing a mother with a son in the RAF. She had been most reluctant to take the part, especially after Norma Shearer, the Oscar-winning Canadian star, had turned it down. They both knew it was career suicide for an actress to play a mother with a grown-up son.

Garson didn't want to be in Hollywood anyway. Her place was in

England, driving an ambulance when not appearing in British films. She had been talked into accepting the part by Lord Halifax, Britain's ambassador to the United States. On a trip to Hollywood, he had persuaded her to put career considerations aside and take the role, grown-up son or not: It would do wonders for Britain's war effort.

Halifax had been supported by Louis B. Mayer, MGM's head of production. Canadian by upbringing, Mayer had brought Garson to Hollywood before the war. He had protected her from her many detractors, who disliked her English snobbishness.

Mayer had reminded her of the debt she owed him when he insisted that she should trust him now when he told her that she was absolutely right for the part: "I brought you along. You were fat, I had no way of knowing whether you could take off that extra twenty pounds. I put my faith in you when others would not accept you. Now you've got to have the same faith in me."[3]

Mayer had appealed to Garson's sense of fair play, but it was the script that had clinched the deal for her. He had read it out to her in his office. Whatever tweaking it might need, Mrs. Miniver was a peach of a part for an actress: a good and decent woman, standing up for England against the Luftwaffe. It would play well all over the free world. Garson had allowed herself to be persuaded.

But the script still needed fixing. It had gone through numerous drafts since the project had first been mooted. With Mr. Miniver at Dunkirk and his son a Battle of Britain pilot, there was ample scope for an action movie, if that was required. Yet the story was supposed to be about the home front, ordinary men and women caught up in a war that was being fought right overhead, instead of somewhere remote and far away. A decision had been taken to concentrate on the female characters instead.

The only German in the film was a Luftwaffe pilot played by Helmut Dantine, an Austrian refugee who had fled the Nazis. As written, he was supposed to be a nice young man, the mirror image of Mrs. Miniver's own RAF son. One draft of the script had her taking pity on him after he had been shot down and offering him something to eat.

Ignoring the script, Wyler had shot the scene differently. He had turned the pilot into a Nazi fanatic determined to destroy England and rule the world. This anti-German bias had gotten him into trouble with Mayer.

Summoning Wyler to his office, Mayer had pointed out that the United States was a neutral country, not at war with anybody and under pressure from isolationists to remain impartial. The Hays Office, the movie industry's self-policing body, had rules about hate films. It had not been shown the changes to the script.

MGM had rules too. With movie theaters all over the world, including two in Berlin, it had a responsibility to its global audience, not to mention its stockholders. As a special favor to the company, the Nazis allowed MGM to repatriate its wartime profits from Germany, but the German consul had made it clear to Mayer that the Nazis expected equal concessions in return.

Mayer had accordingly asked Wyler to tone the scene down, but Wyler had stood his ground: "Mr Mayer, if I had several Germans in the picture, I wouldn't mind having one of them sympathetic. But I've got only one German and as long as I only have one, he's going to be one of Göring's little monsters. That's the way he's been brought up. Maybe it's not his fault."[4]

The two men had reached a grudging compromise. Mayer had allowed Wyler to go ahead, just so long as he didn't overdo it. But Wyler still wasn't happy. The scene was crucial to the picture, yet it was obvious from the rushes that it wasn't working dramatically. Hays Office or no Hays Office, it needed to be shot again, perhaps with Mrs. Miniver slapping the pilot's face.

That wasn't all. In Wyler's view, Mayer was being dishonest with him. The man was quite capable of interfering with artistic considerations behind Wyler's back: "I think I could see what was going through his mind. 'It's just one scene. Let him finish the picture. I can always have another director shoot it over if I don't like it.'"[5]

No way was Mayer going to do that. Over Wyler's dead body would anyone else interfere with the shooting of his movie.

At Warner Bros.' Burbank studio just down the road, the rising star Humphrey Bogart had taken a few days' break from filming and was preparing to fly to St. Louis to speak against the Nazis at a Fight for Freedom rally in the city. On the back of his success in *The Maltese Falcon*, he headed the list of celebrities scheduled to attend the rally in St. Louis's twelve-thousand-seat municipal auditorium.

The Fight for Freedom Committee had recently been set up to counter the efforts of America First, the right-wing isolationists who wanted to keep the United States out of the European war. The isolationists had just persuaded Congress to investigate an alleged prowar bias in Hollywood movies. They were testifying at Senate hearings about a plot to hoodwink the American public into believing that the United States should not remain neutral in the war.

The Fight for Freedom Committee disagreed. They were in no doubt at all that the war against Hitler and his thugs should be America's war too. Bogart supported them wholeheartedly. He had no time for the kind of people who argued that Hollywood was full of Jews manipulating the movie industry for their own sinister ends.

He was on a high after *The Maltese Falcon*'s unexpected success. So was everyone else associated with the project: Mary Astor, Sydney Greenstreet, Peter Lorre, and John Huston, the film's first-time director. Warner Bros. wanted to get them all back together again as soon as possible to cash in with a follow-up movie.

At first the producers had thought of using the same characters again, before deciding that it would be impossible. Mary Astor's character had been destined for the electric chair at the end of the first movie. Casting around for another project, they had decided to shoot *Aloha Means Goodbye* instead.

The new film was a spy thriller. It had begun as a highly popular serial in the *Saturday Evening Post*. Warner Bros. had snapped up the rights and was rushing it into production without delay.

Peter Lorre wasn't available, but Greenstreet, Bogart, and Mary Astor were all on board. So was John Huston to direct. According to the script, however, Bogart would be kissing Mary Astor again, which was a problem for both of them.

Bogart disliked kissing on camera. "It isn't possible to shoot a love scene without having a hairy-chested group of grips standing four feet away from you, chewing tobacco," was his sour view of on-screen romance.[6]

Mary Astor didn't like it either, at least not where Bogart was concerned. A botched operation on his lip had made him a very slobbery kisser, and he sometimes banged her teeth during clumsy takes. She suffered for her art.

But the script looked promising. Set aboard a ship sailing for Honolulu, it involved a plot by the Japanese to blow up the headquarters of the U.S. Pacific Fleet at the American naval base in Hawaii. Warner Bros. felt sure that with the same cast and crew as *The Maltese Falcon*, the project would be a winner.

On the island of Singapore, Lady Diana Cooper was just back from a reception aboard HMS *Prince of Wales*. The battleship had arrived on December 2, along with HMS *Repulse* and four escort vessels. Everyone in Singapore was feeling good about it, that the Royal Navy had turned up in strength at last.

Lady Diana was living in a pretty little house three miles from the city center. Newly appointed to cabinet rank, her husband, Duff Cooper, had been sent to Singapore to assess the Japanese threat and report back to Churchill in London. Diana had gone with him, even though Singapore was the other side of the world and she absolutely hated flying. Some of the journey had been by flying boat. Some of it had been by military bomber, necessitating the wearing of a parachute harness that clipped between the legs, not easy in a skirt.

The Coopers had flown to the United States first, where Duff had had a meeting with President Roosevelt in Washington. From there they had gone to Honolulu, where they had been shocked at the sight of several hundred U.S. Air Force planes lined up wingtip-to-wingtip on a single airfield.

Duff had suggested to the Americans that they might want to adopt the Battle of Britain tactic of dispersing their aircraft around several fields so that not all of them would be destroyed in a single raid. The Americans had curtly informed him that the aircraft were easier to protect from sabotage if they were kept together. They would certainly be dispersed in the event of a war.

Diana had taken to Singapore when they arrived. She loved the colors of the city, and she loved the people. She had disgraced herself only once since her arrival, on a side trip to Rangoon, Burma, when she had asked to visit a famous temple. She had been told that it was impossible because visitors had to enter barefoot, like a native. No Briton could do that.

Diana couldn't see why not. She was the daughter of a duke, the model for Mrs. Stitch in Evelyn Waugh's prewar bestseller *Scoop*, far too assured to worry about what anyone might think. It had been the work of a moment to remove her stockings and enter the temple. The British, including her stuffy husband, had been horrified. They felt she had let the side down.

But they were all together again as *Repulse* and *Prince of Wales* sailed into Singapore on December 2. Along with half the people on the island, the Coopers were there to watch as the two great warships appeared, with all their armaments and firepower. *Prince of Wales* was the Royal Navy's newest, state-of-the-art battleship. *Repulse* was a recently modernized battle cruiser.

Together they made a splendid sight, as Duff Cooper later remembered: "It was a great moment when they came round the bend into the narrow waters of the straits that divide Singapore from the mainland. We were all at the naval base to welcome them, and they arrived punctual to the minute with their escort of four destroyers. They conferred a sense of complete security."[7]

There was supposed to be an aircraft carrier as well. HMS *Indomitable* boasted an armored flight deck and forty-five aircraft, including nine Hurricane fighters. Unfortunately the ship had run aground at the entrance to Kingston Harbor in Jamaica during its sea trials. *Indomitable* had had to put in to the U.S. naval dockyard at Norfolk, Virginia, for repairs. The delay meant that *Repulse* and *Prince of Wales* would be without air cover until the carrier caught up.

The sailors came flooding ashore as soon as leave was granted. They were kept busy all day, loading supplies and overhauling the engines after the long voyage from England. *Repulse* was standing by to sail to Australia, but *Prince of Wales*'s crew were free to go ashore at night.

Few had been abroad before joining the navy. They lost no time taking a bus or taxi into town to sample the delights of the Orient, so very different from life back in Hartlepool or Arbroath.

Miss Venus Chong and the girls of the Happy Cabaret were there to oblige them. So too were the taxi dancers of the New World Cabaret. Liquor flowed. Thirty men had already found themselves in the Alexandra military hospital after a series of punch-ups with Australian troops and Gordon Highlanders from the garrison.

There had also been fights with jealous sailors from other ships. *Prince of Wales*'s captain had had to talk to his crew and warn them not to invite trouble while they were ashore.

It was different for the officers. A reception was held aboard *Prince of Wales* on the night of December 3. All of Singapore's dignitaries were invited—everyone from the governor and Lieutenant General Arthur Percival, the military commander, to journalists, local Muslim leaders, and the Sultan of Johore with his young European wife.

A bosun's whistle piped the guests aboard. The party was held on the forecastle under a canvas awning. White-uniformed stewards served drinks, discreetly topping up the glasses of those Muslims who enjoyed a tipple but preferred not to advertise the fact in public.

"There was a sound of revelry by night": Watching the young officers dancing to the Royal Marine band, Duff Cooper was reminded of Byron's line in *Childe Harold's Pilgrimage* about the Duchess of Richmond's ball in Brussels before the Battle of Waterloo.

Diana was struck by it too: "Brussels ball once again. We danced on the wide decks and quaffed toasts for victory, the red-and-white awnings flapless and everyone dressed overall and grinning with security. Tide turned, wind changed, and beneath my red-and-white dress my heart tolled."[8]

One guest wasn't dancing. Suermasa Okomoto was the Japanese consul-general in Singapore, an alert, bespectacled man in Western evening dress. Glancing casually around the ship, he was far more interested in *Prince of Wales*'s armaments than in idle chitchat with the other guests.

Ten 14-inch guns. Sixteen 5.25-inchers. Thirty-two pom-pom antiaircraft guns, eighty rocket projectors—*Prince of Wales* bristled with hardware.

So did *Repulse*, anchored not far away in the stream. Both ships were sleek with camouflage paint, ready to sail into action at a moment's notice.

Okomoto took it all in. He was in regular contact with Tokyo, reporting on the defenses of Singapore. He made a thorough inspection of the guns and all the new weaponry, not missing a thing as he looked around the ship.

His sailor hosts made sure that he didn't. They wanted him to note all the firepower and then report back to his masters with a message from Great Britain that was crystal clear in its content. Mess with the Royal Navy at your peril.

On the streets of Tokyo, loudspeakers were blaring as the military government broadcast martial music and called on the Japanese to prepare for war. European faces were few and far between as Caucasians remained indoors rather than risk attack.

British and Americans were leaving from Yokohama by the shipload. Those who hadn't gone yet could only hope that they would be treated properly by their Japanese captors, if war came before they too had a chance to get away.

At the Imperial Palace, surrounded by a moat in the heart of the city, Emperor Hirohito was struggling with his conscience as he waited for hostilities to begin. The emperor was not a warmonger. He had expressed his opposition to war on numerous occasions, once producing an antiwar poem written by his grandfather and reading it to a gathering of political and military leaders. He wasn't happy that his people were sleepwalking into a conflict that they couldn't possibly hope to win.

Hirohito was not alone in his concern. The Japanese navy did not want war either. The admirals knew that they must either win a battle with the United States in the first few months or lose in the end.

The country's civilian leaders concurred. Hirohito had summoned a meeting of ex–prime ministers at the end of November. He had gone around the table asking each of them in turn what they thought. Few had given a straight answer, but there had been no consensus for war.

The emperor's brother, Prince Takamatsu, was an officer in the navy. He too had counseled Hirohito against war. He had told the emperor that victory was by no means certain, despite assurances to the contrary.

Yet the army was determined to have a war. General Hideki Tojo had become prime minister in October after the previous incumbent had resigned rather than be a party to such folly. Tojo was convinced that the United States had moved its Pacific Fleet from San Diego to Hawaii in May 1940 because the Americans intended to attack at some point in the future, holding a dagger to Japan's throat. Hirohito was half persuaded that he might be right.

In Tojo's view the Americans wouldn't rest until they had forced the Japanese out of both China and Indochina. They would succeed, too, if their embargo on oil for the Chinese campaign continued for much longer.

If they succeeded, not only would the Japanese suffer a catastrophic loss of face, but their hold on Korea would be threatened as well. The Americans had to be stopped before they could inflict such a lasting humiliation on Japan. They were the enemy now.

The way to stop the Americans was clear to Tojo. A preemptive strike against their Pacific Fleet in Hawaii would put it out of action for at least six months. That would allow ample time for the Japanese to grab the British, Dutch, and American territories whose raw materials they needed for their war effort.

The Japanese would be impregnable by the time the Americans had recovered from the shock and were in a position to hit back. The Japanese would then be able to negotiate a peace settlement from a position of strength.

It was worth a shot, at any rate. The decision had already been taken. At an imperial council meeting on the afternoon of December 1, the emperor had sat on his dais in the east wing of the palace raising no objections while Tojo outlined the case for war. The emperor had then signed the formal document committing Japan to hostilities. The first attacks were scheduled for the morning of December 7 (December 8, Japanese time).

Hirohito remained dubious nevertheless. He felt that his hand was being forced by his military commanders. They were perfectly capable of staging a coup d'état if he stood in their way. They could assassinate him and install one of his brothers as a puppet on the throne. The army had attempted something similar in 1936. The ringleaders had been executed then, but that didn't mean that the army couldn't try again.

The problem was that the generals were much more assertive in making their case than were Japan's civilian leaders, as Hirohito afterward reflected: "I was faced with two sets of opinions. Those who wanted peace were rambling and indefinite about what was to be done. They really had no program, nor any helpful suggestions. Those who wanted war were positive and very strong."[9]

After much soul-searching, Hirohito had decided to go with the army, but he wasn't at all happy about the decision. He was just hoping that it would all work out as Tojo had planned.

While the emperor brooded, Admiral Isoroku Yamamoto, commander in chief of Japan's combined fleet, was on his way back from Tokyo to Miyajima, the shrine island in the Inland Sea near Hiroshima. He had been in the capital for an audience with the emperor, at which he had received his orders for the war. Now he was returning to his flagship, *Nagato*, in Hiroshima Bay. It was from *Nagato* that he intended to mastermind the attack on the American naval base in the Hawaiian Islands that would open hostilities with the United States.

Yamamoto had planned to fly back to Miyajima, but the weather was too bad for that, so he was traveling by train instead. The journey of several hundred miles allowed ample time to reflect on the folly of what was about to happen.

Yamamoto was one of the architects of the plan to attack Hawaii. It was a plan of great skill and daring that would deal the Americans a crippling blow if it was successful. But that didn't mean that Yamamoto wanted to launch a war against the United States.

He was a Harvard man, for a start, a highly educated officer who had attended naval conferences in London and twice served as naval attaché in Washington. He had a higher opinion of Americans than did many of his countrymen, who thought them corrupt and decadent. He was in no doubt that the Americans would fight back with everything they had if the Japanese were foolish enough to attack them without good reason.

Yamamoto had said as much in a letter frequently misquoted against him:

> If hostilities break out between Japan and the United States, it would not be enough that we take Guam and the Philippines, nor even Hawaii and San Francisco. To ensure victory, we would have to march into Washington and dictate the terms of peace in the White House. I wonder if our politicians (who speak so lightly of a Japanese-American war) are confident of the final outcome and are prepared to make the necessary sacrifices.[10]

Shorn of its last sentence, the letter implied overweening arrogance in Yamamoto, a man bent on occupying Washington and dictating Japan's terms to the United States at the point of a gun. In fact he was deeply opposed to a war with the United States, or anyone else either.

Yamamoto had openly deplored Japan's invasion of Manchuria in 1931, the war with China, and the 1940 Tripartite Pact with Italy and Germany. His pacifism had made him so unpopular with Japan's militant nationalists that he received regular death threats in the mail and was a target for assassination.

He had also made an enemy of Prime Minister Tojo. At one point the army had put a guard on Yamamoto, ostensibly for his own protection but in fact just to keep an eye on him. The navy had responded by sending Yamamoto to sea, where he would be safe from assassination. A few militants apart, he was very popular in the navy, perfectly secure among his own kind.

But old enmities had been forgotten as Japan prepared for war. The army and navy were on the same side now that the decision had been taken. Whatever his personal misgivings, Yamamoto was in no doubt that an attack on the American fleet in the Hawaiian Islands could be an outstanding success if it was carried out immediately after the declaration of war, before the Americans had a chance to react.

As his train rattled toward Miyajima, Isoroku Yamamoto had even managed to convince himself that an attack on Hawaii might somehow prove to be "the Waterloo of the war to follow."[11] The admiral certainly hoped so, at any rate.

About 3,500 miles to the east, the weather in the vast emptiness of the Pacific Ocean had turned rough. It was so bad that the destroyers leading the Japanese strike force toward Hawaii were pitching and rolling as much as forty-five degrees in the swell. Men were being washed overboard in the heavy seas, but there was no rescue for them. The task force couldn't afford to stop, now that the decision to proceed with the attack had been made.

The Japanese navy had come a long way in the eighty-eight years since Commodore Perry's squadron had anchored in Tokyo Bay in 1853. Jeering at barefoot Japanese in sampans, Perry's Americans had trained their guns on shore and refused an order to leave Japanese waters at once.

Escorted by several hundred men and a band playing *Hail, Columbia*, Perry had gone ashore instead with a letter from the president of the United States. It was addressed to the emperor of Japan and requested the opening up of the country to American trade and commerce. Perry had made it quite clear to the Japanese that the United States would not take no for an answer.

At the end of his visit, according to Japanese sources, he had presented them with a white flag, telling them that they would need it if they did not do as they were told: "Victory will naturally be ours, and you shall by no means overcome us. If in such a situation you seek for a reconciliation, you should put up the white flag that we have recently presented to you, and we would accordingly stop firing and conclude peace with you, turning our battleships aside."[12]

Despite their outrage, the Japanese had been forced to give in. They had never forgotten the insult. Nearly a century later, the loss of face at the hands of contemptuous Americans still rankled.

But the boot was on the other foot now. Japanese soldiers no longer carried bows and arrows, as they had when Perry's marines came ashore. Their sailors were no longer barefoot natives in sampans. They were as sophisticated and well trained as any sailors in the world.

The strike force made a formidable sight as it headed for American waters. It stretched across the waves almost to the horizon. The destroyers at the head of the fleet were followed at a distance by no fewer than six aircraft carriers in parallel lines, each with a full complement of attack aircraft.

Heavy cruisers protected the strike force's flanks. Battleships covered the rear. There were supply ships, too, oil tankers and support vessels of all kinds. The Japanese were the ones with the firepower now.

The force was scheduled to refuel soon, taking on oil from the tankers at a prearranged spot in the middle of nowhere. The weather was too bad for that at the moment, so the rendezvous had been postponed for twenty-four hours at least.

Once the refueling was complete, the Japanese were due to continue southeast before beginning their final approach toward the islands of Hawaii. They were aiming specifically for the volcanic island of Oahu. The Americans kept their Pacific Fleet there, in a landlocked basin at Pearl Harbor.

THREE

ALL QUIET IN THE PACIFIC

The weather in the Pacific was much calmer next morning, December 5. The sky was still cloudy, but the wind had eased overnight. The swell was no rougher than normal as USS *Nevada* came in toward Pearl Harbor after a routine few days at sea.

The battleship's crew was looking forward to arriving. Friday night in port meant shore leave for most of them, a liberty pass to the bright lights of Honolulu, just a few miles away along the coast. Saturday was the big night of the week in Hawaii's capital, but Friday night was when the weekend began. *Nevada*'s crew had earned a break after all their hard work at sea.

First, though, they had to reach port without mishap. The entrance channel to Pearl Harbor was very narrow, less than four hundred yards wide at one point. It was protected by a torpedo net that could be opened to allow ships in and out. There wasn't much room for the ships to maneuver in the shallow waters.

The gate in the net had already been opened to admit *Nevada*, but the ship didn't enter harbor at once. Priority had been given to the departure at 8:00 a.m. of Task Force 12, a squadron of warships clustered around USS *Lexington*, America's mightiest aircraft carrier.

Nevada hove to accordingly and waited outside for an hour while the task force left harbor. As well as the carrier, there were three heavy cruisers and five destroyers, all heading out to sea for what the crews had been told was a routine training exercise. Together the ships made a formidable sight as they cleared the channel one by one and sallied forth into the wider reaches of Mamala Bay.

The most formidable sight of all was *Lexington*, the pride of the Pacific Fleet. Originally designed as a battle cruiser, "Lady Lex" was almost nine hundred feet long, capable of carrying more than a hundred aircraft, including spares. *Lexington* was one of the most magnificent ships in the U.S. Navy.

Nevada slipped in behind the departing vessels and made port safely. The task force continued out to sea. It was not immediately clear where the ships were going, if indeed they were going anywhere in particular. With so many spying eyes in Hawaii, it was standard practice for U.S. warships to wait until they were out of sight of land before spinning the wheel and setting a course for their true destination.

The task force had been at sea for a couple of hours when a flight of American aircraft appeared over the waves and nosed down toward *Lexington*'s flat-topped deck. Eighteen Vindicator dive-bombers landed in quick succession to join the sixty-five aircraft already on board. They were followed at 11:00 a.m. by a squadron of fighter planes, eighteen Brewster Buffalos equipped with arrester hooks.

Seventeen of the Buffalos landed safely. The eighteenth came in too high, missed the deck arresting wires, and slammed heavily into the barrier farther along. The pilot escaped with cuts to his face, but his machine took a beating. It clearly wouldn't fly again before *Lexington* returned to port.

With space at a premium, the damaged aircraft was a liability on board. The deck was already too cluttered with all the extra aircraft *Lexington* was carrying. It was the work of a moment to dump the Buffalo over the side to allow more room for all the other aircraft that were still airworthy.

Lexington gathered speed again as soon as the remaining aircraft had been secured. The task force assumed formation and set off in earnest. It was heading for a point southeast of Midway Island, fourteen hundred miles to the west, to reinforce the defenses there.

With a Japanese attack imminent somewhere in the Pacific, it was only prudent to move fighters and bombers forward, where they were most likely to be needed. The aircraft would be better placed to counter any threat from Midway, so much closer to Japan.

The carrier USS *Enterprise* had been sent to Wake Island on a similar mission. Moving both carriers forward made perfect sense to the Americans, but the Japanese would have been greatly alarmed if they had known what was happening.

Why would the United States move attack aircraft toward Japan if they did not intend to attack? All the more reason for Japan to strike first and sink the American aircraft carriers in Pearl Harbor before they could do the Japanese navy any serious damage.

While the task force slipped out of port, a man calling himself Tadashi Morimura watched from a few hundred yards away to the north. He was careful not to write anything down, but he missed nothing as *Lexington* put to sea. With the help of the reference book *Jane's Fighting Ships* and a good memory, he knew exactly which American warships were leaving harbor. It was his job to record their movements and report them to his spymasters in Tokyo.

Morimura had been in Oahu since the end of March. Ostensibly he was a junior official at the Japanese consulate on Nuuana Avenue. In reality he was a spy, Admiral Yamamoto's principal eyes and ears on the island. His consular duties were simply a cover for his clandestine activities as Japan prepared for war with the United States.

Morimura's real name was Takeo Yoshikawa. He was twenty-nine years old, a former trainee pilot with the Japanese navy. Invalided out of the service with a stomach condition, he had been recruited as a spy instead and posted to the consulate in Honolulu. He had spent the last eight months familiarizing himself with every army, navy, and air force base in the Hawaiian Islands against the day that the information would be needed when war became inevitable.

Yoshikawa's colleagues at the consulate knew nothing of his spying activities. To them he was just an idle young man, often too lazy to return to work after lunch. He preferred to spend his afternoons driving around the islands instead, like a tourist.

Yoshikawa also spent hours lazing at a Japanese teahouse on Alewa Heights. The place was staffed with pretty girls and had a wonderful view of Pearl Harbor from the front windows. Everything from Ford Island to Hickam Field was plainly visible from the heights, all laid out in a panorama below. The teahouse even kept a telescope for guests wanting to have a closer look.

Sometimes Yoshikawa took a girl with him and went for a trip on a glass-bottomed boat. He pretended to enjoy the underwater tour of Kanoehe Bay, on the other side of the island, which the Americans were said to be considering as an alternative anchorage for their fleet. In reality he estimated the depth of the bay at various points and concluded that it was too shallow for large warships.

He also attended an open day at Wheeler Airbase, noting that three aircraft could take off simultaneously, which meant that fighter squadrons could become airborne relatively quickly. He twice took a tourist flight over Oahu with a geisha girl as cover. Yoshikawa used the first flight to note the direction of the runways at Wheeler and estimate the number of aircraft there by counting the quantity of hangars.

His second flight, on October 13, had confirmed that the Americans were not dispersing their fleet around other anchorages on the island, as Tokyo had speculated. Fearing sabotage from the local Japanese population, the Americans preferred to keep their ships, like their aircraft, close together in one place for better protection.

Yoshikawa's information wasn't always accurate, but he was an effective spy nonetheless. While monitoring U.S. Navy messages in Tokyo, he had received a personal letter of thanks from Adolf Hitler for alerting the Germans to a British troop convoy that subsequently suffered heavy losses.

He was always careful not to arouse suspicion in his work or do anything to draw the attention of the authorities to himself. Nevertheless the Americans had been onto him from the start. He was clearly too young for his diplomatic responsibilities at the consulate. There was no Tadashi

Morimura listed in the Japanese diplomatic register. As a consequence the Americans had tailed him for months, but had never managed to pin anything on him that could lead to his arrest and expulsion from the islands.

Yoshikawa knew nothing of the Japanese plan to attack Pearl Harbor as he watched *Lexington*'s departure that morning, but it did not take a genius to put two and two together. On September 24 the Japanese Foreign Ministry had asked the Honolulu consulate to divide the waters of the harbor into five separate areas and report back on the number and location of warships in each. The ministry had been particularly interested to know the number of battleships moored together in the stream, side by side.

Much more recently, on December 2, Tokyo had sent this message:

In view of the present situation, the presence in port of warships, airplane carriers, and cruisers is of utmost importance. Hereafter, to the utmost of your ability, let me know day by day. Wire me in each case whether or not there are any observation balloons above Pearl Harbor or if there are any indications that they will be sent up. Also advise me whether or not the warships are provided with anti-mine nets.[1]

It could hardly have been clearer that an attack on Pearl Harbor was being considered, even if no decision had been taken.

Knowing what might be about to happen, Yoshikawa watched *Lexington*'s departure with considerable concern. There were now no aircraft carriers left in harbor as the weekend approached. It was normal for two if not all three of the U.S. Pacific carriers to be in Pearl Harbor for the weekend. Most unusually, however, all three were now at sea, at large somewhere on a very wide ocean.

Yoshikawa noted *Nevada*'s arrival after the task force's departure. He stayed to watch as two more battleships arrived later in the day, routinely returning to base for the weekend. Then he hurried back to Honolulu and went to transmit the details to Tokyo.

———

Yoshikawa was not Japan's only spy in Honolulu. Tokyo had another agent, a German national named Bernard Kühn. He was not an active spy, however. He was a sleeper, paid to remain dormant for years until he was needed.

Kühn had served in the German navy during World War I. After an undistinguished postwar career, he had joined the Nazi Party in 1930. He had become friends with SS Reichsführer Heinrich Himmler, who had found him a job in the Gestapo. His son Leopold had become private secretary to Joseph Goebbels.

Kühn's daughter Ruth had outdone them both by becoming Goebbels's mistress at the age of seventeen. She had fallen for the Reichsminister's charm and intelligence, as many women did. It wasn't only actresses eager to further their careers who found Hitler's right-hand man attractive. His club foot somehow merely added to the allure.

But Ruth Kühn had been only seventeen, far too young to become Goebbels's plaything. The affair had quickly become public, adding to the embarrassment. Seeking a way out, Goebbels had learned that the Japanese needed some European faces for their espionage operations. His secretary Leopold had suggested that the rest of the family would make ideal candidates.

The Kühns had moved to Hawaii in 1936, ostensibly for Kühn to study Japanese at the University of Hawaii. He had also started a furniture business and attempted a career in real estate without success. His wife had done better, opening a beauty parlor in Honolulu with her daughter. American wives from all three services had their hair done there, chattering indiscreetly while Mrs. Kühn kept a low profile and said nothing.

The Kühns' daughter, now in her twenties, had also gone out with a succession of American officers desperate for European companionship. Their younger son, Hans, had been only ten when his father first dressed him in a sailor suit and took him for walks along the waterfront. Friendly officers invited the boy aboard their warships, answering all the questions his father had primed him to ask. Kühn himself wisely remained ashore.

His job in Hawaii was to replace Yoshikawa after the outbreak of war.

As a Japanese diplomat, Yoshikawa would be repatriated with the rest of the consulate once hostilities had begun. The plan was for Kühn to move seamlessly into his place, a harmless neutral monitoring all the air and sea movements around Hawaii as the war progressed, and reporting back to Tokyo for cash.

In preparation for his role, Kühn had been given a portable radio transmitter that fitted into a suitcase and had a range of one hundred miles. If war started, he was to send messages to Japanese submarines off Oahu. They would relay his messages to Japan.

Kühn had also just devised a complex system for signaling the movements of American warships in and out of Pearl Harbor. The system comprised everything from cryptic advertisements on local radio to flashing headlights and a yacht rigged up with a star on the sail.

According to the code that Kühn had drawn up, a light shining from the dormer windows of his house between 9:00 and 10:00 p.m. would mean that an aircraft carrier had sailed. A sheet on the clothesline at his beachfront property in Lanikai would indicate that a whole task force had left harbor.

The Japanese at the consulate had been unimpressed by the first draft of the code, which seemed far too elaborate and complex to them. They had told Kühn to go away and simplify it. They were paying him two thousand dollars a month for his services, with big cash bonuses as well, but they had their doubts about his potential as a spy. He seemed far too nervous and amateurish to them.

The Americans had doubts about Kühn too. After his initial business failures, he appeared to have no visible means of support beyond his wife's beauty parlor, yet was still living very comfortably, with two houses on Oahu. The Americans had concluded early in 1939 that "Fritz" Kühn was probably a spy of some kind, working for Japan or Germany or both. They had classified him as a Class A Nazi suspect in July 1940.

Crucially, however, the Americans had done nothing to follow up their suspicions. Hampered in part by peacetime regulations that discouraged excessive snooping, they had not caught Kühn breaking any laws. He had slipped below the radar as the authorities lost interest in him after a while and turned their attention elsewhere.

All that was about to change as Kühn prepared for active service. For reasons that remain unclear, he had recently decided to abandon his sleeper status as war approached. Against all the rules, he had been down to the U.S. Navy Yard at the end of November to scout out the fleet. He had then gone openly to the Japanese consulate to deliver a revised copy of his code and a list of ships in the fleet, which the Japanese knew from their own sources was largely fictitious.

They suspected that Kühn had plucked the figures out of the air rather than risk his neck to get a more accurate picture. He was happy to take their money, in the consulate's opinion, but he lacked the nerve for more dangerous assignments.

Worse than that, Kühn would probably compromise the Japanese by breaking down and confessing everything if the Americans ever arrested him. He wasn't the sort of man to hold out for long. He didn't know it yet, but the Japanese had decided to use him only as a last resort from now on.

On King Street, in the heart of downtown Honolulu, machine-gun posts had just been set up around the railroad station connecting the city to the sugar fields. Others had been established in the clock tower of Kawaiahaʻo Church, known to the islanders as Hawaii's Westminster Abbey. Several more had been placed around the city at strategic locations vulnerable to a Japanese attack.

The guns didn't point out to sea, from where an attack might be expected to come. They pointed along the street instead. The Americans were not expecting trouble from the sea. They were far more worried about an attack from the indigenous Japanese, the Americans with Asian faces who already lived on the island.

There were about 160,000 Japanese in Hawaii, according to the figures, very nearly 40 percent of the population. The vast majority were patriotic Americans, albeit deeply distrusted by the authorities. There were so many of them that the islands would quickly be overwhelmed if ever they turned against the United States.

Most of the Japanese had arrived in Hawaii toward the end of the nineteenth century. The islands had been annexed by the United States in 1898, after which big business had tightened its already strong grip. The Japanese had come to work on the sugar plantations. They had swiftly put down roots in all directions.

Older Japanese, the ones who had been born in Japan, still retained dual nationality under Japanese law, as did their children. The older generation kept up their links with the homeland and often bought Japanese war bonds to fund the war in China, just as Irish Americans once saw no harm in financing the IRA. These Japanese were known as *issei* in Hawaii.

Their children, born in the islands, were known as Nisei. The Nisei, whether born in Hawaii or on the West Coast of the United States, were Americans through and through. They chewed gum, saluted the flag, and entertained impure thoughts about cheerleaders like their counterparts anywhere else in America. The Nisei acknowledged their heritage, but often refused to speak the language at home or wear Japanese clothes at traditional Japanese ceremonies. They were Americans before they were anything else.

If white Americans feared an uprising by the local Japanese population, they had only themselves to blame. They had not behaved well toward the Japanese during the previous half century. The same racial mindset that bedeviled the American South also prevailed in the sugar plantations. The Japanese were no better than Negroes, in the eyes of the overseers.

The authorities had been wary of them ever since Japan's surprise defeat of Russia in 1905. The U.S. government had poured money into Pearl Harbor thereafter, building it up as a bulwark against Japanese expansion in the Pacific.

The Americans had also implemented a number of anti-Japanese laws in the 1920s. They had banned immigration, prohibited Japanese from owning land in many states, and prevented them from marrying whites or becoming naturalized citizens. They had actively discouraged Japanese schools as well, insisting that Japanese children should turn their backs on their own culture and assimilate as one nation under the American flag.

No surprise, then, that many white Americans distrusted the Japanese they had treated so shabbily. They were particularly suspicious of the

Japanese-manned fishing fleet that somehow always seemed to be working near U.S. warships whenever anything interesting was going on. It was only fear of alienating an already unhappy population that had stopped them from making large-scale arrests.

What would have surprised the Americans, if they had known about it, was that Takeo Yoshikawa at the consulate didn't trust the Japanese either. The locals should have been natural allies, but very few of them were, from what he could see. The ones who worked in the cane fields were too stupid to be of any help. More intelligent ones were in no doubt where their loyalties lay, as he afterward complained: "Those men of influence and character who might have assisted me in my secret mission were unanimously uncooperative."[2]

The Japanese on Hawaii weren't America's enemy. Some certainly had divided loyalties, but very few were anti-American. An exception was one of Daniel Inouye's teachers. Later a combat soldier and U.S. senator, Inouye remembered the man telling his pupils in 1939: "When Japan calls, you must know that it is Japanese blood that flows in your veins."[3]

The vast majority disagreed. They shared the view of Masato Doi's father. Asked what the family should do if war broke out between Japan and the United States, he had reminded his son that he had grown up American, not Japanese. "You were brought up by this country," he had pointed out.[4] The Doi family had no obligations to anyone else.

Tens of thousands of Nisei felt the same. The Hawaiian branch of the Future Farmers of America had just spent three thousand dollars of mainly Japanese money to buy U.S. Defense Bonds as a patriotic gesture. And at Kukaiau Japanese School that Friday night, Tadayuki Kato, Toyoko Hamatake, and Yasuko Enomoto were preparing their speeches for a debating competition to be held in both English and Japanese the following evening. The theme of the debate was patriotism.

At Schofield Barracks, in the center of Oahu, the troops were winding down for the weekend. Friday afternoon was the end of the working week for most of them. The officers were planning to spend the next two days playing bridge or golf, socializing at the officers' club, or taking their wives and girl-friends to the beach. The men were going to hit Honolulu.

Schofield was probably the most beautiful barracks in the U.S. Army. It was a sprawling complex of several square miles, elegantly laid out amid tropical palms and flowing green lawns. The accommodation blocks, comparatively new, were arranged in giant quadrangles that allowed everyone plenty of room to breathe.

The rest of Schofield had all the facilities of a small American town, with a lovely view of Mt. Kaala and Kolekole Pass toward the west. There were few more pleasant places for a man to be a soldier in the sleepy peacetime army of the United States.

Despite all the comforts, though, including the cushy job that he had wangled for himself as an assistant company clerk, Private James Jones of the U.S. infantry was not a happy man that Friday as he prepared for the weekend. Never comfortable with military life, Jones had become increasingly disillusioned as time wore on. He was in the army because he needed a job, but that didn't mean that he had to like it.

Jones's ambition in life was to become a writer. Part Cherokee but mostly of Welsh ancestry, he had hitchhiked to Canada late in 1939, intending to join the Canadian army and have a crack at the Germans, as his father had before him. There was bound to be a book in it if the Canadians sent him to Europe to fight the Wehrmacht.

The Canadians hadn't wanted a puny seventeen-year-old with glasses, so Jones had joined the U.S. Army Air Corps instead. If he couldn't fight the Nazis in Europe, he could at least become an American pilot. His eyesight was too bad for that, too, so he had transferred to the infantry a few months after his arrival on Oahu.

Unfortunately the infantry suited him no better. Jones came from a different background than the rest of the enlisted men. Very few of them had finished high school, but it was only lack of money that had prevented him from going to college.

Jones's grandfather had been a rich man after discovering oil on his farm in Illinois, but the money had all been lost during the Depression. There had been no question of college after his parents had been forced to sell their home and move to a rented place instead. Jones felt the loss of social status keenly. He particularly resented the deep divide between enlisted men and officers in the army and regarded himself as "better bred than any of these moronic sergeants."[5]

He was certainly more intelligent than they were. Jones was happy to get drunk with his fellow dogfaces and go whoring with them whenever he had any money, but he preferred to keep to himself as often as not. He spent a lot of time in the camp library, where he had just discovered the works of Thomas Wolfe.

Wolfe was the kind of writer Jones wanted to be. Better than Shakespeare, in his opinion. He would be a happy man if he could ever write books as good as Wolfe's.

Jones had already had an idea for a novel, a half-formed tale about soldiers with venereal disease. It was based on his own experience in a military hospital, where patients with gonorrhea had been treated little better than cattle. He hadn't gotten around to writing it yet, but the idea was still there, fermenting away in the back of his mind.

What he had done instead of a full-length novel was write his first poems and short stories at Schofield. He was sending them off to magazines on the mainland, but hadn't managed to sell anything so far. Everything came back to him with a rejection slip, if it came back at all.

Jones wasn't downhearted, though. All writing begins with rejection. He was finding it difficult to come up with ideas in his barrack block, surrounded by people who were barely literate, so he had decided to work in the orderly room instead. "Now that I'm a clerk in the orderly room, I've been spending all my spare time in there, writing. I have full access to the place, and it's a good place to write: no one can come in and bother me, and I can stay there all night, if I choose."[6]

A desk, a typewriter. Pens, paper, peace, quiet. Private Jones had almost everything he needed in the orderly room to write the great American novel.

The only thing he still didn't have, as the sunlight streamed through the window that Friday evening, was the one he needed most of all: a good subject. History does not record whether Private Jones sucked the end of his pen as he peered out of the window, but authors often do when they're waiting hopelessly for inspiration to strike.

In Honolulu the girls of the red-light district were preparing for Friday night. Every night was busy in the red-light district, but Fridays and Saturdays were the busiest of all. With so many men on Oahu and so few loose women, the area of Chinatown between River, Kukui, Beretania, and Nuuanu Streets never stopped thrumming from dusk until dawn.

There were around twenty brothels in the red-light district, with maybe two hundred girls in all. In theory, the brothels were illegal. In practice, they were tolerated, provided that strict rules were observed. With so many unattached servicemen on Oahu, there was nothing else the authorities could do.

Most of the girls were American, white women from the mainland. Like Sadie Thompson in Somerset Maugham's short story "Rain," they were procured in San Francisco and went back there after a stint on the islands. Meantime they were rushed off their feet, in more ways than one. Some of them were said to be handling a hundred men a day.

Sailors were the biggest customers, drunkenly celebrating their return to port. At peak times there were so many white hats in the red-light district that the line would stretch out of the door and into the street. The sailors were a nuisance, blocking the pavement while they waited their turn, but they would have been even more of a nuisance if they had been roaming around Honolulu instead, roaring drunk with nowhere else to go.

Soldiers were good customers, too, as were the thousands of bachelor Filipinos who had come to Oahu to work in the cane fields. The Americans didn't like to go with girls who went with natives, so the Filipinos and other nonwhites had their own entrances to the brothels and their own waiting rooms, where white men wouldn't see them. The destination was always the same, however, once they had paid the entry fee.

The girls charged the locals two dollars for their services, a full day's wages on the sugar plantations. They charged American servicemen three dollars, which was why James Jones and others like him were always broke.

Jones's favorite whorehouse was the New Senator Hotel. It stood next door to the Wu Fat Chinese restaurant on Hotel Street. Jones scarcely bothered to disguise either of them in his novel *From Here to Eternity*:

> *They came up the lightless stairs of the New Congress Hotel, very dark now after the brightly lighted, almost deserted Hotel Street outside, feeling their way half-drunkenly carefully. They had just left the small bar in the downstairs part of Wu Fat's brightly tropically decorated restaurant next door, and now they carried with them, suddenly, all the unmentionable, unspeakable, pride destroying heart shakiness and throat thickness and breath chokiness of men about to mount women, the same attributes displayed so shamelessly by all the male dogs on the Post as they chased down alleys after reluctant bitches.*[7]

It was all rigorously controlled by the authorities. There were no streetwalkers in Honolulu, and very few pimps. Girls arriving from San Francisco were photographed and fingerprinted as soon as they came ashore.

In the days before penicillin, they were also subjected to a Wassermann test to check for syphilis before they were allowed to work. They had a weekly medical examination thereafter. Venereal disease had been a problem in Hawaii ever since the arrival of Captain Cook and the Royal Navy, but the incidence among U.S. service personnel was astonishingly low.

The control was overdone, in the opinion of the girls. According to the rules, they were not allowed to "visit Waikiki Beach, patronize any bars or better-class cafés, own property or an automobile, have a steady boyfriend, marry service personnel, attend dances, ride in the front seat of a taxi with a man in the back, wire money to the mainland, telephone the mainland without the madam's permission, change from one house to another, or be out of the brothel after 10:30 at night."[8]

The girls couldn't go to the theater either, or visit bowling alleys or golf courses. They weren't allowed to ride bicycles or have any recreation other than an occasional supervised outing. The only beach they were allowed on was at Kailua.

But business was booming nevertheless. For the first time since July, all the Pacific Fleet's battleships were in port that Friday night. Too slow to escort the various aircraft carriers at sea, the nation's largest capital ships had instead been confined to Pearl Harbor for the weekend. They were moored in pairs along Battleship Row.

The crews would be coming ashore soon, thousands of unattached young men, all spruced up for a night on the town. A few drinks later and they would be climbing the stairs to the New Senator, the Rex Rooms, the Service Hotel, and all the other whorehouses east of King Street. Time soon for the girls to stub out their cigarettes, put on their fake smiles, and go to work.

FOUR

JAPANESE FORCES ON THE MOVE

Out in the Pacific, the ships of the Japanese strike force were refueling. The operation took most of the day and was fraught with difficulty. There was an ever-present danger of fuel lines jackknifing across the deck and washing men overboard if they were caught off guard.

When the refueling was complete, three of the strike force's eight oil tankers veered off with an accompanying destroyer and made their way toward a prearranged rendezvous point to await the force's return from Pearl Harbor. The crews cheered one another in a ceremonial farewell as the tankers left.

The rest of the strike force picked up speed again, glad to be on the move once more. There was an increased danger of being spotted when the fleet reduced speed to take on fuel. The plan was for a formal declaration of war on the United States on December 7, to be followed immediately by an attack on Pearl Harbor before the Americans had a chance to respond. It depended on complete surprise for success.

The route to the Hawaiian Islands had been carefully chosen with surprise in mind. Very few ships sailed that part of the Pacific. The Japanese were hoping to proceed unseen and unnoticed, catching the Americans with their pants down on Sunday morning, when golf and a trip to the beach were the priorities for the rest of the weekend.

The Japanese were not pleased, therefore, when a ship appeared on the horizon, probably on December 5, the same day as the three tankers left. It was apparently a freighter of some kind, heading the other way across the Pacific from the United States toward the Soviet Union.

The ship may have been the *Uritsky*, or the *Uzbekistan* or the *Azerbaijan*. Whatever its provenance (the incident was long denied by the Japanese and the details remain obscure), the ship could hardly have failed to notice six aircraft carriers, two battleships, two cruisers, nine destroyers, and a host of support vessels heading across the Pacific toward Hawaii. The crew would have been blind if they hadn't.

Their presence posed a dilemma for the Japanese. One radio message from the freighter and the Americans would be alerted to the strike force's existence, not to mention its course and speed. The secret would be out.

The Japanese had foreseen the risk of being spotted. The orders for Vice-Admiral Chuichi Nagumo, the strike force's commander, had been carefully thought out before the force set sail. They were quite explicit in their instructions.

If the force was seen at any time before December 6 (Japanese time), Nagumo was to turn around and go home. If they were spotted on the sixth, he was free to use his own judgment. If spotted on the seventh, he was to press on and attack anyway.

As arranged, Nagumo used his judgment. If he did see a freighter on the horizon, he decided to ignore it. The strike force pushed on instead.

As a precaution, though, the Japanese began to listen to Hawaiian radio as soon as they were close enough to tune in. If anybody had seen them and raised the alarm, Hawaii's commercial radio stations would surely interrupt their programs with a newsflash to give warning of an attack.

The Japanese kept listening, but no news flashes came. The music of station KGMB played on, its soft Hawaiian melodies undisturbed by any dramatic announcements. If the Americans had wind of an impending assault on their islands and were preparing to defend themselves, nobody was saying so on air.

While the strike force headed for Pearl Harbor, other Japanese ships were also on the move, sailing in different directions across the Gulf of Thailand and the South China Sea.

One force had set out from the Chinese island of Hainan, steaming south along the coast of Vietnam (known then as French Indochina). The force had been joined off Cam Ranh Bay by further warships and backup vessels. Together the combined fleet had continued south past the rest of Vietnam before turning west toward Malaya and the Gulf of Thailand.

The ships were still in the South China Sea when they were spotted by a reconnaissance aircraft of the Royal Australian Air Force, operating at the extreme limit of its range. The Japanese launched a seaplane to intercept it, but without success. Australian aircraft were able to report back that a total of one battleship, seven cruisers, seven destroyers, and forty-six transport ships, almost certainly carrying troops, were heading in the general direction of Malaya or Thailand. The convoys clearly posed a threat to someone.

The question was, who? Japan wasn't at war with Great Britain, so Malaya was theoretically safe. Winston Churchill had promised British help if the Japanese attacked Thailand, but they hadn't struck there either. They hadn't struck anywhere yet.

The British had little option, therefore, but to put their Malayan forces on full alert and await developments. They weren't happy about it, but there was nothing else they could do.

As well as operating at extreme range, their aircraft were hampered by the monsoon, which was blowing in full force. The rain made it difficult to keep track of the Japanese as they sailed around Cambodia Point into the Gulf of Thailand. Having spotted the convoys early, the British then lost sight of them for a long time, searching frantically through the murk for a sight of the warships far below.

While the search continued, other Japanese forces were preparing to strike elsewhere. One task force was heading for Batan Island and Luzon, at the northern end of the American-held Philippines. Another was poised to hit the British territory of Hong Kong, just across the water from mainland China.

If they all struck at once, at the same time as the attack on Pearl Harbor, the Japanese would have complete surprise, right across the Pacific. They would have the British and the Americans exactly where they wanted them. But everything depended on surprise. All sorts of things could go wrong for the Japanese if they didn't have surprise when they attacked.

In Washington, President Roosevelt was well aware that Japanese forces were on the move, likely to attack somewhere within the next few days. The problem for him, as for the British, was exactly whom they were going to attack, and where, and when.

The Japanese had been putting out a variety of false signals to throw people off the scent. For the past week their radio messages had been full of chatter suggesting that the bulk of the Japanese navy was still in home waters around the Inland Sea. Anyone listening in would have been forgiven for assuming that the Japanese navy was comfortably at peace with itself, posing no threat of any kind to anyone else.

The Americans weren't fooled. Among other things, they had managed to crack some of the Japanese codes and were far better informed than they let on. Yet they remained in the dark as to the Japanese navy's real intentions. All they knew for sure was that something was definitely up.

Captain John Beardall, the U.S. Navy's aide to the president, had just said as much in a meeting with Roosevelt at the White House. While showing FDR the intercepts of secret Japanese messages, he had drawn attention to one message in particular.

Dated December 2, 1941, but not decoded until later, the message was from the Japanese government to its embassies and consulates in Washington, Portland, Seattle, Los Angeles, Honolulu, Ottawa, Vancouver, Havana, and Panama. It ordered the destruction of various code books, ciphers, message files, secret documents, and coding machines.

The implications were obvious. The Japanese were about to start a war somewhere in the Pacific. There could hardly be a more innocent explanation.

"When do you think it will happen?" asked the president.

"Most any time," Beardall replied.[1]

There was also the much-disputed winds code, an arrangement that the Japanese had recently put in place for signaling an outbreak of hostilities to their various embassies around the world. According to U.S. code breakers, a message would be hidden in the daily Japanese weather forecast immediately before war began. The words "East wind rain" would mean an imminent break with the United States. "West wind clear" would signal a break with Great Britain, probably including the invasion of Thailand. "North wind cloudy" spelled trouble for the Soviet Union.

Not surprisingly, the Americans had been taking a keen interest in Japanese weather forecasts, with results that have remained shrouded in mystery ever since. A U.S. Navy radioman claimed to have logged the words *Higashi no kaze ame* (east wind rain) on December 4 before transmitting them to the Fleet Intelligence Office at Pearl Harbor.

An officer at Pearl Harbor then claimed to have passed the message to Washington, where everyone denied receiving it. Questioned after the war, the Japanese denied ever having sent the message at all.

Whatever the truth, the arrangements for sending such a message were definitely in place, and that was enough for Roosevelt. It meant that the U.S. economic sanctions against Japan were beginning to bite. Instead of responding sensibly by abandoning their adventure in China, as the Americans wanted them to, the Japanese were planning to escalate the war instead, perhaps as a way of saving face.

Where, though? Against whom? And to what end? With all the resources that were his to command, President Roosevelt had no better idea than anyone else as to which way the Japanese were about to jump.

A letter dictated by him on the morning of December 5 summed up his dilemma. The letter was to Wendell Willkie, the Republican candidate whom Roosevelt had defeated in the 1940 presidential election. Willkie was now an ambassador at large, about to visit Australia and New Zealand on Roosevelt's behalf.

The president wanted to brief him about Japan before he set out: "The situation is definitely serious and there might be an armed clash at any moment if the Japanese continue their forward progress against the Philippines, Dutch Indies or Malaya or Burma. Perhaps the next four or five days will decide the matter."[2]

Roosevelt was right about the next few days being decisive. Right too about Japan's intentions toward the Philippines, the Dutch East Indies, Malaya, and Burma. But that was only the half of it, as he and the rest of the United States were about to find out.

At the Japanese Embassy on Massachusetts Avenue, Ambassador Kichisaburō Nomura and his staff were probably as much in the dark as Roosevelt as to what was going to happen next. Japanese diplomats in Washington were no more in favor of war than was Admiral Yamamoto. By their own account, they had no idea that hostilities were about to commence, although they must surely have had their suspicions.

Nomura was a retired admiral who had served as naval attaché in Washington as a younger man. More recently he had been Japan's foreign secretary. After becoming ambassador in November 1940, he had repeatedly urged his superiors in Tokyo to make concessions to the Americans, enough at least to get the oil embargo lifted, but without success. Tojo's government had no interest in placating the United States.

Nevertheless Tojo had recently sent a career diplomat to Washington to assist Nomura in his negotiations. Saburō Kurusu had married an American woman while serving as Japan's consul in Chicago during World War I. Billed now as the Japanese government's "special envoy," he had arrived in Washington on November 15 and had met President Roosevelt two days later.

Kurusu had asked Roosevelt to stop sending aid to China and to resume the trade relations with Japan that had been frozen since 1940. In response Roosevelt had asked Japan to withdraw all its troops from China, adding that Japan must also sever its tripartite links with Italy and Germany. Roosevelt had made it clear that normal relations could never be resumed unless the Japanese complied.

His officials had gently suggested that peace on American terms had to be better than no peace at all. But the American idea of peace seemed more like an ultimatum to Kurusu: "If this is the attitude of the American Government, I don't see how an agreement is possible. Tokyo will throw up its hands at this."[3]

Kurusu had forwarded Roosevelt's proposals to Tokyo without enthusiasm. He was still awaiting a reply. Negotiations were continuing also with Cordell Hull, the U.S. secretary of state, but again without much conviction. Nobody was optimistic anymore. The opposing positions were far too entrenched for that.

The only remaining hope lay in President Roosevelt's personal appeal to Emperor Hirohito over the heads of the Tojo government. The wording of the appeal was still under consideration. One version was far more conciliatory toward the Japanese than the other. Roosevelt had yet to decide which of the messages to send.

The idea for an appeal to the emperor probably came from Kurusu. According to Gwen Terasaki, the Tennessee-born wife of Hidenari "Terry" Terasaki, a first secretary at the embassy, Kurusu had asked her husband to suggest the idea to the Americans through unofficial channels:

> I think we should approach the President through an intermediary, someone who has the President's ear, and suggest that he send a cable directly to the Emperor appealing for peace. I must warn you that I have already asked permission of Tojo to do this and have been ordered not to. The cablegram must be sent over Tojo's head directly to tennō heika . . . Of course, if your part in it is discovered, it may mean your death and death for your family also.[4]

Terasaki had decided to take the risk. He had approached Dr. Stanley Jones, a Methodist leader who had the confidence of the president. Jones had agreed to be an intermediary, slipping into the White House by the back way to avoid being seen by newspapermen.

With few remaining options, Roosevelt had proved receptive to the idea of a personal appeal to the emperor. At the suggestion of the Japanese Embassy, Jones had warned him not to send the appeal through official channels, because it would be intercepted by the Japanese Foreign Office before reaching Hirohito.

Roosevelt was planning to send it to the U.S. ambassador in Tokyo instead. Joseph Grew had the right of audience with Japan's head of state. He could deliver Roosevelt's appeal straight to the emperor. If the Japanese delayed the telegram to Grew, Roosevelt could release the text to the newspapers and force Tokyo into acknowledging its existence.

One way or another, the appeal would get through. Whether it would have the desired effect was another matter. As a constitutional monarch, Hirohito was very wary of interfering with the decisions of his government.

If he did intervene and make a call for peace, Japanese culture would require Tojo and his military colleagues to acquiesce and back down. But the chances seemed slim as State Department officials pored over the final wording of the president's appeal to Hirohito. From where they were sitting, the Japanese government in Tokyo seemed deaf and blind to all reason.

On the Russian front, the Red Army was fighting back. As the temperature continued to plummet, the Russians were preparing a counteroffensive, a massive assault against the Wehrmacht designed to relieve the pressure on Moscow and force the Germans to back off as winter began to bite.

The attack had been weeks in the planning. Scarcely able to believe their eyes over the past few days, Luftwaffe pilots had reported endless columns of Russian troops advancing toward the front, troops who couldn't possibly exist according to German calculations. Taking an enormous risk, Stalin had summoned his reserves from the Siberian front. He was gambling that the Soviet Union was not about to be attacked by Japan in the rear.

The new troops were equipped for winter as they arrived. They had the right clothing: white camouflage smocks over uniforms properly insulated against the cold. They had the right oil for their vehicles and grease for their guns, lubricants that wouldn't seize up in the cold, as the German equivalents did. The Russians knew all about winter in their country. They came well prepared for it.

Their appearance was an unwelcome surprise for the Wehrmacht. Even if the Germans couldn't take Moscow before Christmas, they had been hoping for a respite in the fighting until the worst of the winter was over. It had never crossed their minds that the all-but-defeated Russians would be capable of mounting a determined counterattack when both sides were exhausted after the bitter fighting of the last six months.

But here the Russians were, in every mood for a fight. After months of running away, nothing but one long retreat after another, they were looking forward to hitting back, carrying the war to the enemy at a time when the Germans were least expecting it.

The attack was officially set for December 6, but some Russian units were already pushing forward in places. Siegfried Knappe, an artillery officer, was sheltering in Peredelkino, not far from Moscow, when the Red Army struck on the afternoon of December 5.

Peredelkino had been a writers' colony before the Wehrmacht came. Boris Pasternak was one of those who had had an official dacha in the village. Knappe and a few other officers were taking refuge from the cold in a peasant's hut when they received an unwelcome surprise from outside:

We were sitting on the stone stove in the middle of the hut, just beginning to thaw out, when we heard the sharp cracks of tank cannons. We had received no warning from our infantry, and we had just got up to investigate when a tank shell crashed through a corner of the hut and exploded.

Shrapnel blasted through the room, scattering broken and bleeding bodies, filling the room with smoke, the smell of burned powder, and the astonished cries of wounded soldiers.

Two people were killed instantly. . . . The blast had knocked me down, and when I tried to get up I fell again. I realized that I had a head wound and had lost my sense of balance . . . Further inspection revealed a piece of shrapnel sticking in the metal insignia of my collar, which had obviously spared me a very nasty neck wound.[5]

Anton Gründer, a medic in the Ninth Army, was west of Moscow as the Russians attacked. He was on duty until 6:00 a.m. on December 5:

As I was making something to eat, all hell broke loose outside. Everything was pulling back, panzers, artillery guns, vehicles, and soldiers—singly or in groups. They were all in shock. There were no more orders, everybody took up the retreat and looked no further forward than what he felt he might reach.

Most vehicles didn't start because of the terrible cold; despite that we were able to take most of the medical supplies with us. We tried to keep together with the remnants of the company so far as possible, but whoever fell out, was lost.[6]

Hans von Luck, a panzer commander, was retreating from the Klin road toward Volokolamsk, west of Moscow, when his vehicle was attacked from behind by Russian aircraft. Two bullets whistled past his shoulder, smashing the windscreen in front of him. Luck and his driver passed dead horses and wounded infantrymen as they fled. The soldiers begged to be shot rather than be left behind for the Russians to find.

Far away in Berlin, the radio was describing the retreat as a straightening of the line, but the generals at the front knew better. The Wehrmacht had gone as far as it could without the means to finish the job. Luck's divisional commander explained it to him thus:

Luck, this was to be expected. Hitler has overreached himself. Now we've all got to pay for it, especially the poor infantry and the grenadiers. Give your men all the support you can. Many of them will get into a panic and try to save themselves at all costs.

The disengagement—don't talk of retreat—must and will succeed if we all keep our heads. We will lose a lot of materiel, but the main thing is to get the men back. In the hands of God, Luck.[7]

Luck was an intelligent man, a student of history. Even so, he had difficulty coming to terms with what was happening:

> *Although catastrophe was looming, I couldn't grasp it. For the first time since the successful blitzkriegs we were going back on disappointing terms. Snow, frost, icy winds, and an opponent who knew this climate and did not give up, had defeated us.*
>
> *The comparison with Napoleon was inescapable. I could see the pictures in my history books, of how the sad remnants of a proud army turned back and crossed the Beresina.*[8]

All along the line it was the same story. The Germans were in disarray, brought to a halt and forced to retrace their footsteps for the first time since September 1939. The great adventure was turning sour at last.

It had all begun so promisingly six months earlier. In many places the Germans had been welcomed with open arms when they invaded the Soviet Union in June. Delighted to be free of Communism at last, village elders and young girls in white dresses had showered the traditional gifts of flowers, bread, and salt on their liberators.

Thousands of girls had been delighted to sleep with the handsome young men who had come to save them from Stalin, but the honeymoon hadn't lasted for long. The forced labor, the requisitioning of food and livestock, the widespread rapes where consent was not forthcoming, and the hanging of teenage girls who had fought with the partisans had quickly soured relations.

At the same time the exhilarating advance across sunlit prairies in pursuit of a fleeing enemy had turned into a dogged footslog through the rain and then stalemate in the snow as the Wehrmacht war machine ground to a halt. Without adequate clothing or shelter for the winter, the Germans had taken whatever the Russian civilians still had left and then turned them out of their own homes into the snow, knowing that they would die there. No one welcomed the Germans anymore.

The soldiers knew it as they hurried westward. While their Japanese allies were steaming across the Pacific, full of enthusiasm for a war of aggression against the United States, the Germans were openly wondering if they had been wise to launch a similar unprovoked attack on the Soviet Union. It would have been much more sensible to have stayed at home instead and to leave the sleeping giant in peace.

FIVE

ADMIRAL NAGUMO HOISTS A SIGNAL

At sea the Japanese strike force refueled again on the morning of Saturday, December 6. Admiral Nagumo wanted to be sure that his ships were fully topped up before beginning the final approach to Oahu.

The refueling was completed just before midday. As soon as it was done, Nagumo gave the order for the remaining oil tankers to peel off from the convoy and await the task force's return after the attack.

Once the slow-moving tankers had gone, the rest of the convoy was able to increase speed significantly. At Nagumo's signal, the entire force turned to starboard and fired up its engines. The pace quickened until the ships were traveling at more than twenty knots. Oahu lay due south of them, just six hundred miles away.

The ships would remain at full speed now for the rest of the voyage. They were at their most vulnerable as they approached Hawaii. Surprise was essential from here on in. Everything depended on not being discovered until their bombers were safely in the air, on their way to attack Pearl Harbor.

ENGLAND EXPECTS THAT EVERY MAN WILL DO HIS DUTY. The Japanese navy was familiar with the famous signal that Lord Nelson had hoisted at Trafalgar in 1805 as the British sailed into battle against the French and Spanish. Admiral Togo had copied the signal at the Battle of Tsushima (the Sea of Japan battle) in 1905. The Japanese navy had gone on to destroy two-thirds of the opposing Russian fleet.

Yamamoto radioed a similar signal to the task force as it turned toward Oahu. His message was read aloud on every ship. Aboard the destroyer *Akigumo*, executive officer Sadao Chigusa never forgot the moment as the signal appeared in flag form:

> *The signals flags "D-G" were gallantly hoisted high on the mast of the flagship, the* Akagi, *meaning: "The fate of the Japanese Empire will depend upon the issue of this battle, so please everyone exert yourself to the utmost." . . . I have heard many times of that order given by the "Z" flag from Admiral Togo in the Japan Sea Battle against Russia in 1905. Now I have actually received the same order myself. . . .*
>
> *We completed all remaining preparations for war and battle which had not been completed in the morning. On receiving the order "Be well dressed," we changed to clean uniforms for battle. After that, both my ship and myself had completed our preparations for attack against the enemy at any time.*[1]

In Tokyo the government had finalized its response to Roosevelt's ten-point peace plan. As Kurusu had forecast, the proposals had been interpreted as an ultimatum rather than a serious attempt to come to an agreement. In Japanese eyes Roosevelt was as arrogant and presumptuous as Commodore Perry had been in 1853 when his men came ashore uninvited, not bothering to conceal their contempt for the natives.

The Japanese framed their response accordingly. They were well aware by now that their military adventure in China had been a costly mistake. It hadn't achieved its goals, and it was very unpopular at home. The Americans were only talking common sense when they suggested that the Japanese should pull out and put the whole disastrous episode behind them.

Yet the Japanese couldn't back down just because the Americans told them to. They would lose face if they did. Their instinct was to fight back instead.

They had decided to reply to Roosevelt's ten-point plan with a fourteen-part response of their own. Their rejoinder was long and wordy, effectively a rehash of everything they had already said many times before:

> The Government of Japan, prompted by a genuine desire to come to an amicable understanding with the Government of the United States in order that the two countries by their joint efforts may secure the peace of the Pacific area and thereby contribute toward the realization of world peace, has continued negotiations with the utmost sincerity since April last with the Government of the United States regarding the adjustment and advancement of Japanese-American relations and the stabilization of the Pacific area . . .
>
> Ever since the China Affair broke out owing to the failure on the part of China to comprehend Japan's true intentions, the Japanese Government has striven for the restoration of peace and it has consistently exerted its best efforts to prevent the extension of warlike disturbances. It was also to that end that in September last year Japan concluded the Tripartite Pact with Germany and Italy.
>
> However, both the United States and Great Britain have resorted to every possible measure to assist the Chungking regime so as to obstruct the establishment of a general peace between Japan and China.
>
> Interfering with Japan's constructive endeavors toward the stabilization of East Asia, exerting pressure on the Netherlands East Indies, or menacing French Indo-China, they have attempted to frustrate Japan's aspiration to realize the ideal of common prosperity in cooperation with these regions.[2]

And so on, for many pages. The Japanese put the blame for the breakdown in negotiations entirely on American self-interest. They accused Roosevelt's government of refusing to yield an inch, sticking to impractical principles and disregarding realities without displaying "in the slightest degree a spirit of conciliation."[3] It was all the fault of the United States that discussions over many months had gotten nowhere.

The final section of the Japanese response was the killer. It was couched in diplomatic language, but the underlying threat was clear:

> *Obviously it is the intention of the American Government to conspire with Great Britain and other countries to obstruct Japan's efforts toward the establishment of peace through the creation of a New Order in East Asia, and especially to preserve Anglo-American rights and interests by keeping Japan and China at war.*
>
> *This intention has been revealed clearly during the course of the present negotiations. Thus, the earnest hope of the Japanese Government to adjust Japanese-American relations and to preserve and promote the peace of the Pacific through cooperation with the American Government has finally been lost.*
>
> *The Japanese Government regrets to have to notify hereby the American Government that in view of the attitude of the American Government it cannot but consider that it is impossible to reach an agreement through further negotiations.*[4]

In other words the talks were about to be broken off. War might easily follow.

As soon as the wording had been agreed, the formal response was sent to the Japanese Embassy in Washington. Ambassador Nomura received a pilot message early on Saturday morning. It alerted him to the imminent arrival of a "very long" memorandum—so long that it would have to be transmitted in fourteen separate parts.

Once the memorandum had arrived, Japanese Foreign Minister Togo wanted Nomura and Kurusu to sit on it for a while before delivering it to the United States government:

> *The situation is extremely delicate, and when you receive it I want you to please keep it secret for the time being.*
>
> *Concerning the time of presenting this memorandum to the United*

States, I will wire you in a separate message. However, I want you in
the meantime to put it in nicely drafted form and make every prepa-
ration to present it to the Americans just as soon as you receive instruc-
tions.[5]

An additional thought arrived a few minutes later. "There is really no
need to tell you this, but in the preparation of the aide-mémoire be absolutely sure not to use a typist or any other person. Be most extremely cau-
tious in preserving secrecy."[6]

Tokyo began to transmit its fourteen-part repudiation of Roosevelt's
peace proposals at about eight o'clock Eastern Standard Time. On a very
busy day for signal traffic, the message took a long while to transmit, let
alone decode. The text arrived in dribs and drabs over several hours, not
always in chronological order.

Japanese officials at the embassy set to work at once to decode the various segments of the message as they came in. So did the U.S. Navy. It had
intercepted the message at the same time as the Japanese Embassy and was
decoding it just as fast, with a little help from the War Department.

While the officials at the Japanese Embassy prepared their government's
lengthy response to Roosevelt's peace proposals, Special Envoy Kurusu had
decided on a last-minute initiative of his own. He had invited an old American friend to come and see him at the embassy with a view to finding a
way through the impasse.

Ferdinand Mayer reached Massachusetts Avenue at about eleven o'clock.
He found a hostile crowd outside the embassy as he went in. A retired diplomat, Mayer had become friends with Kurusu in the early 1930s when both
had been serving in Peru.

The two men were glad to see each other again. After a brief exchange
of pleasantries about old times, they went to the drawing room and got
down to business. They spent the next hour and a half discussing the situation, desperately trying to find a way out of the mess.

As Mayer remembered it, Kurusu was very agitated, longing to unburden himself to someone he could really trust. "He seemed very apprehensive of being overheard by members of the embassy staff, repeatedly turning his head to see if anyone was approaching."[7]

"Fred, we are in an awful mess," Kurusu began.[8] He went on to explain the tensions between the civilian government and the army in Japan. He claimed that the civilians had spent the last few months trying to stop the army from doing anything stupid that would alarm the British and Americans.

The civilian government had only sanctioned the move into French Indochina because the army had been determined to go somewhere. Invading a French colony had seemed the option least likely to offend the Anglo-Americans.

Kurusu wanted Mayer to get that across to Cordell Hull at the State Department. He added that the main problem now was how to get the Japanese out of China without a loss of prestige. As Kurusu saw it, ordinary people in Japan had long since had enough of the war and wanted only peace. He told Mayer that the "show was up in China, that the militarists knew this as well, or perhaps better, than anyone else and that they were all looking for a way out to save their faces . . . the militarists continued to bluster and roar, but this was merely normal face-saving, particularly in the army."[9]

Mayer agreed with Kurusu that the Japanese army was a nuisance, constantly repudiating decisions taken by the civilian authorities. Kurusu concurred, but he was hopeful that the generals had shot their bolt at last: "The militarists were so much on the run and in such a difficult position that, unless hotheads among them upset the apple cart—which might be done at any time—he felt that the better element in Japan was really on the way to control the situation."[10]

The wish was father to the thought. The two men continued their discussion until lunchtime without coming to any conclusion. Mayer was going to dinner that night with another old friend, a retired U.S. ambassador to Poland. He suggested that Kurusu should come too. He wanted his ambassador friend to hear at first hand what Kurusu had to say.

They arranged to meet again that evening. As soon as they had parted,

Mayer hurried to the nearest telephone to brief the State Department about Kurusu's astonishingly candid revelations. If what he was saying was true, the United States ought to put its Far East forces on full alert without further delay.

As the meeting at the Japanese Embassy broke up, President Roosevelt was approving the final draft of his personal appeal to Emperor Hirohito. Secretary of State Cordell Hull disliked the idea of an appeal and had counseled against it, but Roosevelt had decided to overrule him. The appeal was to go ahead.

After drawing the emperor's attention to the good relations that had long prevailed between Japan and the United States, the president warned him of a deep and far-reaching emergency that now appeared to be in formation:

> *Developments are occurring in the Pacific area which threaten to deprive each of our nations and all humanity of the beneficial influence of the long peace between our two countries. Those developments contain tragic possibilities.*
>
> *The people of the United States, believing in peace and in the right of nations to live and let live, have eagerly watched the conversations between our two Governments during these past months. We have hoped for a termination of the present conflict between Japan and China. We have hoped that a peace of the Pacific could be consummated in such a way that nationalities of many diverse peoples could exist side by side without fear of invasion . . .*
>
> *More than a year ago, Your Majesty's Government concluded an agreement with the Vichy Government by which five or six thousand Japanese troops were permitted to enter northern French Indo-China for the protection of Japanese troops which were operating against China further north.*
>
> *This spring and summer the Vichy Government permitted further Japanese military forces to enter into southern French Indo-China for*

the common defense of French Indo-China. I think I am correct in say-
ing that no attack has been made upon Indo-China nor that any has
been contemplated.[11]

Roosevelt pointed out that people in the Philippines, the East Indies, Malaya, and Thailand suspected that they were about to be attacked by these troops. He told the emperor bluntly that a very large number of people in the United States looked askance at this development. He went on:

It is clear that a continuance of such a situation is unthinkable.
    None of the peoples whom I have spoken of above can sit either in-
definitely or permanently on a keg of dynamite.
    There is absolutely no thought on the part of the United States of
invading Indo-China if every Japanese soldier or sailor were to be with-
drawn therefrom.[12]

Having stated his country's position, Roosevelt concluded by making a personal appeal to Hirohito, as one head of state to another:

I address myself to Your Majesty in the fervent hope that Your Majesty
may, as I am doing, give thought in this definite emergency to ways of
dispelling the dark clouds. I am confident that both of us, for the sake of
the peoples not only of our own great countries but for the sake of human-
ity in neighboring territories, have a sacred duty to restore traditional
amity and prevent further death and destruction in the world.[13]

It was a good pitch. It would put Hirohito on the spot, if nothing else. Roosevelt sent the appeal to the State Department when he had finished. He wanted Hull to check the final draft before forwarding it to the emperor.

Hull had spent the morning discussing the reports of Japanese ship movements in the direction of the Kra Isthmus. The figures he had were eight cruisers, twenty destroyers and thirty-five troop transports. Whether bound for Thailand or Malaya, they were certainly going to cause trouble somewhere in the very near future.

The secretary of state and his advisers scrutinized the final draft of the appeal when it arrived from the White House. They recommended a few technical adjustments to make it more accurate and then bounced it back to Roosevelt. He approved the changes and returned the draft to them later in the day. Attached was a handwritten note instructing Hull to send the appeal to the American ambassador in Tokyo without delay:

> Dear Cordell,
> Shoot this to Grew. I think it can go in gray code—saves time—I don't mind if it gets picked up.
> FDR.[14]

While the State Department complied, the U.S. Navy's security intelligence section on Constitution Avenue was busily decoding Japanese radio signals as fast as its people could do so. There had been so many signals that morning, as well as the fourteen-part response to Roosevelt's peace plan, that only the important-looking signals were receiving priority. The rest were being left for a day or two before full decryption and analysis.

The Japanese sent messages in a variety of codes, not all of which had been broken by the Americans. The code used by Japanese consulates was adjudged to carry some of the least important messages. Consular traffic therefore received less attention from the navy's analysts than perhaps it should have.

Translator Dorothy Edgers had a pile of consular messages in front of her that morning. She had only been in the job for a month, but she had grown up in Japan and had a good command of the language. She knew what she was doing as she skimmed through the messages to see if any of them was important enough to merit immediate attention.

One message seemed to be. Already three days old, it had been sent to Tokyo from the Japanese consulate in Honolulu. It appeared to be about the movements of U.S. warships in and out of Pearl Harbor and the exact position of the aircraft carriers in the dock.

Edgers showed the message to the section's senior translator, her brother, Fred Woodrough. She thought it was important enough to be completed immediately. Her brother wasn't so sure, but told her to go ahead anyway. She took the message back to her desk and set to work.

The message was indeed about Pearl Harbor. It was clear from the content that a Japanese spy was transmitting signals from a house on Oahu to Japanese ships offshore. It was also clear that it would take Edgers several hours, if not the rest of the day, to translate the whole of the message and have it ready for the yeoman of signals to read.

It was Saturday. She was supposed to knock off at noon for the rest of the weekend. If she did, the message probably wouldn't be read until Monday at the earliest.

Dorothy Edgers decided to forget about her plans for Saturday afternoon. She remained at her desk instead.

SIX

WHERE ARE AMERICA'S AIRCRAFT CARRIERS?

In Egypt they already knew that the United States was about to be attacked by Japan. A senior British officer had warned the military attaché at the U.S. Embassy in Cairo at ten o'clock that morning that an attack would come within the next twenty-four hours.

Colonel Bonner Fellers had been in Egypt for just over a year. His job was to observe British military operations in the Mediterranean and Middle East and report back to the U.S. government. The British allowed him considerable access and were as open as they could be about their operations. Fellers' reports were read in Washington all the way up to the president.

Perhaps as a result of their openness, Fellers had formed a poor opinion of the British in the Western Desert. In his view the Eighth Army was amateurish in the extreme when compared to the Germans. Its weapons, tactics, and leadership couldn't hold a candle to the Afrika Korps under the redoubtable General Rommel.

It was a reasonable assessment. The British were the first to admit that most of them were just civilians in uniform. Many took a perverse pride in being gentleman-amateurs compared to their professional German counterparts. A few concealed their own professionalism under a cloak of amateurishness that was sometimes lost on American colonels from West Point.

There were plenty of American soldiers in Egypt. More were arriving every week as part of the United States Lend-Lease Agreement with Great Britain. The American public at home was very reluctant to join the fight against the Nazis. Roosevelt had answered Churchill's plea for help by supplying him instead with the tools to finish the job.

He had authorized the setting up of a U.S. North African military mission in September to supervise and coordinate the delivery of American arms and vehicles to the British forces in the Middle East. He also intended to deliver weapons to the Russians via the Persian corridor, an enormous undertaking that required the enlargement of port and rail facilities and the construction of roads in Iran before the deliveries could begin.

As neutrals, the Americans could not do the work themselves. It had to be contracted out to civilians. But an increasing number of U.S. military personnel were needed in Egypt to instruct the British in the use and maintenance of the equipment being supplied.

Much of the equipment was new, untested in battle. The British were duly trying it out on the Germans in the Western Desert. American observers were taking notes from the sidelines before reporting back to the manufacturers at home with suggestions for improvement. If nothing else, the war was proving to be a great boon for American industry.

On the British side, the war was run from an ornate apartment building near the British Embassy in Cairo's Garden City. The army, navy and RAF all had their headquarters there, the offices very close together. Fellers was a frequent visitor, a familiar face to the deskbound staff officers who coordinated Britain's Middle Eastern operations. Nattily uniformed, the officers were known as the gabardine swine to the fighting men farther up the line.

As Fellers remembered it, he walked into RAF headquarters at ten o'clock that morning and found the air officer in command sitting at his desk. Recalling the incident many years later, Fellers thought the officer was Air Marshal Arthur Longmore.

In fact Longmore had returned to England by then, replaced by Air Marshal Arthur Tedder. Whomever Fellers met, the officer was very excited.

"Bonner," he announced as soon as Fellers arrived. "You will be in the war in 24 hours. We have a secret signal Japan will strike the US in 24 hours."[1]

Fellers found that hard to believe. He said so. "I replied the Japanese were having a free hand in the Orient and it would not be to their advantage to strike the U.S. We had a conversation of some minutes. It was clear the Air Marshal was confident the attack would be made and he was elated that at long last the U.S. would be in the war."[2]

Fellers spent the rest of the day wondering if the report was true. He ought to tell Washington at once if the United States was about to be attacked. But if the British in Cairo already knew, then surely Washington did too? He would look like an idiot if he passed the information on and it turned out to be wrong.

After worrying about it until late that evening, Fellers decided to do nothing. He later came to believe, as many Americans still do, that Washington had indeed been warned about what was coming but had chosen to let the attack go ahead anyway, so easing the United States entry into the war. Whatever the truth, Fellers always regretted that he didn't pass the RAF message on while he still had the chance.

In Singapore, Cecil Brown of CBS radio had no qualms about passing such messages on at the first opportunity. It was his job to report the news and get the story out as fast as he could.

Brown was a difficult man by all accounts, perhaps too opinionated to be an ideal reporter. He had been expelled from Italy earlier in the year for a "continued hostile attitude" toward the Mussolini regime.[3] After a brief spell in Cairo, he had then been posted to Singapore, where he had managed to irritate the British almost as much as he had the Italians.

Overwrought and strident much of the time, was one commonly held view of him. Blistering and relentless, was another. Like Fellers in Cairo, Brown didn't think much of the British war effort and never hesitated to say so on the air, if the censors let him. Wherever the British were fighting, there were always plenty of Americans ready to criticize from the bleachers.

Despite their military failings, however, the British were alive to the threat from Japan. After a hiatus of almost thirty hours, their aircraft had reestablished contact with the Japanese ships in the Gulf of Thailand. Men in khaki had been spotted on the decks.

Singapore had already moved to a "First Degree of Readiness," as Brown informed CBS on the afternoon of Sunday, December 7 (Saturday, December 6, in the United States):

> *Strong indications Japanese are moving up ships and troops to launch an imminent attack with landing parties against Thailand with immediate objectives of capturing Bangkok. . . .*
>
> *British aircraft sighted extremely heavy shipping activity less than 300 miles distant from Malaya coming from Saigon and Camranh Bay rounding Cambodia Point which is 400 miles distant from Bangkok . . .*
>
> *I understand British naval patrols are extremely active and units of the Eastern fleet are disposed for immediate action. Aircraft at all Malaya airfields are disposed and fighters are ready to take off. The big question in Malaya is what will the British do if Thailand is attacked.*[4]

The moves were a precaution rather than anything else. Nobody in Singapore was seriously expecting to be attacked. The general feeling was that the Japanese would be mad to invade Malaya in the middle of the monsoon season. British forces just needed to be ready to help if the Thais were attacked instead.

Brown's cable had little impact in the United States. No one took any real notice. Whatever the British were up to, far away across the sea, was nothing to do with them.

In the Philippines, though, the Americans were reacting much as the British in Singapore. They had put their forces on full alert and were waiting to see what happened next.

The Philippines faced a very real prospect of invasion if the Japanese were foolish enough to start a war. The islands lay across the sea from China, south and slightly west of Japan. If the Japanese intended to plunder the resource-rich territories of the Dutch East Indies farther to the south, they would have to secure the Philippines first.

In his penthouse suite at the Manila Hotel, General Douglas MacArthur was acutely aware of the situation as he awaited developments. In common with most Americans, MacArthur imagined that the Japanese would have more sense than to start a war against the United States that they couldn't possibly hope to win. But he was ready to defend the Philippines if they did.

MacArthur had been about to retire in 1935 when the Philippines' new government invited him to form an army for them. They wanted him to have it ready for the islands' independence, scheduled for 1946. Long familiar with the islands, where his father had once been the commanding general, MacArthur had agreed with alacrity.

As military adviser to the Philippines government, he had worked hard to create the army for them, but without the resources that he had been promised. Like peacetime governments everywhere, the Philippines had preferred to spend money on other things. So had the United States, which maintained only a small military force on the islands, and that only grudgingly.

MacArthur was ready to make the best of the forces at his disposal, but he knew that if the unthinkable happened, they would not be able to hold off the Japanese for long. Their best bet was to retreat into the Bataan Peninsula, across the bay from Manila, and hang in there until reinforcements arrived from the United States.

He was also aware that Japanese practice was to begin hostilities by launching a surprise attack at exactly the same moment as they declared war. That was how the Japanese had opened their wars against the Chinese in 1894, the Russians ten years later, and the Germans in 1914. It was probably what they would do again, if they really were intent on war.

There was no way to preempt them. It was imperative that the Japanese should be the ones to strike the first blow. The United States couldn't try to head them off if it meant being seen as the aggressor. MacArthur had instructions to that effect from the War Department in Washington:

> *Negotiations with Japan appear to be terminated to all practical purposes with only the barest possibilities that the Japanese Government might come back and offer to continue. Japanese future action unpredictable but hostile action possible at any moment. If hostilities cannot, repeat cannot, be avoided the United States desires that Japan commit the first overt act.*[5]

The good news for the Philippines was that reinforcements were already on their way. Eight U.S. troop ships were steaming toward Manila that day, bringing guns, ammunition, and much-needed aircraft with them. They would double the size of the American forces when they arrived. It couldn't be a moment too soon for Douglas MacArthur.

Hawaii was too far away from anywhere to feel under much threat that Saturday afternoon. If the Japanese were about to launch an attack somewhere, it was unlikely to be against a tiny spot in the middle of the Pacific. No one saw any need to suspend normal weekend activities because of untoward events elsewhere.

The University of Hawaii had a football game that afternoon. The Rainbows were playing the Bearcats from Willamette University, Oregon. The visitors had arrived on Wednesday to an enthusiastic aloha welcome at the dockside, complete with traditional leis of flowers. Everyone had been afraid that the trip would be canceled at the last minute because of the worries about Japan. They had been relieved to see the Bearcats when they arrived.

On an island where very little happened, a football game against a team from the mainland was a big event. There was hardly a spare seat in the Honolulu stadium as spectators arrived for the start. Almost 25,000 people—10 percent of the Hawaiian Islands' population—were there to see it begin. Kickoff was at 2:30, but fans had been advised to take their seats by 1:15 at the latest if they wanted to watch the parade beforehand.

The marching bands were led by the marines. Another fourteen bands followed them onto the field. They played "Hawai'i Pono'i," one of the islands' most popular tunes, as they went. There were fireworks as well and a pair of miniature parachutes floating down to earth, bearing the Stars and Stripes and the Hawaiian state flag.

The massed bands played "The Stars and Stripes Forever" as the American flag fluttered downward. Not to be outdone, a uniformed soldier brandished a supporting flag with "Ever On Alert" emblazoned on it. His role in the events of the next morning remains unknown.

The Bearcats had easily won the last seven of their eight games on the mainland, but they proved to be no match for the much heavier Rainbows. The home team beat them by twenty points to six in a rather scrappy game. Analyzing it afterward, the Bearcats were inclined to blame their defeat on the heat in the Pacific and the seasickness that some of them had experienced on the way over.

But the game was finished soon enough and the evening lay ahead. The Bearcats were in lovely Honolulu, on an island that looked ravishingly beautiful to their eyes. The first thing to do was to have a shower after the game and run a comb through their hair. After that, the evening was theirs to do with as they wished. It would be a very unusual postgame evening if it didn't involve cheerleaders at some point.

Elsewhere Honolulu was bracing itself for the Saturday-night rush. With so many battleships in port, it was bound to be a busy time. There was going to be a dance later at the Pearl Harbor officers' club, another for the officers and their wives at Schofield. The enlisted men would converge on Honolulu in their thousands.

Tantalizing Tootsies was the name of the variety show on at the Princess Theater. For moviegoers, the new picture at the Waikiki Theater was *A Yank in the RAF*, "a spectacular aviation drama" starring Tyrone Power and Betty Grable.[6]

The movie had been made with British cooperation. It featured Power as a dashing American pilot in the RAF, pursuing WAAF officer and part-time singer Grable in London as the Germans invaded France. Power flew a Spitfire, downing two Luftwaffe fighters with consummate ease before escaping from Dunkirk with the British army and returning to England to get the girl.

The movie had been filmed in Hollywood, but its selling point was the real action scenes spliced into the narrative. The film contained actual footage of the Dunkirk beaches during the evacuation and genuine combat operations over Germany as the RAF took the war to the enemy. In a garrison town like Honolulu, a long way from any possibility of similar action, it was already proving to be a hit.

While the Americans showered and shaved and scrubbed up for the evening, the Japanese diplomat Takeo Yoshikawa had just returned to the consulate after his second visit to Pearl Harbor that day. At Tokyo's request, he had gone first to see if the battleships at anchor were shielded by torpedo nets and to investigate a report that the whole place was protected by barrage balloons.

Yoshikawa had seen neither torpedo nets nor barrage balloons at the harbor. Hundreds of balloons were on order, apparently, but there was currently nothing to stop an aircraft flying overhead without hindrance. "I imagine that in all probability there is considerable opportunity left to take advantage for a surprise attack against these places," was his assessment for Tokyo.[7]

Yoshikawa had only just gotten back to the consulate when he was asked to go out again. The Foreign Ministry wanted precise details of recent fleet movements in the harbor. Yoshikawa returned for another look and then cabled Tokyo just after six that evening:

> *The following ships were observed at anchor on the 6th: 9 battleships, 3 light cruisers, 3 submarine tenders, 17 destroyers, and in addition there were 4 light cruisers, 2 destroyers lying at docks (the heavy cruisers and aircraft carriers have all left). It appears that no air reconnaissance is being conducted by the fleet air arm.*[8]

The message was quickly passed to Admiral Yamamoto on his flagship in Hiroshima Bay. It was just what he didn't want to hear. Earlier reports had suggested that against all the odds there were no aircraft carriers in Pearl Harbor at the moment. Now the reports were confirmed. The American carriers were all at sea.

It was devastating news. The Japanese had been expecting three carriers when they planned the attack. The Americans in the Pacific would be crippled without their aircraft. The main point of the strike against Pearl Harbor was to sink the Americans' carriers and leave them unable to hit back.

Yamamoto's first instinct was to pass the bad news to Admiral Nagumo aboard *Akagi* and tell him to look for the American carriers at sea. On second thought, he decided simply to forward the message and leave it to Nagumo to decide what to do next.

NO CARRIERS REPEAT NO CARRIERS IN PEARL HARBOR. Nagumo apparently threw the message down in disgust onto the chart table when he received it. He understood the implications as clearly as Yamamoto had. All that planning had been for nothing. All those months of preparation and now there were no American carriers in harbor just when the Japanese needed them to be there.

But the Japanese couldn't stop. There would never be another chance if they turned back now. The strike force's destination had been a secret when its ships sailed from different harbors in ones and twos and formed up at Hitokappu Bay in the Kurile Islands, far from prying eyes. The ordinary sailors had only just been told where they were going.

Now that they knew, the secret would be out as soon as they returned to Japan. It had to be now or never for an attack on Pearl Harbor.

Rear-Admiral Ryūnosuke Kusaka, chief of staff aboard *Akagi*, was no fan of the plan to attack Pearl Harbor. He privately considered it amateurish and foolhardy. Nevertheless, he shared Nagumo's view that it was too late to turn back now, as he later recalled:

Most of the U.S. Pacific fleet was in Pearl Harbor. The absence of their carriers in port, however, was our only concern and very regrettable. But I thought that indecision at this moment considering this and that would only result in blunting the cutting effect of a sword swung down from overhead.

Then I made up my mind to concentrate all striking power upon enemy vessels in Pearl Harbor. This meant that I rejected all other ideas including assigning elements of the air forces to search the vicinity to seek out enemy carriers.[9]

Nagumo agreed with him. The task force continued south.

SEVEN

"THE JAPANESE WILL NOT GO TO WAR"

n Washington, Dorothy Edgers had completed her translation of the Japanese consular message from Honolulu just before 3:00 p.m. She was glad that she had decided to remain at work for the afternoon. Consular traffic was usually routine stuff about trade and commerce, but not this time:

> *If the above signals and wireless messages cannot be made from Oahu, then on Maui Island, 6 miles north to the northward of Kula Sanatorium . . . at a point halfway between Lower Kula Road and Haleskala Road (latitude 20° 40' N, longitude 156° 19' W, visible from seaward to the southeast and southwest of Maui Island) the following bonfires will be made daily until your EXEX signal is received. . . .*[1]

Bonfire signals out to sea? To whom? It could only be a Japanese vessel of some kind.

Lieutenant Commander Alwin Kramer, head of the translation section, came in just as Edgers had completed her first draft. She showed it to him at once.

Kramer read the message standing up, but was not particularly impressed.

His mind was on other problems, notably the fourteen-part message from Tokyo to the Japanese Embassy in Washington that had been coming in all day. He told Edgers that her draft would need a lot more work before it was ready.

She volunteered to stay on for the rest of the afternoon to make a fair copy, but Kramer wouldn't allow it. He insisted that she should go home instead. There would be plenty of time to finish the job next week.

The fourteen-part message was the important one. The Japanese were sending it in their "purple" code, which was only used for top secret information between Tokyo and Japanese embassies abroad. The content was still jumbled, but its tone was becoming increasingly clear with every section that came in. The Japanese weren't buying Roosevelt's ten-point peace plan.

The message was being transmitted in English, but still took a long time to decode. Frustratingly, the final, fourteenth part had yet to arrive. The fourteenth part was the one all but confirming that the Japanese were about to break off peace negotiations. It didn't reach Washington until the following morning.

Between them the navy and the War Department succeeded in decoding the first thirteen parts of the message by about 8:30 on the Saturday night. It had been typed up into a fifteen-page document by then and copied into folders for delivery to the select band of names on the "Magic" distribution list. The next problem was how to track down all the names, on a Saturday night in the nation's capital.

Kramer began by telephoning the naval people on the list to say that he had something important to show them that they should see at once. He managed to get through to most of the names, but not all. Admiral Harold Stark, chief of naval operations, was at the theater. Another officer was apparently out walking the dog.

Kramer's final call was to his wife at home. Official cars were in short supply in Washington, so he asked her to stop wrapping Christmas presents and drive him around the capital, delivering copies of the Japanese message by hand to the people on his list.

They went first to the White House office building. The president was in the middle of a dinner party with thirty-two guests and couldn't be disturbed. Kramer handed the White House's copy of the message to Lieutenant Lester Schulz, Captain Beardall's assistant, telling him that the president would want to read it as soon as possible.

A telephone call confirmed this, so Schulz took the locked pouch to the White House and asked to see the president. Roosevelt had left his dinner party after the main course and gone upstairs to his study. He worked in the Oval Room overlooking the south portico (not to be confused with the Oval Office in the West Wing).

Schulz was escorted up the stairs. He found the president in conference with his adviser Harry Hopkins. It took Roosevelt ten minutes to read the message. Hopkins read it too before handing it back to the president, as Schulz recalled: "The President then turned toward Mr Hopkins and said in substance—I am not sure of the exact words, but in substance—'This means war.'"[2]

Hopkins agreed. Schulz was all ears as the two men discussed it, Roosevelt telling Hopkins that he had just sent a message to the emperor requesting in effect the withdrawal of Japanese troops from Indochina.

Hopkins wondered if the United States shouldn't prevent a surprise attack by striking the first blow, if war was inevitable anyway. Roosevelt wouldn't hear of it, as Schulz remembered:

> The President nodded and then said, in effect, "No, we can't do that. We are a democracy and a peaceful people." Then he raised his voice, and this much I remember definitely. He said, "But we have a good record."
>
> The impression that I got was that we would have to stand on that record, we could not make the first overt move. We would have to wait until it came.[3]

Roosevelt decided to phone Admiral Stark. Learning that he was at the theater, the president declined to have him paged for fear of causing alarm. Instead he returned the fifteen-page folder to Lieutenant Schulz, who took it with him when he left the room.

Kramer meanwhile had continued to distribute copies of the Japanese message around Washington. It was after midnight by the time he had worked his way through the list.

His wife then drove him back to his office. He wanted to find out if the fourteenth part of the message had arrived yet. Learning that it hadn't, Kramer decided that he had done as much as he could that night and went home to bed.

In the Japanese Embassy at the same time, the embassy's cryptographers had just finished decoding the first thirteen parts of the message. They were about four hours behind the Americans, perhaps because the message was in English rather than their own language. With no sign of a fourteenth part, they too called it a night and went to bed.

Up in Georgetown, Special Envoy Kurusu had enjoyed a good dinner with his friend Mayer and Mayer's friend Ferdinand Lammot Belin, a former U.S. ambassador to Poland. Kurusu and Belin had never met before, but the Japanese diplomat with an American wife spoke as frankly to him as he had to Mayer that morning.

His openness astonished Belin. Kurusu was disliked and distrusted by many people in Washington, but he seemed to be holding nothing back, revealing confidential information and unburdening himself most undiplomatically to a complete stranger. To Mayer, it seemed clear (perhaps with hindsight) that Kurusu was desperately trying to warn them about something, probably an impending Japanese attack somewhere.

The three men had hardly sat down to dinner when Kurusu got a phone call advising him that President Roosevelt had just made a personal appeal to Emperor Hirohito. It was the first Kurusu had heard of the appeal. He recognized it at once as a shrewd move. Hirohito could hardly turn the appeal down without acute embarrassment. But he couldn't accept it either.

The three diplomats spent the next four hours struggling to find a solution. The one thing they all agreed on was that Japan would have to renounce the Tripartite Pact with Italy and Germany if it wanted to restore good relations with the United States.

Kurusu was the man who had signed the pact, but he claimed to disapprove of it as much as the two Americans did. He was in no doubt that the

Germans would exploit the pact in their own favor and treat Japan as the junior partner in the arrangement. Yet the Japanese would be breaking a formal agreement if they repudiated the pact now. The United States would be less inclined to trust them if they repudiated formal agreements.

The discussion continued long into the evening. Kurusu had ordered his car for 10:00 p.m., but the diplomats kept talking. In the end his chauffeur had to send a message in to him, reminding him that he was expected back at the embassy.

At the American Embassy in Tokyo, Ambassador Joseph Grew learned of the president's appeal to Hirohito from San Francisco radio. Soon afterward he received a triple-priority message from Cordell Hull at the State Department telling him that the appeal was being encoded and would reach him soon.

It arrived in Tokyo at noon but wasn't delivered to Grew until 10:30 that night. Evidence emerged later that the message had been deliberately delayed at the behest of the Japanese army.

As soon as he finally had his hands on it, Grew contacted the Japanese Foreign Ministry to warn them that he might need an urgent meeting with Foreign Minister Togo at about midnight. He wouldn't know for sure until the message from Washington had been decoded.

The Japanese weren't eager. It was far too late for a meeting, and Togo wanted to go to bed. Couldn't it wait until morning?

Grew's people insisted that it had to be that night. They wouldn't have asked if it wasn't very important. The Japanese reluctantly consented. Grew met Togo at his official residence sometime between ten minutes to midnight and a quarter past.

Togo's face gave little away. Like many Japanese, he did not want to fight an unwinnable war and believed that an attack on the United States would be a very stupid move, bound to end in disaster. But he showed no hint of his own feelings as he listened to Grew reading aloud the president's appeal to the emperor.

Grew requested an audience with Hirohito at the earliest possible moment so that he could deliver the appeal in person. From Togo's non-committal reaction, the ambassador wondered if the foreign minister was stalling for time. "The Minister at first said that he would study the document, but when I inquired if that observation implied some doubt as to whether he would ask for an audience for me, he replied that he would present my request to the Throne."[4]

They agreed to leave it at that for the night. Grew left a copy of the president's appeal with Togo and went home to bed.

At Pearl Harbor, Admiral Kimmel's day had begun early, as it always did. As commander in chief of the U.S. Pacific Fleet he was at his desk at fleet headquarters in the submarine base by 8:00 a.m., ready for a string of meetings with his staff.

They were all aware that something was cooking in the Pacific. From the reports of Japanese ship movements, it was obvious that a move was about to be made somewhere in Southeast Asia. Kimmel had received the same message as Douglas MacArthur in the Philippines about the possibility of imminent enemy action. Yet he was no wiser than MacArthur as to where it might happen.

Joseph C. Harsch, a correspondent for the *Christian Science Monitor*, was on his way to the Soviet Union to report on the war against the Germans. Interviewing Kimmel early that morning, he asked him off the record if there was also going to be a war in the Pacific.

Kimmel played it down. He told Harsch that a Japanese offensive in the Pacific was most unlikely while the Red Army remained undefeated by the Wehrmacht. As an ally of Germany, the Japanese wouldn't want to risk fighting on two fronts. They were too intelligent to do that.

Yet the signs were all there. Japanese convoys heading south. Missing aircraft carriers that hadn't been seen for days. Codes being burned, call signs changed. Something was definitely up on the other side of the Pacific.

Kimmel had issued a checklist of things for his staff to do in the event of a war. "Steps to Be Taken in Case of American-Japanese War within the Next Twenty-Four Hours" was not a battle plan, but it was reviewed and updated regularly so that his staff would not be caught napping if the moment came.

The big worry that Saturday morning was the large number of battleships in harbor for the weekend. Kimmel was well aware that the ships would be sitting ducks in the event of an attack. Without carriers to defend them though, they would be even more at risk on the high seas. At least in harbor they had the army's antiaircraft guns to protect them. And they would save fuel if they were in port.

Vice-Admiral William Pye commanded Pearl Harbor's battle force. A cerebral man, he was aboard his flagship, *California*, on Battleship Row that morning when he received a message from Kimmel asking his opinion of the latest Japanese movements south toward the Philippines.

The military assessment was that the Japanese would have to take the Philippines before attacking the Dutch East Indies. But taking the Philippines meant declaring war on the United States. Pye spoke for most people when he boggled at the prospect. "The Japanese will not go to war with the United States. We are too big, too powerful and too strong."[5]

Kimmel's discussions with his staff spilled over into lunch. The meeting broke up toward three o'clock, and the commander in chief went home for a couple of hours. He had left his wife behind in California and lived alone in a new house on Makalapa Hill, a few minutes' drive from headquarters.

He surfaced later to attend a small dinner party on the terrace of the Halekulani Hotel. It was being given by Admiral Herbert Leary and his wife for a few close friends. Kimmel had another invitation as well for later that evening. He had been asked to drop by the Japanese consulate for a glass of champagne.

His instinct was to ignore the invitation. For one thing, this was no time to hobnob with the Japanese. There had been a report only that day of the consular staff burning papers in the yard, perhaps getting rid of their codebooks for reasons that could only be sinister.

Kimmel didn't enjoy Japanese entertainment, for another. The consul liked to throw stag parties for around fifty American officers and businessmen, each provided with his own bottle of whiskey and a geisha girl at his side to pour it. Not Kimmel's style at all.

Yet the Japanese might have invited him for a reason. He might learn something to the United States' advantage if he went. Admiral Milo Draemel advised strongly against it. The Japanese were not to be trusted, in his opinion. He urged Kimmel not to go, and the commander in chief was happy to accept his advice.

Instead, Kimmel left the hotel shortly after nine thirty and was home by ten. He went straight to bed because he had an appointment early on Sunday morning. He was going to play golf with his opposite number in the army, Lieutenant General Walter Short.

In Honolulu it turned out to be a relatively quiet night. Despite all the warships in port, and more than forty thousand soldiers scattered across the islands, there was very little trouble on the streets. The shore patrol made only five serious arrests. The military police picked up fewer than thirty drunken soldiers and dumped them in the cells at Fort Shafter until they had sobered up.

The bars all closed at midnight. No liquor could be served in Honolulu after that time. The band at the Royal Hawaiian Hotel marked the moment by playing "The Star Spangled Banner" as the dancers across the floor snapped to attention.

Elsewhere soldiers and sailors spilled out onto the streets after the pubs had shut. Most found their way safely back to ship or barracks, but more than seven hundred opted to stay the night at the YMCA in Honolulu, where beds were kept available for service personnel who needed somewhere to bunk down. It was heading for one o'clock on Sunday morning before the last of them had drifted away and the streets began to quiet down for the night.

Not everyone had spent the evening in Honolulu. Quite a few sailors had opted to remain aboard their ships or else to spend a few hours ashore at the new Bloch Recreation Center at Pearl Harbor. With the Pacific Fleet stationed at Oahu for the foreseeable future, the center had been opened in August to take some of the pressure off Honolulu. The center offered films, music, billiards, boxing, bowling, and beer—everything that Honolulu did except brothels and clip joints.

There was a music competition at the center that night, the final round of a contest to decide the best ship's band in the fleet. "The Battle of Music" was fought between *Argonne, Detroit, Pennsylvania*, and *Tennessee*. *Pennsylvania*'s band won, after which everyone sang "God Bless America." The dancing continued until midnight.

The fleet was brightly lit up as the liberty men weaved unsteadily back to their ships. Signal lights were blinking from ship to ship. The docks were illuminated on shore. More than one sailor was reminded of Christmas decorations as he headed back to his quarters or waited for the last liberty boat of the night to ferry him across the water to his ship anchored in the stream.

At station KGMB at the same time, they were settling in for an all-night session of Hawaiian music on the radio. They were doing so at the request of the U.S. Army Air Force, which paid them for the service.

A flight of B-17 bombers was due in next morning, flying through the night from California, en route to the Philippines. The air force wanted KGMB on the air so that the bombers could home in on the signal. It was common knowledge on Oahu that if KGMB played music all night, military aircraft were sure to arrive early the following morning.

EIGHT

AN ENGLISHWOMAN DANCES ON DECK

Aboard the task force, there were mixed feelings as darkness fell and the Japanese prepared to attack Pearl Harbor the next morning. The news that there were no longer any aircraft carriers in port had come as a blow, but they were all agreed that it couldn't be helped now. They would just have to press on regardless.

On the carrier *Akagi*, a relief map of Pearl Harbor had been laid out on the hangar deck as soon as the task force's destination had been revealed to the crew. Constructed from plaster of Paris, the model showed every fold and contour of the harbor in great detail. The pilots had spent hours gathered around it, familiarizing themselves with everything they needed to know as they planned their attack.

They had also studied the silhouettes of U.S. warships, playing games with large flashcards until they could recognize every battleship at a glance. A brief glimpse was all the pilots would have as they roared across the harbor to attack the biggest ships before speeding away again under heavy ground fire.

The pilots on the other five carriers were equally well prepared. A total of just over four hundred aircraft stood ready for the raid. The aircraft were a mix of fighter planes and fighter-bombers of various kinds carrying enough bombs and torpedoes to disable anything they came up against in the harbor.

After the U.S. warships had been dealt with, the plan was for a later wave of aircraft to destroy the oil tanks and other installations ashore. If all went well, Pearl Harbor would be knocked out of commission for months while the Japanese army rampaged unchecked through the islands of Southeast Asia.

Morale was high as the airmen prepared for a few hours' rest before the start. After all the waiting, they were glad that the moment had almost arrived at last. In accordance with Japanese custom, quite a few of them had filled an envelope with nail clippings and locks of hair as a memento to be mailed back to their families if they didn't return from the raid. The airmen were under no illusions about the dangers that lay ahead.

Some had a few beers before bed, or a shot of sake to steady their nerves. Others lay on their bunks writing last letters to wives and sweethearts, or had a ritual bath to purify their bodies before battle, like the samurai of old. According to Chigusa aboard *Akigumo*, everyone thought they were going to die before the raid was over.

Some pilots were very gung-ho at the prospect of attacking America— or pretended to be. Others were quieter, more reflective. But all were driven by their duty to their country, personified by the emperor, a duty that they would carry out to the utmost of their ability.

In *Akagi*'s engine room, the stokers had drunk sake and shouted "Banzai!" with the rest when the task force's destination had been announced. "An air attack on Hawaii!" seaman Iki Kuramoti had exulted. "A dream come true!"[1]

Many ordinary sailors in the fleet shared his feelings. In common with fighting men everywhere, they couldn't see beyond the immediate satisfaction of squaring up to the enemy and giving him a hard punch in the nose. The long-term consequences were beyond their comprehension.

Plenty of Japanese had their doubts, however. A substantial number shared Admiral Pye's view that the United States was far too big and powerful to attack. They wondered if the government back in Tokyo really knew what it was doing in sending them into Pearl Harbor.

Commander Kyozo Ohashi was a staff officer aboard the carrier *Shokaku*. In his view, opinions about the impending attack divided into three main categories:

> *First, there were those who were virtually unmoved by the special mission of attacking Pearl Harbor, who considered the operation as their God-given duty, and who faced the immediate future with grim stoicism. Into this class fell most of the older staff officers and key pilots.*
>
> *Secondly, there were those who thought the Pearl Harbor operation would succeed, but who were apprehensive about the final outcome of the war. They wondered what was going to happen after the initial phase was over. Into this class fell the more intelligent of the younger officers who tried to look at things from a long-range viewpoint.*
>
> *Finally, there were those who were nervous and afraid of what lay ahead. This class included the newer officers, the young trainees, and those of the crew who could only glimpse snatches of the overall plan.*[2]

Commander Minoru Genda, aboard *Akagi*, was the operation's leading planner. He had spent most of the summer supervising torpedo runs in the Inland Sea to decide whether an attack in the shallow waters of Pearl Harbor was feasible. By fitting wooden stabilizers to the torpedoes' fins to prevent them from sinking too far into the water, he had established that an attack in shallow seas was indeed possible.

Genda had been as disconcerted as everyone else to learn that the aircraft carriers were no longer in harbor, but his despondency hadn't lasted long. Lieutenant Commander Kanjiro Ono, Admiral Nagumo's intelligence officer, comforted him with the thought that a couple of the carriers might easily return to port at short notice. Genda brightened at the prospect. "If that happens, I don't care if all eight battleships are away."[3]

The attack was to be led by Commander Mitsuo Fuchida, an old friend of Genda's from their days at the naval academy in Hiroshima. Genda was a torpedo man. Fuchida was the expert on conventional bombing.

A gifted airman, with recent combat experience in China, Fuchida had been recommended by Genda for the job. He was to lead the first wave of bombers to the target the next morning. Once they reached Pearl Harbor, he was to decide the order of attack after he had sight of the American fleet and could make a visual assessment of the situation down below.

Genda and Fuchida had worked hard on the details during the ten-day voyage from Japan. The aircrew were as ready as they could be for the attack. The pilots had gone over the plan again and again, rehearsing every possibility until they all knew what to do in any foreseeable situation. The rest was in the lap of the gods.

After supper that night, Fuchida had a final meeting in *Akagi*'s wardroom with his flight commanders and a few key pilots. Then he told them all to get some rest before the early start next morning. He himself turned in at 10:00 p.m., the same time as Admiral Kimmel on Oahu.

By his own account Fuchida was philosophical as he lay down to sleep, certain that everything had been done that could be done. Whatever his fears for next morning, particularly the lack of aircraft carriers in harbor, he didn't allow anything to interfere with his rest. "I slept soundly. I had set up the whole machinery of the attack, and it was ready to go. There was no use worrying now."[4]

While the airmen tried to get some sleep, Japanese submarines were silently taking up positions around Oahu, ready for the outbreak of war.

Traveling underwater by day, on the surface by night, a fleet of more than twenty I-class submarines had crossed the Pacific and then fanned out to cover the Hawaiian Islands and the approaches to the United States from the west.

The I-class submarines were enormous vessels, designed for long-distance, oceangoing warfare. They were so large that they could carry a float plane in a watertight hangar attached to the conning tower. Some could catapult the plane into the sky and retrieve it from the sea with a crane.

A few of the submarines had been converted to carry a midget submarine on deck, instead of a seaplane. Five of these had surfaced off Oahu after dark and were preparing to launch their midget subs in an attack on Pearl Harbor.

The midget submarines were two-man vessels, each carrying two torpedoes. They were small enough to sneak undetected into the harbor and wreak havoc on the American warships at anchor. With torpedo nets stretched across the narrow entrance channel to the harbor, the crews' chances of doing any serious damage were minimal, but they were going to try anyway.

The plan called for the midget submarines to enter Pearl Harbor that night and then lie low until the Japanese air attack in the morning. They were to wait until the bombing started before loosing their own torpedoes.

The idea seemed half-baked to many. For one thing, surprise would be lost if any of the submarines was spotted. For another, they might be sunk accidentally by their own aircraft if they ventured into the target area. The risks of the operation far outweighed any potential benefit that the plan's critics could see.

A skeptical Admiral Yamamoto had originally stipulated that the midget submarines were not to enter the harbor, for fear of giving the game away. He had relented only after being persuaded that the submarines could easily slip through the entrance channel without being seen.

The vessels had been transported across the Pacific on the decks of the larger submarines to within a few miles of Oahu. The lights of Pearl Harbor and Honolulu were clearly visible as the handpicked crews transferred to the smaller craft. They could even see the illuminated twin towers of the Royal Hawaiian Hotel on Waikiki Beach.

Few of them expected to return from the adventure. If they couldn't escape after firing their torpedoes, they had been ordered to destroy their submarines instead so that the machinery couldn't be examined by the Americans.

After that the crews planned to make their way ashore and continue the fight on land. Each of them was armed with a gun and a samurai sword. Wearing white *hashamakis* (the traditional headbands of the Japanese warrior), they intended to emerge from the sea and fall on the nearest Americans, dying gloriously in a hail of bullets and flashing swords, "like cherry blossoms falling to the ground."[5] That would certainly show Roosevelt who was boss.

Out in the darkness to the east, the passengers aboard the Dutch ship *Jägers-fontein* were unaware of what lay ahead of them as they prepared to arrive in Honolulu next morning. After an uncomfortable voyage from San Francisco, they were having a dance to celebrate their last night at sea.

The first three days out from California had been truly awful. Rough seas, gray skies, cold weather. Quite a few passengers had chosen to remain in their bunks with a sick bag handy until the storms had passed.

The fourth day at sea had been much better. The waters had calmed down. Blue skies had replaced gray clouds. The sun had come out, shining brilliantly on a bright blue sea. The passengers had perked up accordingly.

Among them was Joan Fawcett, a twenty-one-year-old Englishwoman traveling with her mother. They were on their way home to India. Joan's mother was ill. Joan had been given time off from her postgraduate studies in Toronto to look after her mother and see her safely back to their home.

She was enjoying the trip, now that the weather was better. There were deck games to play, and table tennis, and fooling around in the netting over the empty pool. A lot of the passengers were missionaries, but there were a few young men as well, enough to make up a party. Joan was shocked at how much Americans drank. She confined herself to a single glass of wine in the evening and then orange soda for the rest of the night.

The dance was on deck, in the moonlight. The passengers had only just been told that the ship was to call at Honolulu next morning. After days out of sight of land, Joan was looking forward to it. She was planning to be up very early next day so as not to miss a minute of their arrival as *Jägers-fontein* rounded Diamond Head soon after first light and came into the harbor at Honolulu.

NINE

A STRANGE PERISCOPE AT SEA

The pessimists on the Japanese staff had been right to worry about the danger of their submarines giving the game away as they approached Pearl Harbor. The first one was probably spotted at 3:42 a.m. on the Sunday morning, a little under three hours before dawn.

Something that might have been a periscope created a modest bow wave at that time as it headed for the buoys marking the entrance to the harbor. The wave was traveling at nine knots and had another thousand yards to go when it was seen by an alert lookout aboard the U.S. minesweeper *Condor*.

The submarine evidently spotted the minesweeper at the same time. The periscope immediately changed course to avoid a collision and veered off in another direction.

Condor blinked the news by signal lamp to the destroyer *Ward* nearby. U.S. submarines were not allowed to submerge in that area, so Lieutenant William Outerbridge, on his first day in command, sounded general quarters.

Ward's crew spent most of the next hour at their stations, scouring the sea in vain for another sight of the submarine. Finding nothing, they radioed *Condor* for more information about the supposed vessel's whereabouts and course.

In replying, *Condor* forgot to mention that the submarine had changed course. The ensuing discussion at cross-purposes was picked up by the radio station on Bishop's Point, but neither the ships nor the radio station passed it any further up the chain of command. Everyone was thinking in terms of a large submarine, not a tiny craft capable of slipping into Pearl Harbor when the gate in the torpedo net was opened. It might not have been a periscope anyway.

The midget submarines were certainly in the area. Once the two-man crews were aboard, the mother submarines had submerged again and the midgets had been released underwater, a complicated business involving the unlocking of the huge metal clamps that held them in place.

One of the midgets failed to launch until just before dawn. Its gyrocompass had malfunctioned, which made underwater navigation much more difficult. After failing to repair it, Ensign Kazuo Sakamaki decided to go ahead anyway, only to encounter problems with the sub's trim as soon as he and Seaman Kyoji Inagaki had detached from the mother ship.

The other midgets launched without trouble and headed for the harbor entrance. As well as the U.S. Navy, they also had to avoid the coral reefs around the entrance channel. Once they reached the channel, they had to find a way of getting past the anti-torpedo net at the entrance.

The net was forty-five feet deep, designed to stop torpedoes, not tiny submarines. The channel was seventy-two feet at the deepest point. If the submarines found the right spot, they might just about wriggle underneath without snagging the net.

Or they could wait for the gate to open and slip through before the net closed again. As if on cue, the gate swung wide at 4:58 that morning to allow another minesweeper to return to base. *Condor* was also due to return shortly. The gatekeeper decided to leave the net open for a while, rather than go to the bother of closing everything up again.

Just over two hundred miles to the north, the pilots of the task force rose in the early hours to prepare for their attack on the harbor.

The men dressed carefully, in accordance with Japanese custom. It was part of the ritual of battle that they should dress for the occasion, like the knights of medieval Europe. The *fundoshi*, a Japanese loincloth, was a popular choice. Commander Fuchida preferred red long johns and a red shirt that wouldn't show the blood if he was wounded.

The pilots also wore the *hashamaki* headband, as samurai warriors of the air. They all had crisp, clean uniforms under their flying suits. They looked the part as they went to breakfast to eat a last meal before taking to the sky.

The food was traditional too. Special occasions demanded special rations. The pilots had been pampered during the voyage, fed milk and eggs not available to everybody. Some now ate a last meal of pickled plums in rice balls wrapped in bamboo leaves.

Others had a ceremonial feast of *sekihan*—rice and red beans—reserved for very important occasions. Aboard *Akigumo*, the whole crew had been treated the day before to cakes, apples, and *ohagi*, a mix of sugar and red beans that was hard to come by and much appreciated now that sugar was rationed by the government.

A shot of sake was available for those pilots who wanted it. Others preferred to spend a few quiet moments at one of the portable Shinto shrines that all the ships carried. Then they reported to the briefing room to receive their last-minute instructions for the attack.

The briefings were brisk and to the point. The pilots were given the latest weather report from Hawaii radio, followed by details of wind speed and direction. The sea was excessively choppy that morning, crashing repeatedly over the bows of the ships. Visibility was just about adequate. There was a strong east wind for takeoff.

Taking all these factors into account, the flying time to the target and back had been calculated to within a few minutes. The diagrams on the blackboards had also been updated to show the last known positions of the warships in Pearl Harbor. The pilots took a final look at their targets, then conferred quietly together before dispersing to their aircraft.

The first wave was due to take off at 6:00 a.m. It comprised forty torpedo planes, forty-nine horizontal bombers and fifty-one dive-bombers, all under the protection of forty-three escorting fighters.

Another large wave would follow later, but without any torpedo planes.

Slow and ponderous, the torpedo planes depended on the advantage of surprise for success. They were all flying in the first wave so that they could drop their torpedoes and get away again before the Americans realized what was happening.

The first wave was commanded by Fuchida. He was the only one allowed to break radio silence. Everyone else was under strict orders to say nothing on the air until they had reached the target. Fuchida's bomber had a red-and-yellow stripe around the tail so that the rest all knew who to follow.

His maintenance crew presented him with a *hashamaki* as he prepared to set off. It was decorated with a rising sun and the slogan "Certain Victory." The crew wanted him to have it to show that they would be with him in spirit over Pearl Harbor.

The signal to go came from *Akagi*. A set of flags flew at half-mast to warn the pilots to get ready. As soon as they were, the flags were hauled to the top of the mast and then quickly dropped again, the signal everyone had been waiting for.

Engines gunned as the aircraft began to take off from all six carriers simultaneously. The fighters went first, because they were lightest and needed the least runway. The takeoff officer on each carrier judged the pitch and roll of the ship to the best of his ability and then waved a green light telling each pilot to go at once.

One flyer didn't make it. Taking off from an aircraft carrier is a fraught business at the best of times, let alone in the dark with a heavy swell running. The pilot misjudged his run and was forced to ditch in the sea. He was picked up by a destroyer, but the plane was lost.

The rest quickly got airborne and formed up alongside the task force, waiting for the other aircraft to follow. They were soon joined by the horizontal bombers: three-man aircraft carrying a one-ton bomb. Some of the bombs had been inscribed with hate messages from the maintenance crews to the people of the United States.

Dive- and torpedo-bombers brought up the rear. In just over fifteen minutes, the entire force of 183 aircraft was airborne and ready to go. The pilots had practiced the speed of this takeoff many times in training. Now they were doing it for real.

All eyes were on Fuchida's lead plane as they took formation. Its glowing orange light led the way as he turned and flew across *Akagi*'s bows. That was the signal for the rest to close up behind and follow him south to Oahu. It was a little before 6:30 and still not light as they set out.

Before they arrived, though, Japan had to declare war on the United States.

The fourteenth part of Tokyo's response to Roosevelt's peace plan arrived in Washington just after seven that morning (Eastern Standard Time, several hours before the Japanese aircraft took off).

U.S. Navy cryptographers began to decode it at once. Just up the road, the Japanese Embassy was considerably slower off the mark. The duty officer wasn't immediately able to raise any of the embassy's code people that early on a Sunday morning.

The Americans grasped the significance of the fourteenth part as soon as they read it. Japan intended to break off peace negotiations. It seemed a fair bet that war would follow.

The Americans weren't taken by surprise. They interpreted the message as confirmation of their suspicions, rather than anything more. The Japanese were about to launch an attack somewhere in the Pacific, almost certainly against American interests.

Their suspicions were redoubled when they intercepted a follow-up message from Tokyo to the Japanese Embassy. "Will the Ambassador please submit to the United States Government (if possible to the Secretary of State) our reply to the United States at 1:00 p.m. on the 7th, your time."[1]

That could hardly have been clearer. Whatever the Japanese were planning was timed for one o'clock that afternoon, Washington time. Less than five hours away.

Colonel Rufus Bratton, head of Military Intelligence's Far East Section, was onto it at once. He didn't have the authority to issue a general alert, so he went in search of a more senior officer who did.

Nobody was in their office on a Sunday morning. Bratton hit the phone and called them at home. He rang the chief of staff, General George C.

Marshall, at around 9:00 a.m., only to be told that the general had gone out for his customary Sunday-morning horseback ride.

Bratton told Marshall's orderly to find him at once and get him to the nearest phone. Bratton also rang Brigadier-General Sherman Miles, the assistant chief of staff, asking him to come in to the office immediately. Marshall would want to see him later.

While Bratton was on the phone, the navy's Alwin Kramer was on his way to a 10:00 a.m. appointment at the State Department. He dropped in at the White House first to deliver the overnight messages to the president's staff.

The fourteenth part of the Japanese response was among them. Captain Beardall took it to Roosevelt in his bedroom.

The president had spoken of war when Lieutenant Schulz had shown him the first thirteen parts the previous night. He was less forthcoming when he saw the fourteenth part that morning. So far as Beardall remembered, he remarked only that it looked as if the Japanese were about to break off the negotiations.

Kramer returned from the State Department to find Tokyo's one o'clock message waiting on his desk. He sat down immediately to calculate what time it would be elsewhere when it was one o'clock in Washington.

In Hawaii it would be seven thirty in the morning, full daylight. Kramer couldn't speak for the army, but in the navy at that hour the hands would be on their way to breakfast, fully awake and ready for the day.

Farther west though, it would still be dark. Everyone not on duty would be fast asleep. The standard time for a surprise attack was in the hours just before dawn, when human beings were not alert and vitality was at its lowest.

Malaya? The Philippines? The Kra Isthmus? They would all be approaching dawn while Washington was having lunch.

Other intercepted messages arrived as Kramer was pondering. Deepest thanks from Tokyo to Ambassador Nomura and Special Envoy Kurusu for all their hard work over the past few weeks in Washington. A cryptic observation that relations with Britain and the United States were not as they ought to be. An order to destroy all remaining codes, cipher machines, and secret documents at the embassy without further delay.

It all added up to something about to happen in the Pacific, something that did not bode well for the United States. The question of when appeared to have been answered by the interception of the one o'clock message that morning. The question of where was still wide open, anybody's guess.

At the Japanese Embassy, the diplomats were preparing a copy of Tokyo's fourteen-part response to Roosevelt's peace plan for delivery to the secretary of state at one o'clock, as ordered. They had no idea that the Americans had broken their code and already knew what was in the response.

The document ran to about thirteen pages in all. It had to be neatly typed before it could be delivered. Tokyo had stressed that its contents were too secret for any of the usual typists to see, so the job had been given instead to Katsuzo Okumura.

Okumura was a first secretary at the embassy. He was a trained diplomat but a far-from-skilled typist. He had been hard at work since the day before, laboriously bashing out Japan's formal response with two fingers in a language and typescript not his own.

Okumura's job had not been made any easier by the arrival of the response in dribs and drabs, often out of order. The fourteenth part was still being decoded as he worked. There had been corrections, too: afterthoughts and minor adjustments from Tokyo that had arrived after he had already typed the relevant section.

To add to his problems, there was now a tight deadline as well. One o'clock didn't allow much time for completing a fair copy. Okumura was the fastest two-finger man in the embassy, but that didn't mean much. There were serious doubts as to whether he would be able to finish the job in time.

Outside Pearl Harbor, another submarine had been spotted at about six thirty that morning, just as the first wave of Japanese aircraft was taking off from the carriers and turning south.

At first glance the submarine appeared to be a buoy in the distance. Through binoculars, it transformed itself into a small conning tower, but not one that matched any American vessel.

The tiny green craft seemed to be shadowing a barge that was being towed into Pearl Harbor through the open torpedo net. It was either having trouble submerging or else didn't realize that it could be seen.

The destroyer *Ward* was alerted. Lieutenant Outerbridge arrived on the bridge in a hurry, clad in a Japanese kimono. He took one look at the submarine and sounded general quarters for the second time in three hours.

The crew raced to their battle stations. Overhead, a U.S. Navy Catalina had seen the submarine at the same time. The craft was in a prohibited area for an American submarine, but the pilots' first thought was that it was there by accident and must be in distress. Seeing *Ward* steaming toward it, they dropped a couple of smoke flares to mark its position.

The submarine continued to trail the barge toward Pearl Harbor. It failed to spot the approaching *Ward*. The destroyer was only a hundred yards away, close enough for the crew to see moss and barnacles on the submarine's hull, when Outerbridge gave the order to open fire.

It wasn't an easy decision to make. The United States was at peace. Plenty of crewmen aboard *Ward* feared that the submarine might be in the wrong area by mistake, an American craft manned by sailors like themselves. They would never forgive themselves if they sank it with friendly fire and killed the crew in error. Nor would their country.

Yet *Ward*'s orders were quite clear. Sink any submarine found in the defensive area without authority.

The target was too close for the gunners to use their sights, so they just aimed toward the hull and fired. The first shot whistled harmlessly over the conning tower. The second, fired at about fifty yards, struck the base of the conning tower at the waterline.

The submarine reeled and began to lose speed. It was so close that *Ward*'s crew could see the glass in the periscope as it vanished beyond the destroyer's stern. Four depth charges followed, primed to detonate at a hundred feet below the surface.

The submarine was crushed in a cascade of exploding seawater.

Overhead, the Catalina joined in after a brief discussion between the pilots. Both men could see themselves being court-martialed if they got it wrong, but their orders were the same as *Ward*'s.

Encouraged by the destroyer's action, the flying boat too dropped depth charges. The two pilots hoped that they hadn't killed any Americans as a large quantity of oil bubbled to the surface. The submarine had evidently gone down in a thousand feet of water.

The action was watched from a distance by sailors on other ships. Most of them failed to appreciate what was happening. They weren't close enough to realize that the action was real. They assumed it was just some kind of early morning naval exercise.

Others had a closer view. The Hawaiian-Japanese crew of a fishing sampan was only five hundred yards away from the submarine when it was first sighted. Sampans weren't allowed in the defensive area, so *Ward* went after it as soon as the depth-charging had been completed.

The sampan hastily departed in the direction of Barber's Point, west of Pearl Harbor. There it hove to while the skipper found something white to wave in surrender. He didn't want to be blown out of the water.

While *Ward* was pursuing the sampan, the destroyer picked up the echo of yet another submarine below the surface. This one too was depth-charged at 7:05 a.m. The resulting oil slick did not impress Outerbridge. It was a common submarine ploy to fake a sinking by releasing small quantities of oil.

At 6:53, he reported his attack on the first submarine back to base. "We have attacked, fired upon, and dropped depth charges upon submarine operating in defensive sea area."[2] Now, just after 7:00 a.m., he radioed again. "Please have coast guard send cutter to relieve us of sampan."[3]

The cutter duly arrived. *Ward* delivered the sampan and went back to patrolling the bay.

At the same time, the two-man crew of the mobile radar station at Opana, on the northern tip of Oahu, were going off duty at the end of their shift.

The early morning shift lasted from 4:00 to 7:00 a.m., the hours when a hostile attack was most likely. It was a dull shift at the best of times, particularly so on a sleepy Sunday morning. There were very few blips to see on the radar screen that morning, even fewer than normal for a Sunday.

The mobile radar station comprised two trucks and a tent for the men to sleep in. It was one of five on the island, all of them linked to the aircraft-warning system at Fort Shafter. Radar itself was brand-new, unfamiliar to the men until recently. It had done wonders for the British during the Battle of Britain.

Private Joseph Lockard operated the screen. Private George Elliott did the plotting on the table. Between them, they recorded nine blips on the oscilloscope in the fifteen minutes before 7:00 a.m., when they were due to stand down.

The blips may all have belonged to the same aircraft. The Japanese had sent a couple of seaplanes ahead of the main force to check out Pearl Harbor and the anchorage at Lahaina from a discreet distance. The pilots had orders to report back at once if they spotted any aircraft carriers anywhere.

The blips were nothing out of the ordinary, certainly not worth reporting. Elliott and Lockard were far more interested in breakfast as they reached the end of their shift. The truck that came to take them back to camp was often late, so Elliott decided to spend a little more time at the oscilloscope until it arrived. He was a novice at radar, eager to learn more.

The more-experienced Lockard sat with him, explaining how to interpret the echoes on-screen. They hadn't been there long when the set picked up something that Lockard had never encountered before:

There was this thing on the screen. It was the largest blip I'd ever seen. At first, we thought something was wrong with the equipment, so we ran it through a series of tests. I checked out the receiver and transmitter to see if there was anything mechanically wrong. There was nothing electronically wrong that we could see, so we started plotting the blip.[4]

Lockard took over the oscilloscope. Elliott returned to the plotting table. The blip quickly became a flight of at least fifty aircraft, 137 miles to the north. They were heading for Oahu and closing fast.

In English war films, a clipped RAF voice would then have announced "Bandits. Fifty plus," and a nice girl in a tin hat would have moved her gambling chips across the table. But the United States wasn't at war with anyone. Lockard didn't think the echo was worth mentioning to the plotters at Fort Shafter.

Elliott disagreed. He thought they should be told. It was 7:06 as he donned the headphones connecting him directly to the plotters. No one answered, so he tried the switchboard on another line and got through to Private Joseph McDonald, who occupied a little cubicle next door to the plotting room.

McDonald didn't think anyone was in that time of day. The plotters had all gone to breakfast. Elliott told him to find someone and pass the information on. McDonald wrote it all down, then turned to look at the clock in the plotting room so that he could log the time of receipt.

Through the open door, he noticed that Lieutenant Kermit Tyler, a fighter pilot, was still at the plotting table. Tyler was there to observe the system and learn how the operation worked. Since nothing was happening, he had spent much of his shift writing letters.

McDonald showed Tyler the message. Neither of them had seen anything like it before. McDonald asked Tyler if they should do something about it, perhaps recall the plotting staff from breakfast. The lieutenant was noncommittal, so McDonald went back to the switchboard and called the radar station at Opana to find out more.

He got through to Lockard, who confirmed that an enormous blip on the radar was heading for the island. It was the biggest electronic cluster Lockard had ever seen on-screen. He asked McDonald to bring Tyler to the phone.

The lieutenant came. Lockard told him what he could see. "We had an unusually large flight—in fact, the largest I had ever seen on the equipment—coming in from almost due north at 130 some miles."[5]

Tyler was pleased to hear it. He knew from the all-night music on the radio that a squadron of aircraft was due to arrive early that morning. They were B-17 Flying Fortresses from California, stopping off at Oahu on their way to reinforce MacArthur in the Philippines. Navigation across the featureless Pacific wasn't easy, even with KGMB's Hawaiian music to guide the bombers in. The Fortresses had clearly managed it and would shortly reach Oahu.

The aircraft carriers were at sea too. If it wasn't the U.S. Air Force on-screen, it could easily be the U.S. Navy. Friendly forces, either way.

"Don't worry about it," Tyler told Lockard, before hanging up.[6]

The breakfast truck still hadn't arrived, so Elliott insisted that they should keep tracking the blip on the oscilloscope. It was ninety-two miles from Oahu at 7:15, forty-five at 7:30. Nine minutes later it was only twenty miles away when Elliott and Lockard lost the echo in the hills around the radar station.

There was nothing they could do to get the signal back. They closed the system down instead and went outside to wait for the breakfast truck. It arrived a few minutes later, and the two of them went off to have something to eat.

TEN

"TORA! TORA! TORA!"

Japan still had to declare war on the United States. The formal rejection of Roosevelt's peace proposals was supposed to be delivered to the State Department at exactly 1:00 p.m., just as the first wave of Japanese aircraft approached Pearl Harbor. Unfortunately Okumura at the embassy hadn't finished typing it yet.

He had bashed it out once, but the result did not look good. There were too many errors and misspellings. Minor errors could be erased and typed over once the correcting fluid had dried. Larger mistakes were impossible to conceal without making a dreadful mess.

What to do? The document was of historic importance. It had to look immaculate when Nomura and Kurusu delivered it to the State Department. Okumura would lose face if it didn't.

Any of the professional typists at the embassy could have made the document look good, if they had been doing it. But none of them had the security clearance to read what it said.

The clock was ticking. A decision had to be taken. Around eleven o'clock, with two hours to go, Okumura decided that there was only one thing to do. He would just have to type all thirteen pages again, making sure he hit all the right keys this time.

By 1:00 p.m., when Nomura and Kurusu were due to present the document to Hull at the State Department, Okumura's fair copy was nowhere near finished. The Japanese had to call and ask for the meeting to be postponed until 1:45.

General Marshall was out riding for the early part of the morning. He returned Bratton's call just before 10:30 and reached the War Department around 11:25. He was immediately shown the fourteen-part Japanese message in its entirety.

Marshall insisted on reading the whole thing aloud while Bratton and Miles tried to draw his attention to the one o'clock message with its urgent deadline. When at last Marshall turned to it, he got the point at once. The Japanese were about to strike somewhere in the Pacific.

Marshall grabbed pencil and paper. The Philippines, Hawaii, Panama, and the U.S. West Coast would have to be warned. He scribbled a hurried message and then telephoned Admiral Stark at the White House to tell him what he was about to do.

Stark was dubious. Several similar warnings had recently been issued, including one the previous weekend. The admiral was reluctant to issue a further alert if it turned out to be another false alarm. He allowed himself to be persuaded, however, asking only that Marshall should copy naval personnel into the warning. Marshall complied:

> *Japanese are presenting at one pm eastern standard time today what amounts to an ultimatum also they are under orders to destroy their code machine immediately.*
>
> *Just what significance the hour set may have we do not know but be on alert accordingly. Inform naval authorities of this communication. Marshall.*[1]

Thrusting the message into Bratton's hand, the general told him to send it out by the fastest secure means available. If there was a question of priority, he wanted the Philippines to be warned first.

Bratton hurried to the code room. Neither the cipher clerk nor the officer in charge could read Marshall's handwriting. Bratton stood over a typist and dictated the message at speed. It was 11:58 as he handed it to the code people for immediate dispatch.

It would be another half hour at least before the message could reach anyone. It was sent to the Caribbean at exactly midday and to the Philippines six minutes later. Unfortunately it couldn't be sent to the Hawaiian Islands because of the atmospheric conditions in that part of the Pacific. There had been no contact with Honolulu since half past ten that morning.

Commercial services were still operating. The message went by Western Union to San Francisco, and then by RCA to Honolulu.

On Oahu, Outerbridge's decoded signal about attacking a submarine outside Pearl Harbor was on Lieutenant Commander Harold Kaminski's desk at naval headquarters by 7:12. Kaminski was a retired officer from World War I, recently recalled to duty. Picking up the phone, he got word of the attack via a third party to the staff duty officer, Commander Vincent Murphy, who was just getting dressed. Then, on his own initiative, he sent a message to the duty destroyer *Monaghan*. "Get under way immediately and contact USS *Ward* in defensive sea area."[2]

Having done that, Kaminski called Captain John Earle, chief of staff to Admiral Claude Bloch, to tell him what was happening.

Earle was skeptical. There had been so many false reports in the past. Whales, flotsam, jetsam. This one sounded a bit different though, if shots had actually been fired and depth charges dropped. He couldn't remember that happening before.

It was difficult to know what to make of it. *Ward*'s report about attacking a submarine had been followed by a routine message to the coast guard about a sampan apparently trying to fish in the wrong place. That rather suggested that the report about a submarine couldn't have been too serious.

On the other hand, the air force had attacked the submarine too. Commander Murphy had just received a message from the duty officer on Ford Island saying that one of its Catalinas had sunk a submerged submarine a mile outside the harbor. Presumably the pilots knew the difference between a submarine and a whale.

The reports were too serious to be ignored. Various senior officers were therefore telephoned at home and asked to come in at once. A search of the waters around Pearl Harbor was the first priority, if only to establish that it had all just been a false alarm.

Admiral Kimmel was telephoned too. He had been up since seven, looking forward to his fortnightly game of golf with General Short. He was unshaven, still in his nightclothes, when Murphy called.

Kimmel shared Earle's skepticism. "We had so many reports, false reports of submarines in the outlying area, I thought, well, I would wait for verification of the report."[3] Nevertheless, Kimmel took no chances. He told Murphy that he was on his way.

At the Japanese consulate in Honolulu, Consul General Nagao Kita was far more relaxed as he arose that morning. He was planning to play golf later, the same as Kimmel. It was just another Sunday, so far as he and the rest of the staff were concerned. If any of them had any inkling of what was about to unfold above their heads, they were making a very good job of concealing it.

No one else had any suspicions. It was business as usual on Oahu as the sun came up over the hills to the east. No one on the island had any reason to expect anything different.

At the Moana Hotel on Waikiki Beach, the defeated Bearcats from Willamette University had put yesterday's football game behind them and were looking forward to a tour of the island later in the morning. A bus was going to take them around Pearl Harbor first, then on to a picnic on the north shore with some girls from the University of Hawaii.

Most of the Willamette boys came from small farms or lumberjacking families in Oregon. San Francisco had been an eye-opener to them, let alone the delights of the Hawaiian Islands. They were determined to make the most of their visit now that the game was over and they could afford to relax for the rest of the trip.

Some got up early and padded across the beach for a swim. Others were preparing for church. Their time was their own until nine thirty, when the bus would be waiting for them at the hotel. They were taking boxed lunches with them and had the whole of the day to see all the sights.

AraBelle Fuller was going on a tour of the island too. A registered nurse, she had only been on Oahu for two weeks and had yet to see much of it beyond Honolulu. She greatly liked what she had seen so far. The weather wasn't as warm as she had expected, but there was always plenty to do, and the island's red dust reminded her strongly of home in South Dakota.

Fuller was still in bed as the light streamed in. After a busy week at the Leahi Hospital, she was looking forward to a lazy day off. She planned to lie in until nine or so and then spend the rest of the day on a leisurely jaunt around Oahu's beauty spots, seeing all the same sights as the Willamette boys.

At Schofield Barracks, in the middle of the island, most of the enlisted men were also enjoying a Sunday lie-in after the working week. Those who didn't have weekend passes to Honolulu were still in their barrack rooms, either dead to the world or quietly surfacing in their own time.

The big event at Schofield that morning was breakfast. It was always special on Sundays because the men were served extra rations, a half pint of milk to be added to all the eggs, pancakes, and syrup. The milk was highly prized and easily stolen if soldiers didn't keep an eye on it. Private James Jones was just one of many who were looking forward to the treat as they made their way to the mess halls for the meal.

At Wheeler Field, the army's fighter base a mile away, not much was stirring either. A total of sixty-two new fighter planes stood in neat rows along the field alongside a number of older ones. The aircraft were bunched tightly together and out in the open so that they could more easily be protected from sabotage by local Japanese agents.

A couple of fighter pilots were awake, but only because they hadn't been to bed yet. Lieutenants George Welch and Kenneth Taylor had come over yesterday from the Haleiwa airstrip for the Saturday-night dance. They had spent the rest of the night playing poker and were now thinking of driving back to Haleiwa for a swim, since it was far too late to go to bed.

The army's bombers were kept on the coast at Hickam Field, a concrete runway by the entrance to Pearl Harbor. The bombers, too, were lined up on the apron to prevent sabotage. They were about to be joined by a dozen Flying Fortresses from California, already on the radar and coming in fast. A medical officer stood ready with a Flit gun to spray insecticide and kill all the bugs as soon as they touched down.

The navy's aircraft were kept on Ford Island, right in the middle of the harbor. The place was looking half empty that morning because only the seaplanes were there. The carrier planes lived on the island when the carriers were in port, but they were all at sea that day, on their way to other destinations.

Eight battleships were still moored off Ford Island. Seven of them were anchored in the channel to the southeast known as Battleship Row. The water stood between Ford Island and Hickam Field on the mainland.

The ships' crews were enjoying the same Sunday-morning routine as the troops on land. For some that meant lengthy discussions about football or girls as they lay idly on their bunks with nothing to do until lunchtime. For others it meant letters and snapshots from home or a last chance to get their Christmas cards written before the final mailboat to San Francisco.

Aboard *Arizona* they were rigging up an awning for church service on deck. On *Honolulu*, Catholics were preparing to go ashore for mass at the base. On other ships people were getting ready for softball, tennis, or an expedition to the beach at Waikiki. It was Sunday morning on a lovely, sunny, peaceful day in the Pacific. The best time of the week.

Out at sea the sun had come up soon after the Japanese aircraft had taken off. It was full daylight as they headed for Oahu in tight formation.

The bombers were flying at 9,000 feet. Their fighter escorts were 6,000 feet above them. The weather below was overcast, so much so that the Japanese only rarely caught a glimpse of the sea. They were homing in on

KGMB, using the radio to guide them to a target that they couldn't see through the cloud cover.

The music was routine, not interrupted by any sudden announcements of impending attack. The weather report was encouraging too. According to the radio, it was going to be partly cloudy over Oahu that day, but most of the clouds would be over the hills. The cloud ceiling was 3,500 feet. There was perfect visibility below that height.

Best of all, some of the music they could hear as they flew was Japanese. One fighter pilot picked up a well-known children's song that haunted him for years afterward. "There happened to come on a lovely teenage girl singing a Japanese song 'Come on a Pony.' Thinking about what would happen to such lovely children and what a change in their lives would occur only an hour and a half later, I couldn't listen to it anymore and had to switch off."[4]

That was a minority view. Another fighter pilot had visited Oahu with his ship and remembered it as a lovely place, full of pleasant people who hardly deserved their fate. Most pilots, however, appear to have had little doubt that what they were about to do to the Americans was right and necessary. Plenty relished the prospect.

Fuchida's three-man bomber with its red-and-yellow markings led the way. The other horizontal bombers followed closely behind. The dive-bombers were flying slightly higher and to Fuchida's left. The torpedo planes flew below and to the right.

Sitting behind the pilot, Fuchida slid the cockpit canopy back as the attack force sped toward Oahu. The ends of his *hashamaki* streamed in the wind as he raised both arms and waved to the other aircraft. Some of the crews saw him and waved back, fellow samurai saluting one another as they rode forward into battle.

Each of them carried a pistol and a knife for personal protection, but they wore no parachutes. The men had cork life vests and a rubber dinghy that could be inflated if they were forced to ditch in the sea, but their chances of being picked up on the wide ocean were slim to nonexistent. They all knew it as they munched on the chocolate and snacks that had been issued to them for the flight.

Their eyes were peeled for a sight of enemy aircraft, but they saw none in the skies around. They heard nothing on the radio either, still no indication that the Americans knew they were coming. Their biggest fear as they drew nearer to Oahu was that they might miss the island altogether, overshooting it somewhere in the clouds below that were still blotting out the sea. It would be easy to do, with the island so small and the surrounding ocean so large.

The Japanese were approaching from due north. Pearl Harbor would be on the right when Oahu came into view, separated from the other side of the island by a range of hills in the middle. The plan was to veer around to the left and fly in over the hills, dropping unexpectedly onto the harbor before the Americans knew what had hit them.

The clouds parted suddenly, and there it was. The little island of Oahu, looking exactly like the relief models they had all studied. The north shore lay directly in front of them, clear blue water and a long line of surf breaking off Kahuku Point. The island was lush and green, with cane fields dotted everywhere and pretty little rooftops of red, blue, and yellow.

Toshio Hashimoto, aboard one of the bombers, was so charmed by the sight that he raised his camera and took a picture. Others had momentary qualms about attacking such an idyllic spot. They wondered if it really had to be done.

Fuchida did not share their reservations. Looking ahead, he saw only the hilltops disappearing dangerously into the clouds. It would be far too risky to attack from the east, with the hills lost to view.

He decided to attack from the north and west instead. The crews had rehearsed two scenarios in advance. The chosen attack was to be signaled by the firing of dark-blue flares known as black dragons.

Surprise or surprise lost? If the Americans had been taken by surprise, Fuchida was to fire one black dragon. The torpedo planes would go in first, before their targets were obscured by smoke. High-level bombers would follow, and then dive-bombers. The fighters would remain overhead for protective cover.

If surprise had been lost, Fuchida would fire two black dragons in quick succession. The fighters and dive-bombers would then take the lead, hitting the airfields and antiaircraft defenses initially to put them out of action. The torpedo planes would follow immediately afterward, sneaking in to attack the battleships while the Americans were fully engaged elsewhere and unable to hit back.

Fuchida had only a minute or two to make up his mind. There was no antiaircraft fire that he could see, no sign of American aircraft coming to head them off. With no reason to believe that surprise had been lost, he fired a single flare from his signal gun.

The torpedo planes and horizontal bombers quickly began to drop down toward the sea, as arranged. The dive-bombers moved up toward twelve thousand feet to gain height for their attack.

The fighters were supposed to move too, but failed to respond. Fuchida assumed they hadn't seen the signal. He waited for a few seconds. When they still hadn't responded, he fired another flare.

The fighters reacted at once. So did the dive-bombers. Seeing two black dragons, they presumed that surprise had been lost and they were to begin their attack without further ado.

Fuchida could only curse as he watched them go. The knowledge that plans rarely survive the first contact with the enemy was little consolation. The attack had begun prematurely. There was nothing he could do to stop it now.

Bowing to the inevitable, he issued the signal "To! To! To!," an abbreviation of the Japanese word for "Charge!" It was 7:49 a.m. as he did so. Four minutes later he radioed the famous code words "Tora! Tora! Tora!" (Tiger, Tiger, Tiger) back to the fleet to confirm that surprise had been achieved. The attack was on and the planes were going in.

ELEVEN

A JAPANESE PILOT GRINS AT JAMES JONES

They all knew what to do. The torpedo planes peeled off at once, heading west and then south across Oahu in two separate echelons. They were to attack the ships off Ford Island from opposite sides of the harbor.

The high-level bombers remained out to sea, wheeling around Oahu to attack Pearl Harbor from the south. They too were aiming for the big ships around Ford Island. They intended to bomb Battleship Row from several thousand feet after the torpedo planes had had their run.

Supported by fighters, some of the dive-bombers went for Wheeler Field first. Their task was to knock out the airfield before the U.S. Army's fighters could take off to retaliate. The rest continued across the island toward Pearl Harbor and other designated targets.

Fuchida went with the bombers out to sea. They kept well clear of the antiaircraft guns around Barber's Point as they waited for the torpedo planes to make their run. The attack hadn't begun exactly as planned, but from what Fuchida could see through his field glasses, it didn't matter much. The Americans on the ground appeared to be fast asleep, not showing any signs of resistance. The Japanese had them at their mercy.

The attack on Wheeler Field was a spectacular success. The dive-bombers came through Kolekole Pass just before eight o'clock and headed straight for the target. A couple of minutes later, bombs began to rain down on the aircraft hangars and tightly packed rows of fighter planes parked on the apron.

The hangars were badly hit. So were the planes. One aircraft after another caught fire as the bombs fell and fuel tanks began to explode. Within a few minutes, the runway at Wheeler was covered in black smoke from burning planes.

After the bombers had dropped their load, the fighters went in, speedy Zeroes strafing the parked aircraft with cannon and machine-gun fire. With nothing to stop them, the Zeroes made three runs over the airfield, hammering away at the helpless fighters on the ground until their ammunition was almost exhausted.

The Americans were powerless to hit back. A sentry ran to a hangar to get a machine gun, but couldn't break the lock on the armory door. Other people just emerged from barracks and married quarters in various states of undress and stood gaping at the sky, not realizing what was happening until it was too late.

Lieutenants Welch and Taylor, the all-night poker players from Haleiwa airstrip, were among the first to catch on. A phone call to Haleiwa assured them that their P-40 Warhawks were still intact. The fighters could be armed and fueled at once. The two pilots leaped into a car and headed there at high speed, pursued for a while by a hostile Zero winging bullets after them as they drove.

At Schofield Barracks, just north of Wheeler, Major General Maxwell Murray hurried to his front door to get the number of the aircraft that was buzzing so close overhead on a Sunday morning. He failed to see the plane's number, but did spot the bomb that it dropped. Others did too and assumed that some army pilot had gone mad.

They were swiftly enlightened. The aircraft overhead were not American. Neither were the machine-gun bullets raking the lines of men on their way to breakfast.

The troops scattered in all directions. One had the presence of mind to grab an air-raid siren and start turning the handle. Some ran for their rifles, smashing open the armory doors with more success than the sentry at Wheeler. Others demanded ammunition from a supply sergeant who refused to issue it because he didn't have the necessary authorization from an officer.

Private James Jones, still seeking inspiration for his first novel, was already at breakfast when the Japanese struck. It took him a while to realize what was happening:

> Most of us were more concerned with getting and holding onto our half-pints of milk than with listening to the explosions that began rumbling up toward us from Wheeler Field two miles away. "They doing some blasting?" some old-timer said through a mouthful of pancakes.
>
> It was not until the first low-flying fighter came skidding, whammering low overhead with his MGs going that we ran outside, still clutching our half-pints of milk to keep them from being stolen, aware with a sudden sense of awe that we were seeing and acting in a genuine moment of history.
>
> As we stood outside in the street huddled back against the dayroom wall, another fighter with the red suns on its wings came up the boulevard, preceded by two lines of holes that kept popping up eighty yards in front on the asphalt. As he came abreast of us, he gave us a typically toothy grin and waved, and I shall never forget his face behind the goggles.
>
> A white silk scarf streamed out behind his neck and he wore a white ribbon around his helmet just above the goggles, with a red spot in the center of his forehead.[1]

Jones learned later that the white ribbon with a red spot was a *hasha-maki*, traditional headgear of the samurai since medieval times. For the moment, all he knew was that Schofield was being attacked by the Japanese. It was just what he needed for his novel.

The assault on Pearl Harbor was even more successful than the one on Wheeler. The dive-bombers and torpedo planes were supposed to attack in separate waves. Because of the mix-up with the signals, they went in more or less together, coming at the Americans from all points of the compass at the same time. It couldn't have gone better if they had planned it that way.

As everywhere else, the Americans were taken completely by surprise. On Ford Island, a color guard was preparing to hoist the American flag at exactly eight o'clock as the aircraft appeared. Similar ceremonies were happening on board ship.

Various officers followed General Murray's example and looked for the number of the offending pilot as "The Star-Spangled Banner" was drowned out by the unexpected roar of low-flying aero engines. They didn't take long to realize their mistake.

Too long, unfortunately. Bombs and torpedoes had already been launched as the men raced to action stations. Plenty of sailors were still in their bunks as the ships were hit. The battleships anchored in a line off Ford Island formed the biggest and most tempting target of all. Unprotected by nets, they were the proverbial sitting ducks.

The torpedo planes came from the southeast, flying in low over navy headquarters on land until they reached the open water leading to Ford Island. Battleship Row lay directly ahead of them. *Oklahoma* was moored beside *Maryland*, *West Virginia* beside *Tennessee*, *Vestal* (a small repair ship) beside *Arizona*. *Nevada* and *California* were anchored alone in the stream, one at each end of the row.

The battleships lay in shallow water, so shallow in theory that a torpedo launched from an aircraft would immediately hit the sea bottom rather than the intended target. In practice, however, the Japanese knew that British aircraft had managed to torpedo three Italian battleships and other craft in very shallow water at Taranto in 1940.

Japan's assistant naval attaché at the Berlin Embassy had visited Taranto soon afterward. The man was a close friend of Fuchida, who had later questioned him closely about the results of his inspection. The attaché had reported to Tokyo that the secret of the British success had been the addition of wooden stabilizing fins to the torpedoes to prevent them from sinking too far. The Japanese had spent months modifying and perfecting their Pearl Harbor torpedoes accordingly.

The torpedo planes were slow, ponderous, and quite deadly as they came in at sixty feet above the waves. With so many battleships in front of them, they were spoiled for choice as they approached. It was the work of a moment to release the torpedo at point-blank range of a few hundred yards and then roar away from the target, relieved of their burden at last. One plane flew lower than the crow's nest on *Oklahoma* as it roared across the deck.

The torpedoes streaked through the water. Their wooden fins kept them on course. American sailors could only watch in horror as the silver fish arrived and torpedo after torpedo found its target and struck home.

Anchored in pairs, it was the battleships on the outside that took the brunt of the assault. *Oklahoma* was hit by the first of five torpedoes, *West Virginia* by the first of six. *Arizona* was on the inside, partly shielded by *Vestal*, but was still hit by two. A little apart from the other battleships, *California* was hit twice as well.

Other ships suffered too. All over the harbor, the torpedoes were going in while dive-bombers and Zeroes attacked the airfields at Hickam and Ford Island. The Americans were fighting back as best they could, filling the sky with antiaircraft fire as they recovered from their surprise and looked to their weapons. They weren't going to take this lying down.

Up above, Fuchida waited with his heavy bombers. He could see the antiaircraft fire through his binoculars and was impressed at the speed of the American reaction. The Japanese navy would have taken much longer to recover from the shock.

He gave the order to join the attack. He had hardly done so when his own aircraft was hit by flak, vibrating horribly as if it had been struck by a club. A quick examination revealed holes in the fuselage and a steering wire half shot through. The pilot still had control, so they flew on regardless.

A few yards away, the plane next to them had dropped its bomb prematurely. Seeing fuel leaking from the extra tank, Fuchida scribbled "What happened?" on a little blackboard and held it up for the crew to see.

They wrote back that the fuselage had taken a hit, indicating in sign language that this had dislodged the bomb. Fuchida told them to disengage and fly back to their carrier. He relented when they asked for permission to remain with the force until the mission was complete.

Thin cloud was covering the target as Fuchida made his first bombing run. His aircraft was circling around for a second attempt when it was rocked by a massive explosion some nine thousand feet below. The explosion was so enormous that it almost sucked his aircraft right out of the sky.

Fuchida was jubilant. "The smoke and flame erupted together. It was a hateful, mean-looking red flame, the kind that powder produces, and I knew at once that a big powder magazine had exploded."[2]

He was quite right. A Japanese bomb had found its target, smashing through *Arizona*'s deck and setting off the forward magazine. The ensuing explosion had killed more than a thousand men.

The fireball shot several hundred feet into the air. The explosion wasn't particularly noisy—more of a *whoomph* than a bang—but the accompanying blast was calamitous. It knocked men off their feet, ripped out their lungs, blew people off other ships, and stalled motor engines on Ford Island. It probably sucked one *Arizona* sailor right through the narrow range-finding port on the antiaircraft system.

The ship immediately began to go down. Sailors from other vessels watched, horrified, as the survivors struggled to escape. The sinking ship was almost completely surrounded by burning oil. The only water not in flames lay toward the stern. Men made their way there, staggering in shock, and hastily cast themselves off as best they could.

Some jumped straight into the sea and struck out for Ford Island. Others found a life raft without any paddles and tried to pull away. Far too many simply slipped into the water and drowned beneath the waves before anyone could save them.

Bombs continued to explode in the sea as the survivors floundered. The bombs had the same effect as depth charges on human flesh. Chests were compressed and lungs fatally imploded as men struggled for breath. Scores of them died before they could get ashore.

Some found the strength to grab hold of a pipeline that stretched from *Arizona* to Ford Island. Others helped one another along as they headed for the island. They were dazed, naked, wounded, and deep in shock as they hauled themselves ashore, more dead than alive, and flopped down onto dry land.

Major Allen Shapley, one of *Arizona*'s marine officers, never forgot the sight as a couple of hundred survivors huddled together forlornly on Ford Island:

> *All burned like steaks, no clothes, just burned like lamb chops. The only thing I could see was their eyes, lips and mouths. Their mouths were reddish; their eyes looked watery. Everything else was black. They were moaning and walking around in a daze.*
>
> *They were in a state of shock and would not suffer deeply until they came out of it. I don't recall anyone keeling over, though many of them may have been dying by degrees.*[3]

Shapley himself was temporarily paralyzed from the explosion and stark naked. The blast had blown his clothes off. Others were crippled with shock, or blind, or choking on oil, or peering uncomprehendingly at the bleeding stumps where their arms or legs had been. Body parts had been flung everywhere by the explosion.

It was a similar story all along Battleship Row. *Oklahoma* was listing rapidly, the port side ripped out by multiple torpedo hits. The great battleship took less than ten minutes to capsize, slowly rolling over until the mast hit the sea bottom and the ship lay helplessly on its side.

California was sinking, too, and *West Virginia*. So was *Utah* on the other side of Ford Island. The ship's port rail was already under water. The deck timbers were cracking up and breaking loose like so much splintered firewood.

Other ships had been badly hit without immediately sinking. Their crews were struggling to control the damage and fight back at the same time as Japanese aircraft continued to pour in. The raid was only just getting into its stride, and already it was the biggest single disaster in U.S. naval history.

Fuchida watched *Arizona* explode from high above the harbor. Admiral Kimmel watched it from his front yard as he waited for a driver to take him to naval headquarters.

Commander Murphy had been on the telephone, telling Kimmel about the destroyer *Ward* and the errant sampan, when a yeoman of signals burst in to announce the Japanese attack. Murphy immediately informed Kimmel, who rushed outside to have a look.

There was an excellent view of Battleship Row from the senior officers' houses on Makalapa Heights. Kimmel lived next door to Captain Earle and his wife. Mrs. Earle came out, too, and stood silently next to the admiral as they watched the disaster unfold.

The Japanese pilots were so low that he and Mrs. Earle could almost see their features as they circled in figures of eight to attack the ships. Kimmel seemed completely stunned to her, his face as white as his uniform as he struggled to take it in.

"Looks like they've got the *Oklahoma*," she told him.

"Yes, I can see they have," he replied.[4]

Mrs. Earle's heart went out to Kimmel as *Arizona* blew up. They saw the ship lift out of the water and then sink back down, settling heavily into the sea amid all the falling debris. Neither of them said anything. There wasn't anything they could say.

Kimmel leaped into his car as soon as it arrived. He reached navy headquarters a few minutes after 8:00 a.m. He soon learned that the situation was even worse than he had imagined. Beside all the sinking battleships, *Maryland* and *Tennessee* couldn't move because they had been boxed in, and *Pennsylvania* was a sitting target in dry dock.

The only battleship still in business was *Nevada*. The ship had already been torpedoed once and bombed twice, but was still afloat in the stream. Various Japanese bombers had been allotted *Nevada* as their particular target. Fuchida's was among them, but they hadn't finished the job yet, although they were still trying.

Kimmel looked increasingly shell-shocked as the reports came in. His air officer, Captain Arthur Davis, knew that nothing could comfort him. "It was a terrible hour for Kimmel and a frightful blow. He loved his ships like any true sailor, and now many of them were gone. But most of all he bitterly regretted and mourned the loss of his officers and men."[5]

The sight from the windows was awful. Kimmel's staff didn't have a good view of the ships, but they could see the torpedoes being dropped, the water-spouts from the explosions, and the clouds of thick black smoke billowing upward. They could hear the noise, too.

One aircraft was shot down over the channel and crashed into the sea. It was scant consolation for all the damage the others were doing. The Japanese were having a field day over Pearl Harbor.

Kimmel was still at the window when a spent machine-gun bullet crashed through the glass and hit the left breast of his uniform. It left a dark stain on the material as it fell harmlessly to the floor. The admiral spoke from the heart as he bent down to pick the bullet up. "I wish it had killed me."[6]

High overhead, Fuchida's four bombers had circled around over Honolulu after seeing *Arizona* blow up and were coming in for another run. Fuchida struggled to identify their appointed target through all the smoke, but couldn't see *Nevada* anywhere. He looked for an undamaged battleship to attack instead.

Maryland appeared to fit the bill. The ship was hemmed in next to *Oklahoma*, taking survivors aboard from the capsized ship. Fuchida needed only one glance to order an attack.

Harlan Eisnaugle was a gunner aboard *Maryland*. From his battle station on the superstructure just below the bridge, he had an excellent view as the Japanese came in:

> *Men were screaming and trying to get aboard our ship and get out of the water. When I got to my gun, there were a few of the others there. . . . After a while we finally got ammo up to our gun. But we had to put it into clips before it could be fired. I don't know how long a time this was, but the* Oklahoma *had rolled over on her side.*
>
> *The harbor was pretty well afire by this time. The smoke and fire was all around us. . . . Then somebody yelled planes overhead. We*

trained the gun around and started firing. One of the planes fell up in front of us off Ford Island. I don't know who hit it, but it was one down. We got a hit in the forecastle from a bomb.[7]

Thousands of feet above, Fuchida's planes had released their bombs. Fuchida lay flat on his stomach to follow their progress through the observation port underneath the engine:

Four bombs in perfect pattern plummeted like the devils of doom. The target was so far away that I wondered for a moment if they would reach it. The bombs grew smaller and smaller until I was holding my breath for fear of losing sight of them.

I forgot everything in the thrill of watching them fall toward the target. They became small as poppy seeds and finally disappeared from my view just as tiny white spurts of smoke appeared on or near the ship. I shouted "two hits" and rose from the floor of the plane.[8]

The bombs had probably hit *Maryland*, although it might have been *California*. It wasn't easy to tell through the smoke of battle.

Fuchida didn't care which. Delighted with the result, he ordered the other three aircraft to break off the action and go home. He himself would stay around to direct operations and assess the damage.

Out at sea, the Flying Fortresses from California had sighted Oahu at last and were coming in to land.

It had been a long journey from the mainland: fourteen hours of non-stop flying. To reduce weight, the aircraft had been stripped of their armor and ammunition and were flying with skeleton crews. Even so, some of the planes were almost out of fuel as they located the island and headed in toward Hickam Field.

The bombers were not in formation. They had been allowed to fly separately from California, each of them doing their own navigation rather than just following the leader. Some came in toward Hickam from the north, like the Japanese. Others came via Diamond Head and Waikiki to the south.

Most of them saw the smoke over Pearl Harbor and assumed it was just a naval maneuver of some kind, or cane fields burning, or some sort of celebration. A few continued to think so as they spotted burning aircraft on the ground and concluded that the practice drill below was looking very realistic. It wasn't until the Japanese air force came at them with machine guns that they began to think otherwise.

Even then, the crew of one B-17 with almost empty fuel tanks were relieved to find themselves being escorted by a dozen red-circled planes as they wobbled toward the runway. They waved gratefully to the stony-faced pilots, but received no acknowledgement in return.

Others quickly realized what was happening and took evasive action, losing themselves in the clouds. One or two were hit as they circled the airfield, guided in by a voice from the control tower telling them which runway to use and warning that there were Japanese on their tail.

One Fortress landed in flames and lost its entire tail section on impact. The rest of the plane skidded down the runway until it came to a stop. The crew hastily abandoned ship and ran for cover. The flight surgeon was machine-gunned by a Zero, but the remainder made it to safety.

Other Fortresses sheered away from Hickam and looked for alternative places to land. They all managed to get down somehow, occasionally under determined fire from their own side. Two of the big bombers braved the tiny airstrip at Haleiwa, where Lieutenants Welch and Taylor were heading for their Warhawks. The Fortresses managed to put down without overshooting the runway.

It was difficult to tell friend from foe in the skies overhead. As well as the Flying Fortresses, a squadron of reconnaissance aircraft from USS *Enterprise* had just arrived from the west. The carrier was returning from Wake Island, but had been held up by heavy seas that had delayed refueling.

The reconnaissance aircraft had flown ahead. Their orders were to sweep the area in front of the carrier and then land at Ford Island. They appeared from the west just as the Japanese came in from the north. Several were quickly shot down, either by the Japanese or friendly fire from the ground.

Even if they managed to land, they still weren't safe. Ground crew yelled at the pilots to get back into the air at once to avoid being strafed. Almost every airfield was under attack. Even for a plane low on fuel, the safest place to be was in the air, rather than parked helplessly on the ground.

To cap it all, another wave of Japanese aircraft had just arrived from the strike force and was about to attack. With the advantage of surprise, the first wave had achieved a spectacular success. Now though, with fuel low and their bombs and torpedoes all gone, it was time to go home.

They were replaced by a second wave of equal strength. The newcomers arrived from the north around 8:40, just as the first wave prepared to depart. This time however, the Japanese didn't have the advantage of surprise. The Americans were pulling themselves together and preparing to fight back.

TWELVE

LORD MOUNTBATTEN'S NEPHEW AND CBS-TV'S FIRST BREAKING NEWS STORY

While the aircraft wheeled overhead, ten-year-old Noel Cunningham-Reid watched fascinated from a house on Alewa Heights. Always an early riser, he had been out in the garden since 7:00 a.m. and had seen the attack from the beginning. He had immediately recognized the aircraft as Japanese from the pictures he had seen in comic books.

There was a good view of Pearl Harbor from the garden, much the same view as the spy Yoshikawa had enjoyed from the Japanese tearoom on the Heights. Noel had had a grandstand seat as the first wave of aircraft went in and the battleships fought back.

Noel was British, the son of a member of Parliament who had been a fighter pilot in World War I. His mother's sister, Edwina, was married to Lord Louis Mountbatten. Mountbatten had spent a week on Oahu the previous September, horrified at the American fleet's lack of preparedness for war.

Noel and his elder brother, Michael, were among many British children who had been evacuated to Canada or the United States to avoid the bombing in Great Britain. They had wound up on ultrasafe Oahu because of their father's close friendship with the tobacco heiress Doris Duke.

Said to be America's richest woman, Doris Duke had a holiday home on Diamond Head, on the other side of Honolulu from Pearl Harbor. Shangri-La was a fabulous place, a fairy-tale palace on a million-dollar estate, much like the Xanadu of *Citizen Kane*.

Duke had agreed to be the boys' guardian during their American stay. Michael was very fond of her, but she had little interest in children and didn't want them in her house while she was away. They had been farmed out to Lieutenant Colonel Evans Whisner and his wife, who lived in army accommodation on Alewa Heights.

Duke was in New York on the day of the attack, planning to fly back the next morning. The Cunningham-Reid boys were getting along fine without her. They were privileged children in England, accustomed to chauffeurs, governesses, and a house full of servants. On Alewa Drive they were just the kids next door, and loving it.

They were enrolled at Punahou School, where Colonel Whisner ran the Junior ROTC (Reserve Officers' Training Corps). He had had a communal bomb shelter dug for his neighbors on Alewa Drive as a precaution against air raids. There were blackout practices too to ensure that no lights were showing.

Noel ran in to tell him about the attack. Whisner confirmed that it was real. He had just had orders to report for duty at once. The colonel departed in a hurry.

Noel decided to alert their neighbor too. Frank Tremaine was the local bureau chief for United Press, covering the news agency's Pacific beat from an office in Honolulu.

Hurrying up the road, Noel banged on the front door. Tremaine had been out late the previous night, attending a dinner dance at the officers' club on Waikiki Beach. He wasn't best pleased to be awoken by a British kid at an ungodly hour on a Sunday morning.

"I've got a scoop for you," Noel told him. "The Japanese are attacking us."

Tremaine was not impressed. He muttered something about naval maneuvers.

"If you just come out of the house, I think you'll see that it's not maneuvers," Noel insisted.[1]

Tremaine came. He saw. He ran back inside to put his pants on.

Noel's brother, Michael, was up by then, wondering what all the fuss was about:

> These strange-looking planes came in, not very fast. They were floating, they had cut their engines, and they all appeared over the hill, masses of them coming down very quietly.
>
> They must have been about 300 feet above us, if that, and every one of the Japanese pilots waved to me as they went over. . . . They were getting smaller and we saw explosions all over the place.[2]

Michael had an invitation to Pearl Harbor that afternoon, a birthday party for an admiral's daughter aboard *Arizona*. Together, he and Noel watched as the venue for the celebration blew up.

Michael burst into tears. His family teased him for the rest of his life that he had been upset about the party rather than the poor men on *Arizona*.

Indoors, Frank Tremaine decided against pants. He was still naked as he called the navy's press officer to find out what was happening.

There was no answer. Tremaine tried several other numbers without learning anything that he couldn't see for himself. His wife, Kay, was still surfacing as he put a call through to the Commercial Cable Company instead.

The Commercial Cable Company was the only wire service that operated on a Sunday. International telephone lines were slow and unreliable. The Cable Company was Tremaine's one real chance of getting the story out to the rest of the world in a tearing hurry.

He asked for flash priority as he dictated his words on the phone. Flash was used only for sensational stories, the ones nobody could afford to miss. "Urgent Unipress Sanfrancisco, Newyork, Manila. Flash Pearl Harbor under aerial attack. Tremaine."[3]

Kay was up by then, watching the attack from the window. Tremaine rang the international operator and booked a phone call to the United Press office in San Francisco. Then he sent some more cables, based on what his wife could see from the window.

They switched the radio on. The manager of KGMB, their friend Webley Edwards, was calling on all service personnel to report to their posts immediately. "Take cover," he kept telling his listeners. "This is an air raid. This is no drill."[4]

Tremaine decided to find out more. Leaving Kay with a pile of notes and instructions to tell San Francisco everything she knew if the phone call came through, he jumped into his car and headed for Pearl Harbor.

He stopped briefly at Fort Shafter on the way and then took the road to the harbor. Everyone else was going there, too, all the servicemen reporting for duty. There was total gridlock on the road as the vehicles inched forward.

Very little was going the other way, so Tremaine pulled out onto the wrong side of the road and drove against the traffic to Hickam Field. He found the place littered with ruined buildings and smashed aircraft, including the Flying Fortress that had broken up on the runway.

Tremaine spent the next hour and a half telephoning eyewitness accounts from Hickam to the UP office in Honolulu. He was strafed once by a Japanese plane and sustained his first and only injury of the war when an airman running for cover trod on his foot. He continued reporting until the navy shut down all radio communication to the mainland sometime after eleven o'clock to prevent Japanese aircraft from homing in on the signal.

Tremaine had done enough by then. His was the first eyewitness account of Pearl Harbor to reach the outside world. Kay had reported it, too, reading his copy down the line to San Francisco and adding her own observations soon after he left the house. Between them they had beaten all the other agencies to get the biggest scoop of their lives.

Their story was quickly picked up by CBS Television, which subscribed to UP's radio wire. The fledgling service operated from a vast office above New York's Grand Central Station.

Still only experimental, CBS-TV worked a six-day week and took Sundays off. The staff were all at home when the story broke. Many learned about it from the radio when they tuned in at 3:00 p.m. for a concert by the New York Philharmonic:

> *The afternoon was fantastic. . . . [Artur] Rubinstein's performance of the 2nd Brahms concerto broken into by repeated bulletins. Manila bombed—denial from a radio correspondent speaking from Manila— the* West Virginia *reported sunk, Hull's indignation at the Japanese reply, so full of malicious fabrications . . . all personnel recalled to Floyd Bennett and Mitchel Fields . . . a broadcast from the news room of the White House with a background hum of voices, and a stutteringly excited broadcaster.*[5]

Bob Skedgell, CBS-TV's lead scriptwriter, raced to the studio as soon as he heard the broadcast. "I just took off. Grabbed a hat or whatever and I ran up Park Avenue until I got to the office."[6] Others did the same, trickling in all afternoon as they hurried to the studio. They were all new to television, uncertain how to play it, but determined to get the story out somehow. Nothing like Pearl Harbor had ever happened before on American television.

The first problem was the backdrop. They couldn't use the existing news set because most of its wall maps were covering the war in Europe. The Pearl Harbor story was clearly going to run for days, if not weeks. It needed a backdrop of its own.

The crew built one from scratch. In just under four hours, they produced a new set for America's entry into the war. It covered nine different geographic areas and was dominated by a map of the world measuring sixteen feet by five.

The set had to be carefully lit and supplied with cameras and microphone cables before CBS could go on the air. It also needed a news feed from the wire services. The latest information was torn from the teleprinter and hurriedly typed up into something that could be read straight to camera, without any preparation time.

No one in the studio had worked this way before—certainly not the two terrified presenters, taking it in turns to ad-lib desperately without a prompt until the next news bite arrived. Yet it had to be done. Pearl Harbor was the first breaking news story in American television history.

In Washington, Okumura had finally finished his typing at the Japanese Embassy. He completed Japan's four-thousand-word, fourteen-part response to President Roosevelt's peace proposals at about 1:50 in the afternoon, Washington time. Ambassador Nomura and Special Envoy Kurusu immediately hurried to the State Department to present the document to Cordell Hull.

They had no idea that Pearl Harbor had been attacked an hour earlier. Neither had Hull, although he soon found out:

> *The Japanese envoys arrived at the Department at 2:05 and went to the diplomatic waiting room. At almost that moment the President telephoned me from the White House. His voice was steady but clipped.*
>
> *He said, "There's a report that the Japanese have attacked Pearl Harbor."*
>
> *"Has the report been confirmed?" I asked.*
>
> *He said, "No."*
>
> *While each of us indicated his belief that the report was probably true, I suggested that he have it confirmed, having in mind my appointment with the Japanese Ambassadors.*[7]

Hull summoned the two men to his office at 2:20. He didn't offer them a seat as he surveyed them coldly. Nomura handed him the Japanese response. Hull pretended to read the document, although he already knew what was in it. Then he looked up and told Nomura what he thought of it:

> *"I must say," I said, "that in all my conversations with you during the last nine months I have never uttered one word of untruth. This is borne out absolutely by the record. In all my fifty years of public service I have never seen a document that was more crowded with infamous*

falsehoods and distortions—infamous falsehoods and distortions on a scale so huge that I never imagined until today that any Government on this planet was capable of uttering them."[8]

Nomura didn't reply. His face was a blank, but he seemed to be under great strain, perhaps privately agreeing with Hull. The two envoys were dismissed with a contemptuous wave of the hand. They slunk out of the room without a word.

The Roosevelts were busy with a lunch party when they learned of the attack. They had invited thirty people to the White House, including a young Englishwoman on leave from the Wrens (Womens' Royal Naval Service).

The president had intended to be there, but decided at the last minute not to join his guests. With so much on his mind, he found large social gatherings a strain. There was always a danger of revealing some secret by mistake that he would regret later.

Instead, leaving his wife to make his excuses, he ate lunch from a tray in the Oval Room. He was having a quiet chat with Harry Hopkins when U.S. Navy Secretary Frank Knox called at 1:40 to pass on a radio message from Hawaii. Knox told the president that Honolulu was under air attack and that it was not a drill.

Hopkins was skeptical, but Roosevelt thought the report was probably true. While waiting to hear more, he telephoned Cordell Hull and told him not to mention it to Nomura and Kurusu when he saw them.

Admiral Stark phoned at 2:28 to confirm the story. He didn't have all the details yet, but it was looking pretty bad. Ships and men had been lost.

A meeting was convened for 3:00 and began shortly afterward. Secretary of War Henry L. Stimson, Hull, Knox, Stark, Marshall, and others crowded into the office to discuss the next move.

When Eleanor Roosevelt saw her husband later, he seemed more serene than he had for a long time, now that the die was cast. Hopkins thought so too:

The conference met in not too tense an atmosphere because I think that all of us believed that in the last analysis the enemy was Hitler and that he could never be defeated without force of arms; that sooner or later we were bound to be in the war and that Japan had given us an opportunity. Everybody, however, agreed on the seriousness of the war and that it would be a long, hard struggle.[9]

Winston Churchill telephoned later to say that he had heard a radio report of the attack. Roosevelt told him it was true. They were all in the same boat now. The two leaders agreed that they would go to their respective legislatures next day to ask for a declaration of war against Japan.

Later still, Ambassador Joseph Grew was summoned to meet Foreign Minister Togo in Tokyo. It was 7:00 a.m., Japanese time, when he got the call. Togo's secretary had been trying to reach him since 5:00, but hadn't been able to get through to the embassy.

Grew reached Togo's official residence at 7:30. Grim and formally dressed, the foreign minister handed the unshaven Grew a copy of Japan's fourteen-part response. He told Grew that he had seen Emperor Hirohito (at 3:00 a.m., as Grew later learned). The fourteen-part response was Hirohito's reply to Roosevelt.

No one mentioned Pearl Harbor. A Japanese official came to the U.S. Embassy at 11:00 that morning to read the formal declaration of war:

I have the honor to inform Your Excellency that there has arisen a state of war between Your Excellency's country and Japan beginning today.
I avail myself of this opportunity to renew to Your Excellency the assurances of my highest consideration.[10]

Privately the official apologized for the declaration, telling the diplomat who received it that his duty was most distasteful. He returned later with a group of equally polite Japanese who confiscated every radio set that they could find in the embassy compound, apologizing again for the trouble caused.

The Americans were prisoners thereafter. They couldn't leave the compound without permission. They were being held for their own protection, among other things. A demonstration of Japanese waving a German swastika had already been headed off as it advanced toward the gates.

Grew threw a party that night for the entire staff of the embassy and consulate. About sixty people gathered for cocktails. Those who had lived outside the compound were going to have to bed down on other people's floors for the next few months, until they could be repatriated. They were all cheerful though, all pitching in together. They had done their best to avert this calamity. Drew knew plenty of sensible Japanese who disapproved of it as much as he did.

He also took some consolation from a telegram he had recently sent to Washington. He had been very prescient in his warning. "Japan would be perfectly capable of an all-out, do-or-die attempt to render herself impervious to foreign economic pressure even if it meant national hara-kiri. We should be ready for any step of 'dangerous and dramatic suddenness.' "[11]

Grew heard later that Togo had not known in advance of the Japanese attack on Pearl Harbor. Whether it was true or not, the U.S. ambassador was certainly inclined to believe it.

The Americans in Tokyo burned all their codebooks and confidential documents as soon as hostilities began. So did the Japanese at the consulate in Honolulu.

The Japanese were in denial for a considerable while. Shortly after the first air raids, reporter Lawrence Nakatsuka of the *Star-Bulletin* hurried around to the consulate and asked Consul Kita if he would care to comment. Kita, all set for a round of golf, insisted that whatever was happening wasn't a Japanese attack. He attributed the gunfire and explosions to military maneuvers.

Nakatsuka wasn't satisfied with that. He returned later in the morning with a copy of the *Star-Bulletin*'s extra edition, fresh off the press. WAR! OAHU BOMBED BY JAPANESE PLANES was the headline.

Kita continued to stonewall. He was still arguing with Nakatsuka when the police at the consulate smelled smoke. Swift investigation revealed the spy Yoshikawa burning documents in a washtub. Others were preparing to destroy five burlap bags full of shredded papers.

The police moved quickly. The fire was stamped out, and a few of the documents were saved. Lieutenant Yoshio Hasegawa, the senior Japanese American among the policemen, then asked Kita the same question as Nakatsuka. Did he know about the Japanese attack?

No, Kita insisted. The consulate in Honolulu still knew nothing of any attack.

While the fighting continued overhead, RCA messenger Tadao Fuchikami was riding around Honolulu, delivering cablegrams on his motorbike. He was finding it hard going, stuck in the same traffic jam as Frank Tremaine.

Among the cables in his bag was one for the commanding general at Fort Shafter. It wasn't marked urgent, so Fuchikami delivered the other cables that were on his way before heading for Shafter.

Dressed in RCA's green-and-khaki uniform, he was disconcerted to run into a national guard roadblock, where he was nearly mistaken for a Japanese paratrooper. He was advised to go home, but decided to deliver the rest of his messages first.

Fuchikami ran into another roadblock on Middle Street. The police told him that only defense workers were being allowed any further. He produced his cable for the general and was waved though.

It was 11:45 by the time Fuchikami delivered the cable to the message center at Fort Shafter. Three hours later the decoded cable was shown at last to General Short. He copied it at once to Admiral Kimmel.

The message was from General Marshall. It was the one he had sent out at midday (Washington time) warning everyone about the Japanese ultimatum and advising them to be on the alert. Kimmel hurled it into the wastebasket.

THIRTEEN

EDGAR RICE BURROUGHS WATCHES THE WAR GAMES

The second wave of Japanese aircraft reached Oahu around 8:54. They had no trouble finding the place. They could hardly miss it with all the black smoke billowing upward from Wheeler Field, Pearl Harbor, and other stricken bases.

The Japanese had no option but to attack in two waves. The original plan had been to send all the aircraft in together, but that had proved to be impractical. The first aircraft to take off from the carriers would have used up too much fuel by the time the rest had joined them and were ready for the journey south.

There were no torpedo planes in the second wave. Just fighters, bombers, and dive-bombers looking for opportunity targets that hadn't already been destroyed. The Japanese sought them out through a hail of antiaircraft fire as some very angry Americans recovered from their initial surprise and made it clear that the Rising Sun was not welcome over Oahu.

The Americans were airborne too. Lieutenants Welch and Taylor had managed to take off from Haleiwa and were fighting back. They took off so hurriedly that their fighters weren't fully armed. After a quick foray in search of the Japanese, they had to land at smoke-filled Wheeler to take on more ammunition.

Welch and Taylor were aloft again by nine and succeeded in shooting down several aircraft as the first wave of Japanese departed. Other American pilots were in combat too, often flying obsolete planes that were no match for the enemy. The best aircraft had already been destroyed on the ground.

Down below, *Nevada* had been torpedoed in the port bow but was still afloat. Burning oil from *Arizona* was drifting toward the battleship, so *Nevada*'s acting captain decided to get under way before the vessel was engulfed.

It wasn't easy with a huge hole in the bow and the forward compartments flooded. The captain was ashore, and there were no tugboats to help. It was pure chance that there happened to be enough steam in *Nevada*'s boilers for the great battleship to swing out into the stream and set off past its crippled sister ships toward the narrow channel that led to the open sea.

The sight galvanized all those who saw it. *Nevada*'s mighty superstructure could hardly fail to impress as the great ship got under way. The American flag flew unbowed and undefeated as *Nevada* steamed forward through the smoke of battle and headed out to sea.

Unfortunately the battleship made an obvious target for the Japanese overhead. Dive-bombers from the second wave homed in as *Nevada* headed for the exit. If they could sink the ship in the channel, they could block it at once, putting Pearl Harbor out of action for months.

Fuchida willed them on as he watched from above. "Ah good. Now just sink that ship right there."[1] High explosives whistled down. Fires quickly broke out aboard *Nevada* as the bombs found their mark. There was nothing the battleship could do to avoid them.

Ashore, Admiral William Pye saw what the Japanese were trying to do. A string of signal flags was promptly hauled to the top of the navy's water tower, ordering *Nevada* not to head for the channel. The danger of being sunk was too great.

Nevada obediently steered to port, heading instead for Hospital Point, just short of the entrance to the channel. The ship was still under attack as it ran aground and dropped anchor in the mud.

The navy's oil storage tanks lay on Hospital Point, an easy target for the bombers above. If they had gone for the oil instead of *Nevada*, they would have put the U.S. Navy out of action for the several months that the Japanese army needed to have the Pacific at its mercy.

Yet the smoke from burning oil would have obscured other targets. The pilots' orders were to hit the ships first. They could have crippled the Americans just as easily if they had managed to sink a ship in the channel.

Up above, Fuchida wasn't too bothered that they had failed to sink *Nevada*. The ship had run aground with a hole in the bows, and that was good enough. *Nevada* wouldn't be back in service any time soon.

Nor would any of the other battleships. *Arizona* had blown up, *Utah* and *Oklahoma* lay on their sides, *California* and *West Virginia* were slowly sinking. The rest were badly damaged. It was all looking very satisfactory from where Fuchida was sitting.

While Fuchida assessed the damage, the Dutch liner *Jägersfontein* was coming in to Honolulu harbor. Most of the passengers were at the rail to watch as the pilot came aboard at nine o'clock to help guide the ship in.

Joan Fawcett had been on deck since eight, enjoying the view as they approached Diamond Head from the south. Like everyone else, she failed to appreciate what was happening at first:

> I noticed a few puffs of grey smoke in the sky, just over the harbour, and as they seemed queer clouds I asked the boys what explanation they could give and we decided that they were the puffs from anti-aircraft fire. By this time there were many grey spots and soon we could hear the report of the guns. We thought it was just a practice manoeuvre and a welcome salute for us. . . .
>
> By nine o'clock we had had breakfast and were all up on deck watching the planes fly over. We did see things drop into the water, and one only fifty yards away, but thought nothing more of it.
>
> Later we heard eight bombs were aimed at our ship. We made a beautiful target for we were entering the harbour, and being in the

mined area could not swerve left or right in the cleared channel. We were thoroughly enjoying the display.[2]

Tom Yarborough, an Associated Press correspondent en route to the Middle East, enjoyed the war game, too. "The passengers crowded the decks and applauded the navy for timing it for our arrival. A bomb hit the water about 100 yards away and a passenger said, 'Boy, what if that had been a real one!'"[3]

It wasn't until *Jägersfontein* had docked that the passengers learned the truth. The agent hurried aboard and told them to disembark at once in groups of twenty. Joan and her mother were about to do so when more Japanese planes appeared and they were hustled down to the lower deck instead.

They got ashore eventually and learned of the sinkings at Pearl Harbor. It was deemed too dangerous for them to return to the ship, so they were taken later to the Moana Hotel on Waikiki Beach. Despite all the drama, Joan had time to assess her new surroundings. "What a beautiful spot: just as you always have pictured Honolulu—the white surf, the water varying from green to deep blue as you look out to the horizon, sunshine, waving palm trees and always a breath-taking sunset. At night the sky is a mass of stars."[4]

Jägersfontein's crew hurried to Queen's Hospital to give blood. So did many of the passengers, along with Hawaiians of all kinds: Koreans, Chinese, Japanese, people of every race and creed answering the call for help on the radio. Some of the prostitutes from the red-light district went too. Like Belle Watling—the brothel-keeper in *Gone With the Wind*—they wanted to do their bit for the cause.

The Willamette footballers watched the attack from the roof of the Moana. In common with the passengers on *Jägersfontein*, they had assumed at first that it was just a naval exercise, maneuvers of some kind. Most of them had been having breakfast when spent antiaircraft shells began to rain down on the sea outside the dining-room window.

A waiter assured them that the splashes were just whales spouting. The boys trooped outside for a closer look. It didn't take them long to realize that more than whales were spouting out there. Between the sirens, the aircraft overhead and the smoke from Pearl Harbor along the coast, the navy was conducting a very lifelike war game around the island.

George Constable, a Bearcat tackle, was one of those who went to the roof for a better view. "We were on the roof of the Moana, watching what we thought were some pretty realistic maneuvers. We heard shells, saw splashes, but were kind of oblivious. Ironically, I had a Kodak box camera in my room, but I wasn't about to go get it just to take snapshots of practice runs."[5]

Earl Hampton was out in front of the hotel, where the bus was supposed to collect the team for their tour of the island:

> Down the street there was a big explosion about two blocks away. I guess a Japanese plane dropped its last bomb as it was leaving. We didn't know exactly what was going on until later, when we picked up news on the radio. Then Coach Spec and some military personnel came by and they had rifles with bayonets stacked in the lobby of the hotel.
>
> They told us that they were expecting the Japanese to attack the island and that Waikiki would be a likely place. They were digging trenches out by the beach, while some of us helped them.[6]

Spec Keene called the team together for a meeting. Most of the boys wanted to enlist on the spot. They ended up doing emergency guard duty at Punahou School, haunted by the thought that hundreds of the servicemen who had watched them playing football on Saturday afternoon had been killed less than twenty-four hours later.

Edgar Rice Burroughs, the bestselling author of the *Tarzan* books, watched the attack from the tennis court of the Niumalu Hotel on Waikiki Beach. He had risen early, as usual on a Sunday, to get a few games of paddle tennis in before the heat of the day. He and his son, Hulbert, heard the firing as soon as they got up, but thought nothing of it as they went to breakfast.

Burroughs was living on Oahu because it was cheaper than California. He had made a mess of his finances and was going through a difficult divorce. His lawyer had advised him to remain on the island until the details had been settled and the divorce was final.

Burroughs had been living in a bungalow at the Niumalu until his wife left him. After that he had moved into the hotel proper, with a bedroom, bathroom, and sitting room, where he tried to write whenever he could.

Alarmed at health reports suggesting that his father might be dying, Hulbert had recently come from California to join him. They were both pretending that Hully was there for a holiday. In reality he was keeping an eye on his father at a bad time and slept on a trundle bed in the sitting room next to Burroughs's bedroom.

Like many people, they weren't bothered by the shooting that morning because the newspaper had warned that heavy guns would be firing from various points across the island over the next few days. The sound of blasting was also quite normal as building contractors blew up mountainside lava to make way for the navy's many new construction projects.

Nevertheless, Burroughs realized something was wrong as soon as he and his son walked out to the tennis court after breakfast:

> There is an area of sand for sun bathers beyond the ocean end of the tennis court, and soon a great many of the hotel guests were congregated there watching the show. Bombs were falling on Pearl Harbor. We could hear the detonations and see the bursts quite plainly.
>
> Anti-aircraft shells were bursting, fighting ships at sea were firing. We could see them plainly. Bombs were falling in the ocean not far from us . . .
>
> For several hours we alternated tennis while watching the show they were putting on before we learned definitely that it was the real McCoy. Even the truth did not interfere with our tennis.[7]

They kept playing because they had nothing better to do. The radio was repeatedly telling civilians to stay at home, keep off the streets, remain calm, and avoid using the telephone. Burroughs and his son did just that until the attack was over.

It wasn't until after lunch that a call came for able-bodied men at the hotel to report to Pier 2 on the waterfront. After considerable chaos, Burroughs and his son were given Springfield rifles and a few rounds of ammunition. They were initially assigned to guard a few Japanese fishermen at a tuna-packing plant and then spent the rest of the evening in the rain patrolling the road leading inland from Fisherman's Wharf.

Nurse AraBelle Fuller spent the day rather more actively. Like the Willamette boys, she quickly abandoned her plans for a jaunt around the island on her day off. Instead, with KGMB calling on all trained personnel to report for duty, she headed to Leahi Hospital to help with the wounded as they came in.

They took a while to arrive, so Fuller spent the morning making dressings instead. She was snatching an early meal break when what was probably a stray antiaircraft shell fell nearby:

> *I was eating lunch when a bomb dropped near our home, wrecking a Jap store and a number of houses. Our dishes went up in the air and me under the table, where I wouldn't be alone. It's interesting under a table. Oh yeah, I have just climbed out from my newly created dog house and decides to finish my dinner, but by 11:36 I'm under again, but I brought my plate with me, something funny about war, it gives me an awful big appetite.*
>
> *The others stated they weren't hungry so I eat some of theirs too. Anyhow I'm under the table this time on account of another boom nearby, which hit a school . . .*
>
> *No noise for a few minutes so I crawls out and goes back to dear ole Leahi surgery room where I am to make more dressings.*[8]

According to Japanese records, the second wave had gone by then, but the Americans didn't know that yet. They didn't find out until Japanese accounts became available after the war.

At the time Oahu still appeared to be under attack at 11:30. The sounds

of battle could still be heard through the smoke. The sky was full of uniden-
tified aircraft, some of them American planes shooting at one another.
Puffs of smoke followed as antiaircraft gunners blazed away indiscriminately
at anything that moved.

Some of the fallout landed on Honolulu. It was impossible to distinguish
spent flak from bombing, thus reinforcing the perception that they were
all still under attack, as many eyewitnesses insisted they were. Whether the
Japanese were still there or not, Fuller went to the roof porch for a better look:

> *The day is still beautiful, only the sky has a lot of black puffs in it, caused
> from anti-aircraft fire no doubt. With our field glasses we can see Hickam
> Field and Pearl Harbor, they are aflame and clouds of smoke are now
> settling down over the once peaceful isle. I am beginning to realize things
> are dangerous when Jap planes fly over Diamond Head and almost hit
> us. Very peculiar, the planes have a flatter, rounder wing, but the lead-
> ers have our emblem on them.*
>
> *Anyhow, thought they were ours until they started their machine
> guns a poppin'. They should be more careful; don't they know they may
> hurt someone? Anyhow, we watched the whole battle from our perch,
> we had the radio on.*[9]

Betty McIntosh, a *Star-Bulletin* reporter, was hurrying to work earlier when
she ran into an attack near Punchbowl Crater:

> *The blue sky was punctured with anti-aircraft smoke puffs. Suddenly,
> there was a sharp whistling sound, almost over my shoulder, and below,
> down on School Street, I saw a rooftop fly into the air like a pasteboard
> movie set.*
>
> *For the first time, I felt that numb terror that all of London has
> known for months. It is the terror of not being able to do anything but
> fall on your stomach and hope the bomb won't land on you.*

McIntosh was assigned to the emergency room in the hospital. She
watched, horrified, as the first casualties of the raid were brought in:

Bombs were still dropping over the city as ambulances screamed off into the heart of the destruction. The drivers were blood-sodden when they returned, with stories of streets ripped up, houses burned, twisted shrapnel and charred bodies of children.

In the morgue, the bodies were laid on slabs in the grotesque positions in which they had died. Fear contorted their faces. Their clothes were blue-black from incendiary bombs. One little girl in a red sweater, barefoot, still clutched a piece of jump-rope in her hand.[10]

On the other side of the island, Chief Aviation Ordnanceman John Finn had been having a Sunday morning lie-in when the attack on Kanoehe naval air station woke him. Zero fighters from the first wave were strafing the row of Catalina flying boats drawn up along the water's edge.

The planes were in flames by the time Finn arrived, but he didn't hesitate for a moment. Grabbing a .50-caliber machine gun, he mounted it on a tripod and dragged it across to one of the aircraft ramps beside the shore. He was completely exposed as fighters and dive-bombers from the second wave arrived to complete the work of their predecessors.

Finn should have been terrified as the Zeroes came for him. In fact, as he admitted later, he was too angry at the Japanese to think about it. He simply continued firing as other sailors kept him supplied with ammunition. "I got that gun and I started shooting at Jap planes. I was out there shooting the Jap planes and just every so often I was a target for some. In some cases, I could see their faces."[11]

Finn took a bullet in the foot and was hit by shrapnel in the shoulder and several other places. He carried on firing for as long as he had something to shoot at.

Later, after receiving first aid, he insisted on returning to duty to oversee the rearming of the only undamaged Catalinas. The three flying boats had been out on patrol during the attack, narrowly avoiding destruction as they flew back to base.

Finn's heroism was the stuff of Hollywood movies. He was later awarded the Congressional Medal of Honor, one of fifteen conferred for the action that day. Only five of the winners had survived the attack to receive it in person.

———

Dorie Miller was awarded the Navy Cross. He was a mess attendant on *West Virginia*, doing one of the few jobs then open to African Americans in the U.S. Navy. He had just served breakfast in the junior officers' wardroom when the first of several torpedoes hit the battleship and the crew scrambled to their battle stations.

Miller's station had been destroyed by the torpedo. He was sent to the bridge instead. A large man—heavyweight boxing champion aboard *West Virginia*—he helped to shift the dying captain before grabbing a .50 caliber antiaircraft gun like Finn and firing back at the Japanese as they came in to attack.

Miller wasn't a trained gunner, but he kept firing until he ran out of ammunition. *West Virginia* was in flames by then, sinking fast. Miller waded through oil and water to rescue several wounded men and carry them up to the quarterdeck, where they had a better chance of surviving when the order came to abandon ship.

He was decorated "for distinguished devotion to duty, extraordinary courage and disregard for his own personal safety," according to the citation. More important, as the first African American to win the Navy Cross, Miller also slew the myth—widely believed in the America of the time— that people of color would be no good in a fight. African Americans had been underestimated by white Americans in the past, just as the Japanese had been. It wasn't a mistake that anyone would make again.

High in the sky, Fuchida decided it was time to leave as *West Virginia* floundered below. The second wave had dropped all its bombs and was ready to go. Fuchida had made notes of the damage to the American fleet and had taken photographs of the airfields for later analysis. There was nothing to detain the Japanese over Pearl Harbor any longer.

The midget submarines did not join them as they turned away from the target. After successfully sneaking into Pearl Harbor, one had been sunk off Ford Island around 8:45. It had launched both of its torpedoes but had

(Above) This map room in London lay at the center of Britain's war effort. Japan's progress across the Pacific was charted hour by hour as the reports came in. *(Courtesy of Imperial War Museum, London)*

(Left) The scene between Greer Garson and a Luftwaffe pilot in *Mrs. Miniver*. The script was hastily rewritten after Pearl Harbor to turn the German into a die-hard Nazi. *(Courtesy of Corbis)*

A Japanese view of Ford Island and Battleship Row during the attack. *(Courtesy of National Archives, Washington, DC)*

Against the odds, USS *Nevada* managed to get under way and head for the open sea without the aid of a tug. *(Courtesy of National Archives, Washington, DC)*

Tarzan author Edgar Rice Burroughs watches the action from the grounds of the Niumalu Hotel. *(Courtesy of Edgar Rice Burroughs, Inc.)*

Japanese pilots were surprised at the speed with which the Americans recovered from their initial shock and began to fight back. *(Courtesy of National Archives, Washington, DC)*

For the first time since July, all of the Pacific fleet's battleships were in harbor on December 7. There was always a long line for Hotel Street's brothels when the sailors were in town. *(Courtesy of National Archives, Washington, DC)*

Ensign Sakamaki's midget submarine later toured the United States as part of a sales drive for war bonds. Sakamaki reportedly burst into tears when reunited with it in Texas in 1991. *(Courtesy of National Archives, Washington, DC)*

Shorn of her superstructure, USS *Arizona* has now lain at peace for many years. *(Courtesy of National Archives, Washington, DC)*

Naval officer Jack Kennedy was driving home from a game of touch football in Washington when he heard the news of Pearl Harbor on the radio. *(Courtesy of Corbis)*

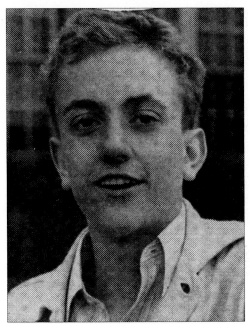

Kurt Vonnegut was in the bath at Cornell. He jumped out at once and ran down the street to remake the front page of the *Cornell Daily Sun*. *(Courtesy of Indiana Historical Society)*

On the set of *Yankee Doodle Dandy*, James Cagney called for a short prayer after listening to President Roosevelt on the radio. *(Courtesy of Corbis)*

Marlene Dietrich was preparing for a Hollywood dinner party. She was delighted that Japan had bombed some sense into the Americans at last. *(Courtesy of Getty Images)*

U.S. pilots from one of the RAF's Eagle squadrons. They sought a transfer to their own air force on December 8. *(Courtesy of Imperial War Museum, London)*

Lady Charles Cavendish (Fred Astaire's sister, Adele) bought a fighter plane for the RAF and later entertained U.S. servicemen in England. *(Courtesy of Getty Images)*

The first mass gassing of Jews took place at Chelmno, Poland, on December 8, 1941, in a van like this one. *(Courtesy of Yad Vashem)*

A Jewish woman writes a last letter before deportation to Chelmno for extermination. *(Courtesy of United States Holocaust Memorial Museum)*

Dropped from ten thousand feet, a Japanese bomb killed about fifty people when it hit HMS *Repulse*'s catapult deck. *(Courtesy of the Aldridge family)*

Adolf Hitler declares war on the United States, December 11, 1941. *(Courtesy of Mary Evans/ SZ Photo/Scherl)*

managed only to hit the island before being shot, rammed, and blasted with depth charges set to explode at only thirty feet.

Others may have penetrated Pearl Harbor, but if they did they were never seen again. Not one of the five submarines returned safely to their mother ships after the operation.

The only man to survive was Ensign Sakamaki. His malfunctioning submarine had drifted around the island toward Bellows Field on the east coast before he and Inagaki abandoned ship. Inagaki drowned. Sakamaki made it ashore, only to become the United States' first prisoner of the war.

Fuchida knew nothing of this as he gave the signal to go home. He knew only that the assault from the air had been an outstanding success. It had gone much better than anyone had dared hope.

Fuchida lingered to round up the stragglers as the aircraft of the second wave pulled away from Oahu and headed for their rendezvous off the island's northwest coast. The bombers led the way because their three-man crews were better able to navigate than the fighter pilots. Once they were all assembled, they would fly back to the carriers in a group so that nobody got lost.

It took a while for everyone to reach the agreed spot. Ahead lay a long flight across the featureless ocean in search of a task force that had moved since they last saw it at dawn. It would be after midday before the last of the returning planes swooped through the clouds and touched down on the flight deck amid rolling seas.

After that Fuchida would have an immediate discussion with his bosses about the possibility of a further attack that afternoon. There was still plenty to do at Pearl Harbor. A third or perhaps even a fourth wave of bombers could finish off the battleships and destroy the remaining aircraft, so completing the work of the morning. They could destroy the oil tanks too, and maybe even the missing aircraft carriers, if the U.S. Navy had summoned them back to base.

FOURTEEN

FUTURE U.S. PRESIDENTS REMEMBER THE MOMENT

While the second wave attacked Oahu, the United States was waking up to what was happening. President Roosevelt dictated the official announcement for release to the press at 2:30 p.m., Washington time. The news was on the radio by three o'clock, still only midday on the West Coast.

Over the next few hours, newspapers all over the country rushed out extra editions with banner headlines. Radio stations ran with the story. Word of mouth did the rest.

By early evening, there was hardly a person in the country who didn't have some inkling of the news. People all over America never forgot the day Pearl Harbor was attacked, the day their country's story changed forever.

Among them were several of the nation's future commanders in chief. Senator Harry S. Truman was far away from Washington when he learned of the attack. He was in Missouri, his home state, seeing family and attending to political business.

Exhausted after a hectic schedule, Truman had just surfaced from an afternoon nap at the Pennant Hotel in Columbia. He was in his room, leafing through the morning's newspapers, when Deputy U.S. Marshal Roy

Webb rang, as Truman later related to his cousin Ethel Noland. "The boy who drove me down left about noon and at three o'clock called me from Cross Timbers (I bet you never heard of it) and told me that the Japs had bombed Honolulu."[1]

Dropping his newspapers, Truman leaped into action. Columbia was a terrible place to be at a moment of national emergency. There was no way that he could get himself back to Washington in a hurry. He immediately telephoned TWA's St. Louis office and told the airline staff that he had to be in Washington next morning. But St. Louis's airport was 130 miles away, and Truman had no car or driver.

Fortunately, Columbia had a tiny airport right across the street from Truman's hotel. The manager quickly arranged for a plane to take the senator to St. Louis. He took off from Columbia at 4:50 and touched down at St. Louis less than an hour later on the first leg of what turned out to be a very fraught return to Washington.

Ensign Jack Kennedy of the U.S. Naval Reserve had rather less of a journey. He was returning to his apartment after a game of touch football near the Washington Monument when he heard the news on the car radio.

Kennedy had been in uniform since October. As the glamorous son of a former ambassador to the Court of St. James, he had featured on a newsreel amid a blaze of publicity when his name was called for the draft. He had failed the medical for the navy, but strings had been pulled by his father. Kennedy had been commissioned into the reserve without even the need to go through officer training.

As the author of the bestselling *Why England Slept*, the twenty-four-year-old Kennedy had been sent to Washington to join the foreign intelligence branch of the Office of Naval Intelligence. While Alwin Kramer and others were preoccupied with the latest signals from Japan, the young Kennedy busied himself with the preparation of daily and weekly intelligence bulletins for distribution to the secretary of the navy, shore stations, and ships at sea.

It was dull work. Kennedy and five others—most of them former journalists—sat at typewriters in the same room all day, bashing out reports and summaries. Kennedy was good at the job and did it conscientiously, but it didn't stretch his mind. He worked a six-day week, taking only Sundays off.

Washington was fun, though. Kennedy's sister Kathleen was a reporter for the *Times-Herald* and introduced him to lots of girls. He was having an affair with one of her colleagues, a Danish divorcée who had once shared a box with Hitler at the Munich Olympics.

Sunday was Kennedy's day of rest. He was spending it with LeMoyne Billings, an old school friend from Choate. Lem Billings wasn't keen on sports, but Kennedy enjoyed nothing better than a game of touch football if one was going. He liked to find a game and then ask if he could join in.

They spotted one easily enough, as Billings remembered. "On that particular Sunday we found a game near the Washington Monument. We'd just finished the game and were driving back to his apartment. All of a sudden the news came over his car radio that the Japanese had attacked Pearl Harbor."[2]

Crowds were forming outside the White House as they drove on. Smoke was rising from the Japanese Embassy. Nomura's staff were burning their codebooks, now that they didn't need them anymore.

Lyndon B. Johnson was in the navy, too. The congressman from Texas had been a lieutenant commander in the U.S. Naval Reserve for several months. He had loudly proclaimed his patriotism during an unsuccessful run for the Senate in June 1941. "If the day ever comes when my vote must be cast to send your boy to the trenches, that day Lyndon Johnson will leave his Senate seat and go with him."[3]

The message had sounded so good that Johnson had repeated it endlessly during his campaign. He hadn't succeeded in becoming a senator, but it was the kind of fighting talk that Texans liked to hear. And he was still a congressman.

Johnson was as good as his word when he learned of Pearl Harbor. Four days later he asked for indefinite leave of absence from Congress so that he could transfer to the navy's active service list and fight the Japanese. Without any actual naval experience, he was disappointed to be given unglamorous administrative work instead.

Dwight Eisenhower was having an afternoon nap when the phone rang. Newly promoted to brigadier general, he was chief of staff of the Third Army at Fort Sam Houston in San Antonio, Texas. He had been in his office all morning, catching up on paperwork. Around noon he told his executive officer that he was dead tired and going home for a snooze.

Eisenhower was a coming man in the army. After years of uneventful service, he had made his name in the Louisiana maneuvers of August and September 1941, when 240,000 men of the Third Army had invaded Louisiana, defended by 180,000 troops of the Second Army. It had been the biggest war game the peacetime troops had ever undertaken.

As chief planner, Eisenhower had received the credit for outflanking the Second Army and forcing it to retreat. He had been promoted as a result and had begun to see his picture in the papers. Eisenhower had never seen a day's action in his life, but he was becoming known throughout the military as an outstanding staff officer.

His wife, Mamie, was there when he got home. He told her that he didn't want to be bothered by anyone wanting to play bridge and went for a nap. He was fast asleep when his executive officer called with news of the Japanese attack. Summoned to Washington a few days later, Eisenhower promised his wife that he would be back soon. He didn't return for years.

George H. W. Bush was a seventeen-year-old high school senior at Phillips Academy, in Andover, Massachusetts. He was due to follow in his father's footsteps to Yale in a year's time. His father was one of the directors of a bank that had had dealings with the Nazis in the past.

Bush was known as Poppy. Rich and gilded, he sent his laundry home from school every week for the servants to wash. He was very active at Andover: captain of baseball, captain of soccer, president of the senior class, and secretary of the student council. He was the insider's insider, an eager networker determined to make the right connections and get on in life.

Bush was not particularly academic, but he made up for it in relentless determination. No one was in any doubt that he would succeed at whatever he set out to do.

The advice after Pearl Harbor was that it was likely to be a long war. Plenty of time to go to Yale first and get a degree. But George Bush wasn't having that. He decided to enlist as soon as he turned eighteen. He wanted to join the navy and learn how to fly.

Jimmy Carter was at Georgia Southwestern, a junior college in Americus. Though without family money, he too was hoping to join the navy. Small and combative, he was studying hard, concentrating on the subjects recommended in the Naval Academy's guide for entrance to Annapolis.

Carter's uncle Tom Gordy was already in the navy, an enlisted man who regularly sent him postcards from foreign ports and once gave him a model of a sampan. Tom was currently stationed on the little island of Guam, one of a small band of specialists maintaining the navy's radio links across the Pacific.

Carter had already told his friends that he planned to become governor of Georgia one day. That Sunday afternoon, though, he was forced to put his plans on hold. A group of Southwestern students stood discussing the Japanese attack on the steps of their dormitory. Carter told the others that his immediate aim now was to become a submarine commander instead.

Gerald Ford had just graduated from Yale Law School. After a football scholarship at the University of Michigan, he had turned down the chance to play professionally in favor of a coaching job at Yale. It was a full-time position, but Ford had managed to persuade the law faculty to take him on as a student as well.

Ford had campaigned for Wendell Willkie in the 1940 presidential election. He had supported the America First Committee at Yale, an isolationist group opposed to sending U.S. troops overseas. An unexceptional student, he had worked hard to graduate as a lawyer with decent but far from remarkable grades.

He had also fallen in love with a very pretty girl. Phyllis Brown was a New York model and cover girl. She had taken the handsome Ford for a photo shoot at a ski lodge in Vermont. The resulting pictures had been spread across five pages of *Look* magazine in March 1940.

The affair had fizzled out after Ford's graduation. The fork in the road had led two ways. Either Ford could follow a lovely girl to the bright lights and metropolitan life of New York City, or he could go back to his home town of Grand Rapids, Michigan, and set up as a dull, small-town lawyer. Ford had opted for the law.

It was hard work, starting a practice from scratch. Ford was preparing for a court appearance the following Tuesday when he learned of the Japanese attack. "I was in the office that Sunday afternoon and didn't hear the news until I flicked on the radio while driving home that night."[4]

Abandoning the law soon afterward, Ford joined the navy early in 1942.

Richard M. Nixon was in Hollywood. Like Gerald Ford, he was a small-time lawyer who had campaigned for Wendell Willkie in the 1940 presidential election. But his life was about to change. He had just accepted a job with the Office of Price Administration in Washington.

The job was nothing much, but Washington was exciting. Nixon was looking forward to seeing the workings of government at first hand. With a new life ahead of them, he and his wife, Pat, were in a good mood that afternoon as they set off for Hollywood to see a movie, as Nixon recalled:

> On the way we stopped for a visit at her sister Neva's house. When we arrived, Neva's husband, Marc, said that he had just heard on the radio an unconfirmed report that the Japanese had bombed Pearl Harbor. I said I was sure that it was just one more of the frequent scare stories we all had been hearing, and we went on to the matinée.
>
> Shortly before the film was finished, the theater manager interrupted

with an announcement that all servicemen had been called to their units immediately. When we left the theater, I saw the headline: Japs Bomb Pearl Harbor. The newsboy held up the paper as I walked over. He said, "We're at war, mister."[5]

Ronald Reagan was in Hollywood, too, apparently fast asleep as the Japanese attacked. They had evidently known what they were doing in timing their raid for a lazy Sunday morning in the United States.

Reagan was on the brink of major stardom after a string of recent movie successes. Warner Bros.' *International Squadron*, about American pilots in the RAF, had just come out, six weeks ahead of Twentieth Century–Fox's *A Yank in the RAF*. British audiences burst into laughter at the plot's inaccuracies, but the film had been a big hit in the States and a major boost for Reagan.

He had also just completed *Kings Row*, alongside Ann Sheridan and Robert Cummings. According to Reagan, Cummings had regularly greeted him on set with the line, "Someday I'm going to vote for this fellow for President."[6]

Reagan's performance in *Kings Row* would be the nearest he ever came to winning an Oscar. Warner Bros. was so pleased with it that they offered him a seven-year contract at a much bigger salary before the movie even came out. His agent Lew Wasserman was still hammering out the details when Reagan's older brother, Neil (nicknamed Moon), phoned to tell him about Pearl Harbor.

Reagan was known to his friends as Dutch. According to Edmund Morris, whose authorized biography of Reagan contained some scenes recreated in the author's own words, he was in bed when his brother called:

> *I've quizzed a lot of people here, including Dutch, who confesses that he was asleep. Well whaddya expect on Sunday morning, at the crack of noon? Typically, it was his brother who called him: nothing Moon enjoys more than scaring the shit out of people.*
>
> *Dutch, equally typically (ain't it marvellous how emergencies establish people's priorities?), called Lew Wasserman for career advice.*

Lew, in turn, listened quietly, then hung up on him—whether in shock or sudden grief for a client demonstrably headed for military service, we will never know.[7]

Reagan's poor eyesight would preclude him from active service, but he was a reserve officer in the cavalry nevertheless, liable to be called for duty at any moment. The Japanese couldn't have struck at a worse time, just when his career was taking off.

Robert Carson shared his dismay. The Japanese couldn't have struck at a worse time for him either, just as his story *Aloha Means Goodbye* was going into preproduction as a major Hollywood movie.

Carson was a scriptwriter. He already had an Oscar under his belt for *A Star Is Born*. But that was ancient history now. His thoughts were focused on the new movie, adapted from his *Saturday Evening Post* story about a Japanese attack on Pearl Harbor.

Bogart, Greenstreet, and Mary Astor were all on board. John Huston was to direct. Yet they couldn't go ahead with it now, not after what had happened. The real story was far more dramatic than anything in the movie.

Unless . . . maybe they could rework it. Move the action elsewhere. A Japanese plot to destroy the Panama Canal might work. Something, anything, that didn't involve the Hawaiian Islands and an attack on Pearl Harbor.

Huston was playing tennis in Bel Air when he heard the news. William Wyler had invited him around for a game before lunch. The two directors were good friends. They were planning a trip together after Wyler had completed *Mrs. Miniver*, a boys-only expedition to China with their fellow director Anatole Litvak. They all wanted to get away from Hollywood for a while, see a bit of the world across the Pacific.

They were on court when Wyler's wife, Talli, came dashing out to tell them about the attack. Someone had just called with the news. The two men reacted like millions of other Americans, as she afterward remembered. "Everyone immediately started talking about how fast they could get into the army. There was no way, with their natures, that they could sit out this war."[8]

They drove to Malibu that afternoon to see Anatole Litvak. They had arranged to meet a travel agent there to discuss the China expedition, but that was off the agenda now. The only topic was the war and how quickly they could complete their movie schedules before getting into it.

The script for *Aloha Means Goodbye* would have to be rewritten, which probably meant shutting the movie down for a while. *Mrs. Miniver* would have to be rewritten too, now that America was no longer neutral in the war.

The crucial scene between Greer Garson and the Nazi flier, the only German character in the film, could be redone completely in the light of developments. There would be no more pussyfooting around, pretending he was a nice boy. The scene would work much better dramatically if he wasn't.

The end speech could be rewritten too, the bit where the vicar mourned the dead and told the British what they were fighting for. There was no longer any need to mollify the Germans or placate the Hays Office and the isolationists. Wyler was free to tell it how it was, now that his hands had been untied.

Some Hollywood people were already in uniform. Drafted in 1940, James Stewart had managed to enlist in the Army Air Corps after bulking up to meet the minimum weight requirement for a man of his height. He was busy logging the flying time necessary to become an officer.

Director John Ford was in the navy, recently transferred at his own request from the reserve to active duty. With *Stagecoach*, *Young Mr. Lincoln*, and *The Grapes of Wrath* behind him, Ford was already a double Oscar winner with another to come. He had volunteered for active service because he was sure the war would reach America soon.

Ford had been stationed in Washington for some time. He was the front man for the Naval Volunteer Photographic Unit. He had recruited the personnel himself, Hollywood professionals quietly preparing to record the war on film once it got started.

Ford had been invited to lunch that Sunday by Rear-Admiral Andrew Pickens and his wife. They lived in an eighteenth-century house in Alexandria, a few miles south of the city. The guests were sitting around the table when a maid called the admiral to the telephone.

Pickens returned to the room with dramatic news. "Gentlemen, Pearl Harbor has just been attacked by the Japanese. We are now at war."9

The lunch party broke up soon afterward. As the guests dispersed, Mrs. Pickens showed Ford a bullet hole in the wall. She told him it had been there since the days of the American Revolution. "It's no use getting excited. This is the seventh war that's been announced in this dining room. I never let them plaster over that."10

Clark Gable was in the stables of his Encino ranch in the San Fernando Valley. He was grooming his horses when his wife, Carole Lombard, burst in. Together they went back to the house and stayed close to the radio as the story unfolded.

Carole Lombard was due on the radio herself that evening. She was scheduled to appear live on *The Jack Benny Program*, promoting their new movie *To Be or Not to Be*. NBC called later to say that normal services had been suspended for a while. The broadcast would be rescheduled later.

Charlton Heston was at home near Chicago, writing an essay about *Macbeth* in his bedroom. A nerdy teenager, too shy to attend his high school prom, he had blossomed since winning a drama scholarship to Northwestern's School of Speech. He had already appeared in a student film of *Peer Gynt* and was all set to become an actor after he graduated.

Marlene Dietrich was in Beverly Hills, preparing for a Hollywood dinner party. Her daughter, Maria, learned of the attack from the radio. In common with many others, she thought it was a spoof at first, like Orson Welles's 1938 broadcast of *The War of the Worlds* from the Mercury Theater. She telephoned her mother as soon as she discovered otherwise.

According to Maria, Dietrich was delighted to hear that the United

States had been attacked. "What? They bombed ships? Finally! So, it took the *Japanese* to bring the Americans to their senses? Good! *Now* they will fight! Now it will all be over soon—like when they came into the war the last time, before you were born."[11]

Marlene Dietrich was German, a Prussian to her beautiful fingertips. Her mother and sister still lived in Berlin. Her cousin was fighting on the Russian front. She loved her family, but she had taken American citizenship before the war because she couldn't bear to be a German anymore. She hated what the Nazis were doing all over Europe.

Dietrich had been a vigorous supporter of the British in the dark days of 1940. She had packed Bundles for Britain (non-military supplies of food, clothing, and medicine) and had listened to Ed Murrow's calm tones night after night as he reported the Blitz on London, with real air-raid sirens and bomb explosions in the background. She had supported the British against her own kith and kin because they were the only ones doing anything to keep the Nazis at bay.

But the Americans were in it now. They had to be, if they had been attacked by Hitler's ally. If the Americans were in it, Dietrich was too. Even with family in Germany, she was going to campaign vigorously for an Allied victory.

Meantime, as her daughter recalled the conversation, Marlene Dietrich needed more butter for her dinner party.

The radio was America's big disseminator of information. In a vast and sprawling country, it was the quickest, most efficient way of telling the people in the heartland what had happened. The announcers remained at the microphone all afternoon, passing the news on as soon as they had it, giving continual updates to an audience of many millions desperate to know more.

Ernest Hemingway was crossing into Texas when he picked up a news flash. He and his wife, Martha Gellhorn, were on a road trip. They had driven down from their home in Idaho to see the Grand Canyon. Now they were driving southeast, heading for the Gulf of Mexico.

Hemingway was riding high as they drove. His latest novel, *For Whom the Bell Tolls*, had been a huge success, selling more than half a million copies so far. He was due to receive a gold medal from the Limited Editions Club for his efforts. He was a happy man until he switched the radio on and heard about Pearl Harbor.

He and his wife had spent some time on Oahu during a trip to China. They had not been impressed by the sight of so many U.S. warships crammed into Pearl Harbor with Japanese sampans all around. Hemingway hadn't been impressed by the aircraft at Hickam either, packed so closely together that they were sitting ducks from above. As a noncombatant, he had seen exactly the same mistake made in Europe during World War I.

He was boiling with rage by the time they reached their hotel in San Antonio. While Dwight Eisenhower was abandoning his afternoon nap at Fort Sam Houston, Hemingway was settling down to write a series of angry letters insisting that whoever had been in charge at Pearl Harbor ought to be shot forthwith.

At his apartment in New York's Bedford Hotel, John Steinbeck completed what he hoped was the final draft of *The Moon Is Down* that morning. It was a play-cum-novella about a European town under occupation by the Germans.

Steinbeck was writing it for the Foreign Information Service, a government body that had recently been set up to combat German propaganda. Fresh from his success with *The Grapes of Wrath*, he was one of several writers who had been recruited to fight the Germans with a pen. Steinbeck had jumped at the chance.

He had set the first draft of the story in an anonymous American town, hoping to bring the realities of Nazi occupation home to an American audience. But the FIS had disliked the implication of American defeat. They thought it would backfire if it demoralized people.

Steinbeck had accordingly relocated the story to a town somewhere on the coast of occupied Europe. He imagined his unnamed country as: "Cold and stern like Norway, cunning and implacable like Denmark, reasonable like France."[12] Steinbeck was hoping that the play would go into production as soon as he completed it. He already had a contract for it to be published as a novella the following spring.

Unusually for him, he had decided to dictate the story to a secretary, rather than write it himself. He had hired a large and rather forbidding court reporter. She sat at the dining table, tapping away at her typewriter while Steinbeck paced the room, dictating revisions as he went along.

Unfortunately, he had had to fire the woman after a while. Instead of typing exactly what he told her, she had made significant changes of her own, often leaving out entire passages about the Germans that she didn't like. Steinbeck discovered later that the woman was a Nazi sympathizer. She belonged to a group of New Yorkers actively supporting Hitler in the war.

Eighteen-year-old Norman Mailer was at Harvard that Sunday. He was too young to be a writer yet, but he was on his way. He had won a national story-writing competition in June and was already receiving attention from publishers who wanted to see more of his work.

Mailer's idol was Ernest Hemingway. He had written a story about German antiaircraft gunners cowering from a British bombardment in imitation of the master. Mailer's Jewish girlfriend, later his first wife, was in no doubt that the United States ought to be in the war, helping to fight the Germans. Mailer heartily agreed, just so long as he wasn't involved in the fighting.

In common with most Harvard undergraduates, he was very excited by the attack on Pearl Harbor, but for different reasons. Like James Jones, only a lot farther away from the action, Mailer was sure that there would be a novel in it somewhere:

> *I may as well confess that by December 8th or 9th of 1941, in the forty-eight hours after Pearl Harbor, while worthy young men were wondering where they could be of aid to the war effort, and practical young men were deciding which branch of the service was the surest for landing a safe commission, I was worrying darkly whether it would be more likely that a great war novel would be written about Europe or the Pacific.*[13]

Kurt Vonnegut was in a bathtub at Cornell. He leaped out as soon as he learned of the attack, tearing down the street to the office of the *Cornell Daily Sun*, the student newspaper. Vonnegut was a night editor at the *Sun*, responsible for laying out the news pages and composing the headlines before the paper went to press.

He was a bad student, at Cornell only because his parents insisted on it. He would much rather have skipped college altogether and gone straight into journalism. The best thing about Cornell was working on the *Sun*, in Vonnegut's opinion.

His family was of German origin, strongly opposed to any American intervention in the European war. Vonnegut was a cadet in the Cornell ROTC because it was compulsory, but he too was an isolationist. He thought it would be an act of supreme folly for the United States to take up arms against Hitler.

Vonnegut had stoutly defended the aviator Charles Lindbergh, probably America's most famous isolationist, in an opinion piece for the *Sun*. Many Americans had turned against Lindbergh because of his intemperate attacks on President Roosevelt, but he had had Vonnegut's full support in the paper:

> *The United States is a democracy, that's what they say we'll be fighting for. What a prize monument to that ideal is a cry to smother Lindy. . . . Lindy, you're a rat. We read that somewhere, so it must be so. They say you should be deported. In that event, leave room in the boat for us.*[14]

But Lindbergh and the isolationists were irrelevant now. There was only one story in town as Vonnegut hurried to the *Sun*'s office above a grocery store on State Street. "I tore down to the office, and we laid out a new first and last page, keeping the stale insides of the previous issue. . . . We took whatever was coming off the AP machine, slapped it in, and were, I still believe, the first paper in the state to hit the streets with an extra."[15]

Charles Lindbergh himself was on Martha's Vineyard that afternoon. He had recently rented a house on the island in an attempt to escape the attention that followed him and his family everywhere.

Much of the attention was Lindbergh's own fault. As a leading light of the America First Committee, he had been a relentless critic of Roosevelt. He had accused the president of planning to put an end to free speech, elections, and other liberties, plotting to go way beyond his powers and take America into the war against the express wishes of his own people.

Lindbergh had said as much on October 30 to a crowd of twenty thousand at Madison Square Garden in New York, one of the few venues still prepared to offer a platform for his rabble-rousing. He had received a six-minute ovation from his supporters, many of them openly pro-Nazi. Millions of other Americans had been sickened at the spectacle.

Lindbergh learned about Pearl Harbor from the radio, like so many people. He was far from alone in wondering how on earth the disaster could have happened. "How did the Japs get close enough, and where is our Navy? Or is it just a hit-and-run raid of a few planes, exaggerated by radio commentators into a major attack?"[16]

Whatever the details, Lindbergh's duty was clear. Isolationism was at an end. No matter what they thought of it, Americans of all kinds had to get behind Roosevelt and fight for their country. They were all in the war now, whether they liked it or not.

Ed Murrow was in Washington, playing a round of golf. He and his wife, Janet, had been invited to dinner with the Roosevelts that evening.

Murrow was CBS's star broadcaster, the second most famous radio voice in the land, after the president himself. Following a long stint reporting the Blitz from London, he had come home for three months' rest. Roosevelt wanted to meet him to hear about the Blitz at first hand.

Murrow was glad to be back in the United States, but he saw his own country through new eyes after his time in England. The contrast between glitzy New York and the smashed buildings and blacked-out streets of rationed, war-torn London could not have been greater.

After so long away, Murrow felt more comfortable among the uniformed men and women of Britain, all of them focused on the war, all quietly determined that Hitler wasn't going to win. He couldn't warm to peacetime New York:

> It was a shock to see so many well-dressed, well-fed, complacent-looking people—shop windows crowded with luxury goods—the chamber maid in the hotel wearing silk stockings—a big formal Bundles for Britain ball . . . fat chorus boys with marcelled hair dressed in sailor uniforms singing nautical songs—little boxes in expensive night clubs marked "Tin Foil for Britain"—wealthy friends moaning about ruinous taxation . . .
> My mind would not work—still have a curious feeling of being suspended between a skyscraper and a bomb crater. . . . Maybe it was a mistake for me to come.[17]

Murrow abandoned his golf after learning about the Japanese attack. He hurried to CBS's Washington office to find out more. Janet Murrow phoned the White House, expecting dinner to be canceled. She was assured by Eleanor Roosevelt that it was still on. "We all have to eat. Come anyway."[18]

While Murrow abandoned his golf, Bill Bullitt was touching down in Trinidad, on his way to Egypt by Clipper.

Bullitt was a former U.S. ambassador to France and the Soviet Union. He was on a fact-finding mission to the Middle and Far East. President Roosevelt had asked him to assess the military and political situation in various countries and report back to him in person.

Flying from Miami, Bullitt had heard nothing about Pearl Harbor as he landed in Trinidad. It wasn't until he arrived at Government House that he found out:

> I drove to the residence of the British Governor, Sir Hubert Young. As I entered the residence I was welcomed by the sounds of someone banging

on the piano as hard as he could and shouting some kind of song. It was
the Governor who rushed forward with his hands outstretched and said,
"The Japs have attacked Pearl Harbor."[19]

Full of enthusiasm, the governor led Bullitt into the garden. A band was
playing hymns and patriotic tunes as they talked. After a while the governor summoned an aide-de-camp before turning back to Bullitt:

"I have been forbidden until this moment to have played together my
national anthem and your national anthem and now I can as we are
allies!" Then he gave orders to his aide-de-camp to have played "The Star
Spangled Banner" and "God Save the King."

We stood at attention while the band played "The Star Spangled
Banner", filled with emotion. Then the band played "Roll Out the Bar-
rel." The Governor grew purple and exploded.[20]

Like so many of his fellow Britons, Sir Hubert Young was delighted to
hear that the United States was now entering the war.

FIFTEEN

BRITAIN CHEERS THE NEWS

Across the Pacific, Fuchida arrived back at the task force sometime after midday. After a long flight, the carrier *Akagi* was a welcome sight as his aircraft touched down on the rolling deck and came to a halt at last.

His friend Genda was there to meet him. Fuchida immediately asked how many planes had been lost in the attack. Genda reckoned about thirty. In fact twenty-nine had been downed over Oahu. Another ten or fifteen were so badly shot up that they had been pushed overboard as soon as their crews were safe. A further forty or so had been hit and would have to be repaired before they could fly again.

The returning aircraft were being refueled and rearmed as Fuchida jumped out of the cockpit. The fighters had to be ready to take off again at short notice to defend the task force if the Americans found it. Now that they were no longer needed, many of the horizontal bombers were being hurriedly converted to carry torpedoes, which were much more effective than bombs at sea.

Fuchida was summoned to make a report. He made his way to the bridge, where Admiral Nagumo and his staff were waiting.

Fuchida told them that four U.S. battleships had been sunk. He had seen them with his own eyes. He thought another three had been badly damaged. The eighth battleship had also been hit, although less seriously, from what Fuchida had been able to make out.

They gathered around a berthing chart of Pearl Harbor. Fuchida took them through the attack, showing where the ships had been hit. When he had finished, Nagumo asked him the crucial question. Could the American fleet use Pearl Harbor for the next six months?

Not in Fuchida's opinion. Small ships maybe, but a large force would be unable to leave port. In the short term, the Americans were stymied.

That was what Nagumo wanted to hear. By some accounts, Fuchida pointed out that there were still undamaged cruisers in harbor. The dockyards and the fuel tanks were there for the taking. He thought they should be attacked that afternoon, along with the airfields again and the battleships still afloat. The Japanese should finish the job while they had the chance.

Nagumo wasn't convinced. They had already done enough, in his opinion. The task force itself was the target now. His first duty was to protect his ships before the aircraft from America's missing carriers found them.

Genda tried to persuade him to look for the U.S. carriers and sink them first. The carriers had always been the main target, but Nagumo wasn't having it. The gods had been with them so far. He didn't want to tempt fate any further.

He gave orders for the afternoon's attack to be canceled. A little later *Akagi* hoisted the withdraw signal from the masthead. The task force turned toward the northwest and headed away from Hawaii.

The attack had been an outstanding success by anybody's standards, but it was not the only triumph the Japanese enjoyed that morning. Within a few hours of their assault on Pearl Harbor—Monday, December 8, across the international date line—they also attacked Hong Kong, Malaya, Thailand, and the Philippines. The results were more gratifying than they had dared hope.

As with Pearl Harbor, there was no declaration of war. The Japanese attacked Hong Kong soon after first light, bombing the airport while battle-hardened troops from the Chinese war advanced from the mainland. Their forces outnumbered the defenders by almost four to one.

The British fought back, but the outcome was never in doubt. The British had long ago concluded that the waterless island of Hong Kong would be impossible to defend in a war. They fought fiercely, but they knew it would only be a matter of time before they were forced to surrender.

The attack on Malaya began with a naval bombardment of the beach at Kota Bharu, just south of the border with Thailand. Japanese troops in landing craft were already heading for shore as their aircraft approached Pearl Harbor.

The British knew the Japanese were off the coast. They had done nothing about it to avoid providing them with an excuse to start a war. Now that the gloves were off, the British immediately returned fire, inflicting heavy casualties as the Japanese came ashore.

The Japanese also attacked Singapore, at the other end of Malaya. Several squadrons of bombers arrived over the brightly lit city just after four in the morning. They hit the harbor and the airfield, but without the spectacular results achieved at Pearl Harbor.

Japanese forces also invaded Thailand. They came by sea, swarming ashore at various points along the Kra Isthmus and occupying Bangkok with barely a shot fired. Powerless to prevent them, the Thais agreed to a ceasefire within hours.

MacArthur in the Philippines was less compliant. He had been forewarned by the attack on Pearl Harbor, but was still unable to stop the Japanese from landing on Batan Island or destroying half his aircraft on the ground before they could take off. Despite these setbacks, he was determined to defend the Philippines and fight a stiff rearguard action until reinforcements could arrive from the United States.

The war had gone global at last. The United States was in the fight now, the largest industrial power on earth. The implications were obvious as news of the attacks flashed around the world. It was going to be a long, hard road, a road strewn with far too much blood and treasure, but nothing now could prevent an Allied victory in the long run.

Winston Churchill was spending a weekend in the English countryside when news of Pearl Harbor reached Europe. He was at Chequers, the prime minister's official country home just outside London.

He was having dinner with, among others, John Gilbert Winant, the U.S. ambassador, and Averell Harriman, the president's Lend-Lease envoy to Britain. Both Americans were having extramarital affairs with Churchill's womenfolk, Winant with his daughter Sarah, Harriman with his daughter-in-law, Pamela. Churchill turned a blind eye just so long as the Americans' pillow talk was relayed back to him.

Churchill was gloomy at dinner—tired and depressed, according to Harriman. He said little during the meal, keeping his own counsel, sometimes with his head in his hands. At 9:00 p.m. the butler came in with a portable radio that had been given to Churchill by Harry Hopkins, and placed it on the table.

Churchill liked to listen to the BBC's nine o'clock news because it usually had a full summary of the day's events. He lifted the lid to switch the radio on. The lead story was about the counterattack on the Russian front, followed by a British tank battle in Libya. There were also a few sentences about an attack on American shipping in Hawaii:

> *The news has just been given that Japanese aircraft have raided Pearl Harbor, the American naval base in Hawaii. The announcement of the attack was made in a brief statement by President Roosevelt. Naval and military targets on the principal Hawaiian island of Oahu have also been attacked. No further details are yet available.*[1]

The item made no immediate impression on Churchill, but the Americans' ears pricked up at the mention of Pearl Harbor. They wondered if they had heard right. One of the other guests thought it was the Pearl River that had been attacked, not Hawaii.

The butler came in again to say that it was quite true. The United States had been attacked by Japan. Churchill's principal private secretary came in too to add that the Admiralty wanted to speak to him urgently on the phone. Ambassador Winant never forgot the moments that followed:

We looked at one another incredulously. Then Churchill jumped to his feet and started for the door with the announcement, "We shall declare war on Japan." There is nothing half-hearted or unpositive about Churchill—certainly not when he is on the move. Without ceremony I too left the table and followed him out of the room.

"Good God," I said. "You can't declare war on a radio announcement."

He stopped and looked at me half-seriously, half-quizzically, and then said quietly, "What shall I do?" The question was asked not because he needed me to tell him what to do, but as a courtesy to the representative of the country attacked.[2]

They telephoned Roosevelt to get the facts. He confirmed the story but didn't go into detail over an open telephone line. Churchill's mind was racing as the president hung up. "We then went back into the hall and tried to adjust our thoughts to the supreme world event which had occurred, which was of so startling a nature as to make even those who were near the centre gasp."[3]

Parliament was not due to meet until Tuesday. Newly invigorated, no longer despondent, Churchill swiftly put the wheels in motion to recall both houses for a joint session on Monday. He also called the Foreign Office to prepare the ground for a rapid declaration of war on Japan.

He was hard at work when word of the attack on Malaya arrived. Churchill arranged for it to be forwarded to King George VI, who had learned of Pearl Harbor from the nine o'clock news at Windsor.

He then dictated several messages to foreign leaders. One of them was to Chiang Kai-shek in China. Another was to Eamon de Valera, the prime minister of southern Ireland.

In common with the United States, southern Ireland had remained stubbornly neutral in the war, although privately helpful to the British. Churchill urged de Valera to abandon that unpopular stance. He told him that the Irish should do the right thing now and join the fight against Hitler and his cohorts.

It was well into the small hours before Churchill finished dictating telegrams and making telephone calls. Despite his earlier gloom and all the night's calamitous news, he was a happy man as he went to bed at last. "So we had won after all. . . . Hitler's fate was sealed. Mussolini's fate was sealed. As for the Japanese, they would be ground to powder. All the rest was merely the proper application of overwhelming force. . . . I went to bed and slept the sleep of the saved and thankful."[4]

In Ireland, it was just after 2:00 a.m. as Sir John Maffey, Britain's official representative to the country, arrived in the Dublin suburb of Blackrock. De Valera lived on Cross Avenue. Maffey knocked at the front door and was admitted at once.

De Valera was waiting for him. He had been warned that Maffey had a very important message from Churchill that couldn't wait until morning.

De Valera was wary. He knew that the British desperately wanted him to allow them the use of Irish ports in their fight against the U-boats. He speculated that Churchill's man was calling to deliver some sort of ultimatum as a result of the attack on Pearl Harbor.

After seeing Maffey, de Valera made a note of what had happened. "He said that he had got a message from Mr Churchill which he was asked to deliver. I gathered from his introductory remarks before handing me the paper that he was rather surprised at the message; that he regarded it as Churchillian."[5]

In the event, the typewritten text which Maffey then handed to de Valera had nothing in it that couldn't have waited until morning. It was just an exhortation for the Irish to join the war in which so many of their people were already fighting. "Following from Mr Churchill for Mr de Valera. Personal. Private and Secret. Begins. Now is your chance. Now or never. A nation once again. Am very ready to meet you at any time. Ends."[6]

"A nation once again" was a popular Irish slogan. De Valera read more into it than Churchill intended. He thought Churchill was implying that Irish reunification would follow if the south joined the war.

De Valera didn't believe that for a moment. He sent Maffey away with a promise that he would think about it, but without any intention of doing anything. Pearl Harbor may have changed the situation for the United States, but Ireland under Eamon de Valera was not about to join the fight against the Nazis.

While de Valera waited up, Anthony Eden was on his way to Russia. The British Foreign Secretary was going to Moscow to discuss and coordinate the war effort with Stalin. He was taking the Russian ambassador with him, and Sir Alexander Cadogan from the Foreign Office, together with various military advisers and officials. They had all left London on the afternoon train, heading north for Scotland and a warship to Murmansk.

Their departure was a closely guarded secret. Ivan Maisky, the Russian ambassador, had gone for his usual morning stroll in Kensington Gardens near the embassy before sneaking into the Underground and traveling incognito to join the others at Euston Station. They were well on their way to Scotland before they learned of Pearl Harbor, as Maisky afterward recalled:

> At about six p.m. we hurtled through some small station and noticed there was great excitement on the platform. There was an unusually large number of people there, hurrying, gesticulating, and apparently hotly arguing. At the next small station, through which the train likewise passed without stopping, we saw the same picture. This interested us, but we could not understand what was the matter?
>
> One thing only was clear, that something important had happened. Thereupon, on Eden's instructions, a short halt was made at the following station. One of Eden's staff jumped out and came back with a shattering piece of news a few minutes later. Japan had attacked the U.S.A.
>
> The station-master at this small place had heard the news on the

radio, but could not tell us of any details, and in particular did not know where and how the attack had taken place: but there was no doubt about the fact of the attack.[7]

It wasn't until late that night that they learned more. They stopped at a larger station and heard that it was Pearl Harbor that had been hit. Stricken with gastric flu, Eden wondered if he should cancel his Russian trip and return to London if he was needed there. Maisky told him no, his visit to Moscow was now more important than ever.

Eden was still sick when the train reached Invergordon next morning. A doctor came to see him, followed by a naval officer who said that Churchill wanted to speak to him on the phone. Eden was feeling dreadful as he followed the officer to naval headquarters. Churchill, on the other hand, was full of beans when they spoke:

Mr Churchill told me what he knew of the Japanese attack on Pearl Harbour. He was quite naturally in a high state of excitement. I could not conceal my relief and did not have to try to. I felt that whatever happened now, it was merely a question of time. Before, we had believed in the end but never seen the means, now both were clear.[8]

The American ambassador shared Churchill's ebullience:

Gil Winant came on the line. It was good to hear the relief in his voice as he acclaimed our decisions and wished me God speed. I knew that in his heart he was acclaiming something else too. The United States and Britain were now allies in the war against Japan.[9]

Eden's party boarded a destroyer for Scapa Flow, the naval base in the Orkney Islands. Ahead lay a long journey by ship and train to Moscow. The Russians learned of Pearl Harbor in the middle of the night. Eden and Stalin would have a great deal to discuss when at last they met in the Kremlin.

While Churchill was at dinner and Eden was on his way to Scotland, Lance-Corporal Dirk Bogarde of the Royal Corps of Signals was sitting gloomily in his hut at Catterick Camp in Yorkshire. He had just returned to the army after a spell of home leave and wasn't at all glad to be back.

As a lance corporal, Bogarde had a little cubicle to himself at the end of the hut. He was due to go for officer training soon, after which his life would change dramatically. For the moment, though, the only consolations of a bleak military existence were the occasional concert parties and performances at the garrison theater that brightened Bogarde's life.

He had made only one friend at Catterick, an illiterate Irishman who had just deserted from the army and gone home to Cork. But he was on good terms with Worms, a skinny youth with a prodigious sex life. It was Worms who told Bogarde about Pearl Harbor that Sunday evening while he was busy unpacking his kit bag after his return from leave:

> *There was a sudden commotion through the partition in the hut. People started clapping, and cheering. I was putting everything neatly away in my locker when Worms shoved open the door, his face scarlet.*
>
> *"You heard, did you?"*
>
> *"What?"*
>
> *"The Japs."*
>
> *"What about them?"*
>
> *"They've gone and bombed some bloody harbour in Hawaii. The Yanks are in!"*[10]

Malcolm Muggeridge was an intelligence officer at V Corps headquarters near Salisbury. He was listening to the radio in the officers' mess at Longford Castle when the attack was announced by the BBC.

"That settles it. We're bound to win now," another officer remarked complacently.[11] Muggeridge just hoped he was right.

Across the country tens of thousands of servicemen echoed the officer's sentiments as the good news spread. The overwhelming reaction as the details became clearer was neither outrage at the Japanese attack nor sympathy for the American dead. It was relief, plain and simple. Relief that the United States was joining in at last.

Few people were more pleased than the American officers in the RAF. The three squadrons of volunteer fighter pilots from the United States had long since identified Britain's war as their own. Now it was their country's struggle as well. The airmen couldn't have been more delighted to hear it.

No. 71 Squadron, the first of the three Eagle Squadrons to be formed, was based at North Weald in Essex. Spitfire pilot Harold Strickland had opted for an early night when the news broke:

After the final mission over the minesweepers and dinner, I turned in early and was reading in bed when the batman pounded on the door, entered and shouted "PEARL HARBOR HAS BEEN ATTACKED BY THE JAPANESE!"

He told me that the news had just been announced by the BBC and added that most of our battleships had been destroyed. I jumped into my clothes (literally) and headed for the bar (in the officers' mess) where pandemonium was in progress.[12]

No. 133 Squadron was being rested from operations at Eglinton, near Londonderry in Northern Ireland. Denver Miner was listening to the BBC when a calm voice interrupted the program to announce the Japanese attack. Miner was ecstatic as he hurried to tell the other pilots:

I let out a yell that could be heard all the way to Derry. . . . I gave them the news I had just heard. . . . That was the start of a bash to end all bashes—with unashamed tears running down their cheeks and patting each other on the back and buying drinks for each other.[13]

Many of the Eagle pilots had volunteered for the RAF only after failing to qualify for their own air force. Some had enlisted in the Royal Canadian Air Force while retaining U.S. citizenship. Whatever their origins, they immediately began to think of transferring to the U.S. Army Air Force now that pilots were needed to fight the Japanese.

The Eagles all had combat experience. They were trained and ready to go. They were looking forward to fighting for their own country now that they finally had the chance.

The Eagles' enthusiasm was echoed by noncombatant Americans as they contemplated their country's sudden entry into the war. Chicago-born Henry "Chips" Channon had taken British citizenship in 1933 before becoming a member of Parliament, but he remained American in origin. Together with his friend Geoffrey Lloyd, a government minister, he was spending the weekend at Leeds Castle in Kent as a guest of Sir Adrian Baillie and his Anglo-American wife while Pearl Harbor was under attack.

Channon had gone to bed when something prompted him to switch on his portable radio and listen to the news:

> I was flabbergasted to hear that Japan had declared war on the United States and Great Britain, and that bombing of Honolulu had already begun. So this vast war spreads. America's participation of course ensures final victory for the Allies . . .
>
> I rushed to Geoffrey Lloyd's room, and awakened him with the startling news, then I told Adrian and Olive Baillie who were still up . . . much talk, and finally to bed again about 2 a.m. this morning. An historic hour.[14]

Channon's astonishment at the turn of events was shared by Virginia-born Nancy Langhorne, better known to the British as Lady Astor. Like Channon, she was a member of Parliament, the first woman to take a seat in the House of Commons.

Nancy Astor understood at once how the Americans felt about Pearl Harbor. Her own constituency in Plymouth had taken repeated poundings from the Luftwaffe in the past couple of years: almost sixty separate raids as the Germans tried to flatten the dockyards and put the Royal Navy out of business. When the details of Pearl Harbor became known, American howls of pain over a single paltry air raid in the Pacific had very little resonance in bombed-out Plymouth.

Fred Astaire's sister had been bombed for the first time in April. Adele Astaire had given up their song-and-dance act after marrying the Duke of Devonshire's younger son in 1932. She had moved to southern Ireland, where she and her husband looked after battle-fatigued RAF pilots at Lismore Castle.

Now Lady Charles Cavendish, Adele could have seen out the war quite comfortably in a neutral country. But the cataclysmic events of June 1940, when France had surrendered and the British had stood alone against a mighty enemy, had prompted her to a different path:

I realize how small and frivolous and utterly unimportant my life has been (especially in the past seven years) compared to the greatness and history-making period of the past eight months of this world war—it's staggering how everything is pale and transparent by comparison.[15]

Eager to help the British out, Adele had bought a fighter plane for the RAF. It flew into battle with "Adele Astaire" painted on the side. She had also begun to make increasingly long visits to London to be nearer the action and participate in the war.

After her first experience of bombing in London, she had written to Fred in Hollywood to say that as opening nights went, it had been pretty shattering. In Adele's view, though, it was much better to come under attack than sit and do nothing. Her countrymen were just beginning to find that out.

Irish-born Chaim Herzog, the son of a Sinn Fein–supporting rabbi, had just graduated from the University of London. He was killing time until he was called up by studying for the lawyers' bar exam at Lincoln's Inn.

In common with Adele Astaire, Herzog had come to admire the courage of the British as he observed them rising to the challenge of the Blitz.

"I saw a very great people in a very great time of crisis."[16] While drilling with the Home Guard (local volunteers ineligible for military service), he had once watched spellbound as the RAF pitched into the Luftwaffe during an enormous daylight raid over London. Some of the pilots had been teenage classmates of his only a few months earlier.

As a resident of Palestine—he had served in the Haganah before the war—Herzog was under no obligation to join the British army. With family in France, Poland, and Latvia, he had volunteered nevertheless and was waiting for his joining instructions.

Like so many others, Herzog saw at once that Pearl Harbor would make all the difference in the long run. The more pressing question for him, though, was whether an Allied victory would arrive in time for all his relations in German-occupied Europe.

For Queen Wilhelmina of the Netherlands, the most immediate concern was the future of her country's colonial possessions in the Far East. Java and Sumatra had yet to be attacked. They surely would be soon, if the Japanese needed oil and rubber.

Queen Wilhelmina was living in a country house near Maidenhead, a few miles from Windsor Castle. She had taken the difficult decision to go into exile after the German invasion of her country in 1940. Holland had been forced to surrender at home, but the Dutch abroad had abandoned their neutrality to join the Allies and were still very much a part of the war.

Holland's government had accompanied Wilhelmina to England, operating from a London base near Piccadilly Circus. Most of the Dutch navy had gotten away too, as had the country's large merchant marine (including *Jägersfontein*, under attack in Honolulu Harbor). There were Dutch airmen in the RAF and Dutch troops attached to the British army.

Wilhelmina was as shocked as any of them when she heard what had happened in the Pacific. "Nobody foresaw an event like Pearl Harbor. The news of the bombing of the American fleet by the Japanese came as a complete surprise."[17]

The queen grasped the implications at once. If the Japanese took

Malaya, the Dutch East Indies would be next. The small Dutch garrisons in Java and Sumatra had gone onto immediate alert after Pearl Harbor, but with no hope of serious reinforcement from home. They would be on their own, powerless to resist for long if the Japanese came looking for them.

Fifteen miles south of Maidenhead, Hitler's former deputy Rudolf Hess had nothing to say when he was told about Pearl Harbor. If he had any thoughts about the extraordinary turn of events, he chose not to share them with his British captors.

Hess was being held prisoner at Mytchett Place, an ugly old house in Surrey owned by the British army. He had been there since May, a few days after flying to Scotland on an apparent peace mission to end the war. The British were keeping him at Camp Z, as they called it, while they interrogated him further and debated what to do with him.

Mytchett Place had been heavily fortified before Hess's arrival. Trenches had been dug and machine guns posted in case anyone found out he was there and tried to kill him. Plenty of Polish soldiers in Britain would have been delighted to cut his throat if they had the chance.

Hess's personal quarters had also been bugged in case he said anything important in conversation or blurted out German secrets in his sleep. Microphones had been placed under the floorboards and hidden up chimneys so that nothing would be missed. Hitler had disowned Hess after his flight, but he was still Britain's most important prisoner from the Third Reich.

He had been kept under close observation since his arrival. Medical opinion was divided as to whether he was insane or merely pretending to be. He was certainly mentally unstable, prone—like so many Nazi leaders—to delusions that had no base in reality.

For his part, Hess had rapidly come to the conclusion that the British were trying to drive him mad before killing him. They were torturing him with the noise of air-raid sirens that sometimes went off four times in a single night. He had just requested a visit from the Swiss ambassador to air a long list of similar grievances.

In addition, Hess had now decided that the British intended to poison him before he had a chance to complain to the ambassador. They were undoubtedly putting something in his food to destroy his memory. There was no other explanation for a succession of meals that Hess found utterly disgusting. "The food tasted interchangeably of soap, dishwater, manure, fishodor, petrol and carbolic acid. The worst was the secretion from camel and pigs' glands from which even the starchy foods were not safe."[18]

Thousands of British troops shared Hess's suspicion of army cooking, but there was nothing sinister in it. Hess's many genuine ailments included acute hypochondria.

He had parachuted into Scotland on his own initiative, without bothering to consult Hitler first. He apparently wanted to negotiate a peace deal allowing the British to keep their empire in return for giving the Germans a free hand in Europe—the same offer that had been made to Neville Chamberlain before the war.

If Pearl Harbor had dashed his hopes, Rudolf Hess gave no sign of it. His minders watched him closely but noted no discernible response when he was told of the attack.

His reactions may have been delayed, however. According to the report, Hess was "in a very bad state" next morning, and "rather tearful" the day after.[19] Three days after that, he hinted to the Swiss ambassador that in spite of everything he still hadn't entirely abandoned hope for his peace mission.

SIXTEEN

OPINION DIVIDED IN EUROPE

Across the English Channel, the news of Pearl Harbor did not reach mainland Europe until much later that night. It was almost midnight before Adolf Hitler was informed at the Wolf's Lair in East Prussia.

The Führer had not had a good day. After the recent reverses on the Russian front, he was reluctantly coming around to the idea that the retreating Wehrmacht could advance no farther that winter. The troops would have to dig in, just as his generals had been telling him, hunkering down until the spring. It had been a bad mistake not to order warm clothing for them when the going was good.

Hitler's women secretaries were with him as he tried to put his cares aside after dinner. So were Walter Hewel, the Foreign Office man on his staff, and a few other functionaries. They were chatting quietly in the bunker when Otto Dietrich, Hitler's press chief, asked to speak to the Führer.

Dietrich remembered it as follows:

I was the first to receive the Reuters report on Pearl Harbor. I promptly went to Hitler's bunker and sent in word that I was bringing an extremely important message. That very day Hitler had received depress-

ing reports from Russia. He received me with an unfriendly question. He obviously feared more bad news.

When I made haste to read the flash, his look of surprise was unmistakable. His face cleared. His expression became one of extreme excitement and he asked quickly: "Is this report correct?"

I said it definitely was, for a minute before, while I was waiting in his anteroom, I had received a telephone message from my office to the effect that confirmation from another source had come in.

Hitler snatched the sheet of paper from my hand, strode out of the room and walked unaccompanied, without cap or coat, the hundred yards to the bunker of the Chief of the High Command of the Armed Forces. He was the first to bring the news there.[1]

Hitler's behavior was unprecedented, as Field-Marshal Keitel recalled:

Jodl and I were both present that night as—the only time during the war— he came bursting in to us with the telegram in his hand. I gained the impression that the Führer felt that the war between Japan and America had suddenly relieved him of a nightmare burden; it certainly brought us some relief from the consequences of America's undeclared state of war with us.[2]

The attack had come as a complete surprise to Hitler. His Japanese allies had told him nothing in advance. Delighted that they were actively joining in the war, he apparently closed his mind to the fact that they were bringing the United States into it as well.

Back in the bunker, Hitler announced—quite correctly—that this was the turning point of the war. He could hardly restrain his enthusiasm as he told Hewel that nothing could stop Germany now. "It is impossible for us to lose the war. We now have an ally who has never been vanquished in three thousand years."[3]

In Berlin, the diplomats at the American Embassy learned of Pearl Harbor around eleven that evening. George Kennan picked the story up very faintly from a U.S. radio broadcast and immediately alerted Leland Morris, the chargé d'affaires. They summoned several officials by phone and sat up late at the embassy, planning their strategy if Germany now declared war on the United States.

The Japanese Embassy learned of the attack at the same time. Ambassador Hiroshi Ōshima promptly hurried around to see Joachim von Ribbentrop, Germany's foreign secretary. The two of them had been negotiating for months about a joint declaration of war if Japan should ever fight the United States.

By his own account, Ribbentrop was horrified to hear what Japan had done. He was all for Japan joining the war. He had encouraged the Japanese to attack the Russians in the rear. He was also happy for them to engage the British in Singapore if it dissuaded them from attacking the Americans in the Philippines. But he was appalled that Japan had elected instead to launch an all-out assault on the U.S. fleet in the Pacific.

Ribbentrop's immediate reaction was that Germany was under no obligation to join Japan's fight against the Americans. It was the last thing the Germans needed when they were already at war on two fronts. He knew, though, that the Tripartite Pact would be dead if they didn't.

Ribbentrop therefore swallowed his misgivings and assured Ōshima that Germany and Italy's participation could be assumed as a matter of course. With Ōshima sitting beside him, he got on the phone to Rome and told Italy's foreign minister, Count Galeazzo Ciano, the same thing, as Ciano recorded in his diary next day:

> *A telephone call at night from Ribbentrop. He is jumping with joy about the Japanese attack on the United States. He is so happy, in fact, that I can only congratulate him, even though I am not so sure about the advantage.*
>
> *One thing is now certain. America will enter the conflict, and the conflict itself will last long enough to allow all her potential strength to come into play. This is what I told the King this morning, when he too expressed his satisfaction. He ended by admitting that in the long run I could be right.*

Mussolini was also happy. For a long time now he has been in favor
of clarifying the position between America and the Axis.[4]

Ciano couldn't share their enthusiasm. He was Mussolini's son-in-law, but no fan of the war or the Nazis. Far from plunging deeper into the conflict, the Italians should disentangle themselves from the fighting and get out of it as soon as they realistically could, in Ciano's sober assessment.

Ezra Pound was in Rome that day, making a broadcast on Italian radio. The American poet had a regular slot on the radio, promoting the views of Fascist Italy to the English-speaking world.

Pound had lived in Italy since the 1920s. He had a small apartment at Rapallo on the Gulf of Genoa, but was a frequent visitor to Rome. He was convinced that the carnage of the Great War had been caused by the failings of unfettered capitalism. Fascism was the answer to the problem, in his opinion.

The Italians were happy to indulge this maverick American so long as he promoted their point of view in return. They allowed him to say anything he wanted on the radio, always understanding that he wouldn't say anything incompatible with his U.S. citizenship.

Pound was not popular in his own country. His Fascist leanings and undisguised anti-Semitism had long since brought him to the attention of the State Department. An extension to his passport had recently been restricted to six months to enforce his return to the United States. Pound's response had been to remain firmly in Italy.

He hadn't heard about Pearl Harbor when he arrived at the radio studio on the Via Asiago. He took the microphone at 6:12 p.m. and for the next twelve minutes gave a typically rambling talk that covered everything from Confucius, the Jews, and the urgent need for financial reform to the hopeless state of England, among other topics. "Roosevelt is more in the hands of the Jews than Wilson was in 1919 . . . Lord knows I don't see how America can have Fascism without years of previous training."[5]

News of Pearl Harbor didn't arrive until after Pound had finished his broadcast. It came via Frank Tremaine's UP report, relayed from New York. Eleanor Packard, wife of Rome's UP correspondent, immediately telephoned George Wadsworth, the chargé d'affaires at the American Embassy, to tell him what had happened.

Wadsworth and his wife lived in a suite at the Grand Hotel. They quickly set up a council of war in their rooms with various diplomats from the embassy. Eleanor Packard kept them supplied with updates from UP as they huddled around the radio and waited to hear more.

Italy had played no part in the attack, but it was obvious to them all that war with the United States would surely follow. Their task now was to burn the embassy's codebooks and oversee the safe evacuation of all the Americans in Italy who wanted to leave. Most, including almost all the reporters, had already gone.

But not Ezra Pound. He apparently tried to join the exodus, but was refused passage aboard the last trainload of Americans heading for Lisbon. Whatever the truth, he returned to Rapallo and stayed there. He continued to make broadcasts on Fascist radio for the rest of the war.

In France, the American ambassador to the Vichy government heard the news of Pearl Harbor at 9:00 p.m. As a professional sailor, Admiral William Leahy guessed at once how it had happened. The fleet had been enjoying the traditional lazy Sunday in port that was routine in the peacetime navy. The Japanese had literally caught them napping.

The town of Vichy lay in the unoccupied part of France, halfway between Paris and Marseilles. The U.S. Embassy was temporarily housed in a modest building on the Avenue Thermale. Leahy had been in his post since January. His brief was to liaise with the Vichy government and do whatever he could to prevent France's collaborators from taking their country into a formal alliance with the Nazis.

The admiral was the right man for the job, but he had an uphill task. Most ordinary Frenchmen would have preferred a British victory if it meant defeat for the Boches, but a substantial number hated the Anglo-Saxons.

They couldn't forgive them for letting France down at Dunkirk, as they saw it, and then refusing to surrender at the same time as the French had.

The government of Marshal Philippe Pétain—France's World War I hero—had nominal control of the two-fifths of France not under German occupation. The more Leahy saw of the old man, the less he was impressed. Whatever fire had once burned in Pétain's belly had long since been extinguished, in Leahy's assessment.

He had used the word "jellyfish" about Pétain more than once in dispatches to the U.S. government. Pétain's colleagues were just as bad, in Leahy's view, increasingly linking themselves to a German victory because they knew they were doomed without it. He was glad of Pearl Harbor, if it would bring the situation to a head and enable his recall to the United States.

The embassy had already made contingency plans for a rapid escape. The staff would leave by train if possible. If not, they had quietly hidden supplies of food and gasoline along the roads to Marseilles and the Spanish border to enable a getaway by car. They were ready for all eventualities.

Leahy's only regret was that he would no longer enjoy his agreeable dinners with the Japanese ambassador. Sotomatsu Kato was a highly civilized man. They had last dined together two nights before. There would be no more of that for the remainder of Admiral Leahy's time in Vichy France.

In Madrid, the Spanish dictator General Francisco Franco welcomed the attack on Pearl Harbor as soon as he was informed of it. He saw it as yet another success for the German-Italian-Japanese Axis to which he had all but hitched Spain's colors. In common with Hitler, Franco presumed at first that an American entry into the war would be confined to the Pacific, with few implications for the fighting in Europe.

Ramón Serrano Suñer, the foreign minister, agreed. He immediately ordered his staff to deliver cards of congratulation to the diplomats at the Japanese Embassy. A government telegram was also sent to Tokyo, congratulating the Japanese on their achievement in sinking the American fleet. Well done, Japan, was the official view from nonbelligerent Spain.

―――――

At the other end of Europe, the American ambassador in Budapest had just declared war on Hungary when he learned of Pearl Harbor. Herbert Pell had done so on behalf of the British, who no longer had diplomatic relations with the country.

Hungary was a reluctant German satellite. The British had little quarrel with a small country that meant them no real harm. They had been bounced into declaring war by their Russian allies, who resented the presence of a few token Hungarian troops on the Russian front.

British affairs in Hungary were handled by the American Embassy. It had therefore fallen to Pell to deliver Britain's formal declaration of war to the Hungarian government. The State Department had cabled him on Saturday, December 6, with instructions to tell the Foreign Ministry at once.

Pell hurried to the ministry. He found it closed for the weekend, without even a skeleton staff on duty overnight. Persuading a guard to let them in, he and his Hungarian-speaking secretary prowled the deserted corridors until they saw a light above a door.

Inside they discovered a Hungarian consular official who lived in his office in winter because it was drier than his apartment. Clad in a red-and-blue robe from the Racquet and Tennis Club of New York, the man was cooking a fish for his supper over a kerosene lamp.

Pell solicited his help in declaring war. The official obligingly picked up the phone and tracked down László Bárdossy, who was both prime minister and foreign minister of Hungary.

Accompanied by a hastily assembled honor guard of four soldiers, Bárdossy duly arrived at the Foreign Ministry in evening dress. Pell served Britain's notice of war on him while the soldiers smartly presented arms.

A week later, six days after Pearl Harbor, the two men met again at the Foreign Ministry. This time it was Bárdossy's turn to do the honors. At Germany's insistence, he tearfully informed Pell that Hungary was now at war with the United States as well.

―――――

While American diplomats gathered around their radios, CBS reporter Howard K. Smith had managed to escape from Germany at last. He had just arrived in Switzerland after an overnight train journey from Berlin.

Smith had been trying to get away for months. Closely monitored by the Gestapo, constantly prevented from saying what he wanted to on the air, he had applied for an exit visa long ago, only to be told that he couldn't leave Germany unless CBS provided another reporter to replace him. The Germans wanted a hostage to prevent Smith from speaking out once he had left the country and was beyond their control.

The Americans were no longer regarded as neutrals in Germany. Their country's shiploads of armaments to Britain had not gone unnoticed. Nor had the food parcels and the fund-raising drives in support of the British. Americans were sometimes beaten up in the street simply for speaking to each other in English.

Smith's telephone had been routinely tapped by the Gestapo, giving off telltale sounds as he spoke down the line. He had been kicked out of his smart office at the radio station, allotted a cubbyhole instead and a broken typewriter while an assistant to Lord Haw Haw, the American-born renegade broadcasting for the Nazis, moved into his old room. Smith had been lucky not to have been thrown out of the building altogether, as some of the Germans wanted.

His apartment in Berlin had become increasingly shabby as the war progressed. Smith was well funded by CBS, but there was nothing to buy in the shops. No furniture, knives, forks, crockery. He had only one drinking glass, impossible to replace. When friends came around, they all sat on the floor.

His clothes were even worse. With everything needed on the Russian front, it was virtually impossible to replace a frayed shirt or buy a new pair of socks in Berlin. Smith had been forced to accept clothes from departing colleagues instead.

William L. Shirer had given him an old sweater as he left. Steve Laird of *Time* magazine had bequeathed him a suit. The wife of the *New York Times* correspondent had brought him some shoes from Sweden. The wife of a Gestapo official had sold him an overcoat. Even with their help, Smith was almost in rags as he finally managed to obtain an exit visa and left immediately for Switzerland before the Germans could change their minds.

He set off from Berlin on the night of December 6. He shared a sleeping compartment on the train with a friendly German who told him that nobody in Germany wanted war with the United States. Peering through the blackout curtain as they went south, Smith managed to make out the fortifications of the Maginot Line on one side of the Rhine, and the Siegfried Line on the other.

At Freiburg next morning, he bought a copy of the *Völkischer Beobachter*, the Nazi propaganda newspaper. It announced that the German army on the eastern front was halting its advance for the moment and shortening its lines in response to an unprecedentedly early winter in Russia.

Smith reached Switzerland later that day. After the drab gray of Berlin, he could hardly believe his eyes as he saw all the goods in the shops, the colorful displays, and wonderful choice of things to buy. He counted fifty-two different entrées on the station restaurant's menu at lunch. There was only ever one in Berlin.

That night Smith stayed at a hotel in Bern. Feeling a bit naked in the brightly lit city, so different to the permanent blackout in Germany, he treated himself to several whiskeys and a giant T-bone steak before going to bed.

He had just turned out the light when the reception desk called from downstairs. UP's man in Berlin wouldn't be able to join him in a couple of days, as they had planned, because no more Americans were being allowed out of Germany. The Japanese had just bombed Pearl Harbor.

While Howard Smith enjoyed his steak, BBC reporter Richard Dimbleby was in Turkey, expecting to leave for Singapore at any moment. He had asked London for the transfer, arguing that the Far East was the place to be if the Japanese were about to launch an attack somewhere.

Dimbleby was the BBC's Asia Minor correspondent. As well as Turkey, he covered Iran, Iraq, Syria, and Afghanistan from hotel rooms in Ankara and Istanbul. He was enjoying Turkey—full of spies and intrigue—but it wasn't where the action was. Singapore had to be a better bet.

There was a strong German presence in Turkey. The host country was neutral in the war, with an unofficial British bias. Franz von Papen, the German ambassador, had carelessly let slip that Nazi policy for the control of the conquered territories in Europe depended on "starvation and massacre."[6] The Turks accordingly favored a British victory in the Western Desert to keep the German army away from their gates.

The Nazis were on a propaganda mission to change their minds. Scarcely a week passed without some German delegation or other arriving in Ankara or Istanbul to further German interests. As with Howard Smith in Switzerland, the first thing they did when they arrived was gobble a lavish meal of the kind that they couldn't get at home anymore. Dimbleby had seen them do it:

> All of them did the same thing as soon as hotel and police formalities had been dealt with. They ordered and consumed gargantuan dinners, shovelling into piles of meat or fish and rice, vegetables and rich sweets as though they had not eaten squarely for months.
>
> Then they settled down to the various jobs that had brought them to Turkey. There were many "attached" to the staff of the German Embassy in Istanbul for various ill-defined duties that left them free to concentrate on propaganda and espionage.[7]

One mission from the German Foreign Office moved into Dimbleby's Ankara hotel and demanded a whole floor to themselves. Dimbleby refused to move, leaving the Germans to occupy the space all around him.

The room next to his bathroom was taken by one Dr. Schmidt, the group's leader. Fat and unattractive, Schmidt was visited by a young woman one evening. Dimbleby put his ear to the wall, hoping to pick up some useful information about the war. He discovered that Schmidt and the girl had business together of an entirely different nature.

The Germans usually gave him a polite greeting when they bumped into him, but Dimbleby wasn't fooled. He had heard too many stories from refugees in Istanbul, terrible accounts of atrocities in the Balkans and children starving to death in the streets of Athens. He had seen the real Germany in a photograph of a grinning corporal standing over the broken body of a Serb partisan who had been flayed alive for daring to stand up to the Nazis.

Despite their bluster, though, Dimbleby sensed a growing loss of confidence among the Germans as the campaign in Russia ground to a halt. The ones his sources spoke to never dared to say anything openly, but it was obvious from their evasive responses that they wondered what on earth Hitler had gotten them into. Dimbleby had said as much in a dispatch to London.

With no actual fighting to report, he spent much of his time on an endless round of embassy cocktail parties, discreet dinners with military attachés, and trips to nightclubs to watch Dr. Schmidt dancing sweatily while his companions asked the band to play "Die Wacht am Rhein." He had once enjoyed the sight of the British and German ambassadors' wives arriving at a government banquet at the same time, both wearing an identical gown bought from the same shop.

Pearl Harbor changed all that. Dimbleby had had no response from the BBC about his request for a trip to Singapore. He cabled again as soon as he learned of the attacks. If the BBC moved fast, he could get to Singapore almost at once, taking the flying boat that left on Wednesday.

SEVENTEEN

THE RESPONSE IN THE FAR EAST

It was late in the evening when news of Pearl Harbor reached Europe. In the Far East it was still only morning. General Tojo's wife in Tokyo learned of the attack from the radio soon after her husband had left for work. Other Japanese heard the loudspeakers playing martial music in the streets and knew that something was up.

Their suspicions were confirmed by the sound of handbells and wooden clappers as newspaper sellers appeared with special victory editions of *Asahi*, *Nichi Nichi*, and *Yomiuri*, Tokyo's daily newspapers. The headlines were much the same as the American ones—"Japs Bomb Pearl Harbor"—but with a different resonance in Japan. The papers quickly sold out as people gathered around to find out what had happened.

Many of them were shocked at first, then delighted. They sang the national anthem in the streets before joining the crowds heading for the emperor's palace. There they all bowed low as they called on the spirits of their ancestors to help them in the coming struggle. The servicemen among them were already reporting for duty, just as their counterparts in America were doing.

Other Japanese were less enthusiastic. They asked the same questions as

Americans about the purpose of the attack. They wondered how on earth Japan was going to defeat the mighty United States, short of marching on Washington and seizing control of the capital.

Had they known it, some very far-fetched ideas were indeed under consideration by the Japanese high command. Plans existed for the printing of occupation currency to be used by Japanese forces in Hawaii and Australia. There was even a scheme for the amalgamation of Alaska, Alberta, British Columbia, and Washington State into a single new country under Japanese control after the war had been won.

But ordinary Japanese knew nothing of this. Dissenting voices were rapidly hushed into silence as a wave of patriotism drowned them out. "A hundred million people, one bullet" was the Japanese way. Swallowing their misgivings, the people of Japan got solidly behind the emperor as they gathered around their radios and loudspeakers to hear the official declaration of war.

Hirohito himself appears to have been ambivalent about his country's aggression. He was well disposed toward the British, particularly their royal family. He was also outraged to learn that Pearl Harbor had been bombed before Japan's formal declaration of war on the United States. The muddle in Washington had caused a serious loss of face for his country.

Yet Hirohito was a patriot before anything else. He considered himself under an obligation to follow government policy, even if he didn't always agree with it. Dressed in naval uniform, he showed no emotion when Tojo told him of the success at Pearl Harbor, but later confided to his aides that he could feel the goodwill of the gods. He remained in a splendid mood for the rest of the day.

Hirohito's declaration of war was broadcast on the radio a few hours after the first attack:

> We, by the grace of Heaven, Emperor of Japan, seated on the throne of a line unbroken for ages eternal enjoin our loyal and brave subjects. We hereby declare war on the United States of America and the British Empire . . .
>
> Eager to realize their inordinate ambition to dominate the Orient . . .

both America and Britain have obstructed our peaceful commerce by every means possible and resorted at last to direct severance. . . . To defend its very existence, our Empire had no option but to resort to arms.[1]

That was the official explanation for Pearl Harbor from the government in Tokyo. Allegedly at the emperor's request, a sentence was added to make it clear what he personally thought of the matter. "Now, unfortunately, it has come—truly unavoidable and far from Our wishes—that Our Empire has to cross swords with America and Britain."[2] Historians still argue about whether Hirohito meant what was said in that final paragraph.

In the Philippines, word of Pearl Harbor reached the U.S. Army in Manila sometime after three that morning. A signals officer woke up Brigadier-General Dick Sutherland, chief of staff to Douglas MacArthur, and told him what had happened.

Sutherland immediately telephoned MacArthur's suite at the Manila Hotel. MacArthur was incredulous. His initial reaction was to observe to Sutherland that Pearl Harbor was America's strongest base in the Pacific. "Its garrison was a mighty one, with America's best aircraft on strongly defended fields, adequate warning systems, anti-aircraft batteries, backed up by our Pacific fleet. My first impression was that the Japanese might well have suffered a serious setback."[3]

Confirmation of the attack arrived at 3:55 a.m. via a telephone call relayed from Admiral Kimmel. It was followed around 4:30 by General Marshall's message from Washington warning everyone to be on the alert for something about to happen.

By 5:00 a.m., MacArthur and his staff had assembled at their headquarters, 1 Calle Victoria, a house next to Manila's old city wall. Troops were sent to their posts, civilian services were taken under military control, orders were given for Japanese nationals to be rounded up to prevent sabotage.

The work was under way when another cable from the War Department arrived at 7:30. It announced that hostilities between Japan and Britain, Holland, and the United States had definitely begun.

Twenty-five minutes later, a brigadier rang from Washington to ask if the Philippines had been attacked. MacArthur said no. His forces were ready, though. He told the brigadier that their tails were in the air.

Around 9:30, a force of Japanese bombers was spotted apparently heading for Manila. Fighter squadrons were scrambled to intercept them. As a precaution, the seventeen B-17 Flying Fortresses at Clark Field took off too, so as not to present a target on the ground.

The Japanese aircraft changed course, leaving Manila alone. The Flying Fortresses therefore returned to base to refuel. The fighters returned as well. Everyone was having lunch when more Japanese aircraft were detected shortly after 11:30. The bombers were just over a hundred miles away and closing fast.

Much confusion followed. Conflicting reports were misinterpreted. Wrong orders were given. Right ones were not received. The result was that the Japanese arrived over Clark Field to find some American fighters and almost all of the Flying Fortresses still on the ground.

They couldn't believe their luck. Within minutes fifteen of the Flying Fortresses and quite a few fighters had been damaged or destroyed. MacArthur lost half his air force by lunchtime on the first day of the war.

In Singapore the war began at 4:00 a.m. with a Japanese air raid across the sleeping city. The streets were brightly lit as the Japanese arrived. Air-raid sirens failed to sound because the Air Raid Precaution system wasn't operative on weekends.

The first wave of bombers flew straight over the city at twelve thousand feet without dropping any bombs. Searchlights and antiaircraft guns were still following them when a second wave arrived at four thousand feet to attack the harbor and the airfields beyond.

The noise woke Lady Diana Cooper, who was sick with dengue fever. She and her husband had been roused at three to be informed of the Japanese landings in the far north of Malaya. They had gone back to sleep before being disturbed again by the noise of the attack on Singapore.

A survivor of the London Blitz, Lady Diana took this new development in her stride:

> *To my great surprise I felt nothing. Was this unusual calm due to the dengue drugs or to an attitude I had settled to adopt when the bombing started—the veteran's "O well, after London, you know"—having become part of me? That first raid they dropped a bomb bang in the middle of Raffles Square, a bull's-eye.*
>
> *I felt, when I first saw this pretty feminine rococo town, so graceful and flimsy with its frail pink and robin's-egg-blue arcades and quays garlanded with nameless fruit and flowers and paper intricacies, that a modern world would not let it survive. Either friendly ferro-concrete or barbarian hands would get at it, so it's for the rubble heap.*[4]

Cecil Brown of CBS radio was in his room at the Raffles Hotel when the first bombs fell. Dressing hurriedly, he grabbed his typewriter and rushed out to the rickshaws outside the hotel. It was a thirty-cent ride to the press office in the Union Building.

The rickshaw man asked him sleepily what all the noise was. Brown told him they were being bombed. The bombs were falling in the direction Brown wanted to go, so the man politely refused the fare.

Two dollars changed his mind. The harbor was ablaze with lights as they passed. Brown arrived at the press office to be informed of the Japanese landings in north Malaya as well as the bombing of Singapore. He cabled the story at 4:45 a.m.

Back at his hotel, Brown tuned in to San Francisco radio before breakfast and heard about Pearl Harbor. He spent the rest of the morning updating his reports and trying to figure out how to get to Kota Bharu in a hurry, if that was where the fighting was.

He was lunching at Raffles with O. D. Gallagher of the *Daily Express* when the press officer asked if they would like a four-day assignment aboard HMS *Prince of Wales*. The great battleship was about to sail. The two reporters could go too if they wished, but they would have to hurry.

Brown was horribly torn. The big story was in Singapore. He might lose his job if he wasted four days splashing about at sea, unable to cover the fighting on land. But the Royal Navy had already sent a car for them. Grabbing clothes, typing paper, and camera film from his room, Brown accepted the assignment and set off at once for the naval dockyard.

When they arrived, he and Gallagher were furious to discover that there was no room for them aboard *Prince of Wales*. There had been a misunderstanding amid all the confusion. The two reporters had been assigned to the far less glamorous *Repulse* instead.

They very nearly turned around to return to Singapore. Instead, swallowing their disappointment, they took the launch to *Repulse*, anchored offshore in the stream. Lieutenant Geoffrey Hulton of the Royal Marines was waiting to look after them as they came aboard. Brown swiftly bearded him:

> *"What the hell are we going to do for four days?" I asked of the lieutenant, still very much worried that I had done the wrong thing by leaving Singapore—and the coverage of the war—for four days.*
>
> *"Oh, we may have something. We might even have movies. We had a picture last night aboard."*
>
> *I asked what it was and he said, "Arise, My Love, with Claudette Colbert."*[5]

After the morning's disaster at Pearl Harbor, *Prince of Wales* was the only friendly battleship still in business in the Pacific. Accompanied by *Repulse* and their four destroyers, but still without the aircraft carrier that was supposed to protect them, the great vessel pulled out into the Straits of Johore toward evening. Still fretting that he was going to miss the real action, Brown was on deck as the task force set off:

> *We moved at half speed. It was a beautiful evening, that twilight of Monday, December 8th. The bright red sunset silhouetted the palms on the shore. Within minutes the* Prince of Wales *drew up alongside and passed us.*

The crews of each ship stood at attention. Captain William Tennant on our bridge waved his white hat. Two men standing on the bridge of the Prince of Wales *waved their hats. They were Admiral Tom Phillips and Captain Leach.*[6]

Slowly leaving Singapore behind, the task force proceeded around the bottom of Malaya and then turned northeast toward the Anambas Islands in the South China Sea. Somewhere ahead lay the invasion fleet that had landed Japanese troops on the coast that morning. The Royal Navy was looking forward to catching up with it as the engines picked up speed and the warships surged forward. The king's ships were at sea.

In China, a radio report of the attack on Pearl Harbor reached Generalissimo Chiang Kai-shek's Chungking headquarters at 1:00 a.m. An aide phoned to tell him as soon as the story had been confirmed.

Chiang reacted quickly. As commander of the Chinese forces resisting the Japanese invasion, he summoned his advisers for an 8:00 a.m. meeting to determine China's strategy in the light of this new development. They would need to coordinate their efforts if Britain and the United States were now fighting the Japanese as well.

The Chinese had already been at war with Japan for four years. They had been at loggerheads with each other before that, Nationalists under Chiang fighting Communists for control of China's future. An uneasy truce in the civil war was just about holding as they all concentrated on beating the Japanese instead.

Japan had counted on a quick victory in divided China. Chiang's forces had suffered hundreds of thousands of casualties in the unsuccessful defense of Shanghai and other cities, but had always survived to fight another day. After their initial defeats, they had withdrawn into China's vast hinterland, stretching the enemy's supply lines and tying up large numbers of Japanese troops in the process.

The consequences for the Japanese had been nothing if not predictable.

Far from a victory in three months, Tojo and his generals were now desperately seeking an exit strategy that would allow them to get out of China without losing face.

Chiang had moved China's provisional government to Chungking (now known as Chongqing), a provincial city in the remote southwest of the country. Its population had risen fivefold to more than a million as a result of the war. Refugees from elsewhere were crammed into the walls of the old city. The open sewers poured into the Jialing River, which joined the Yangtze at Chungking.

Chiang kept a town house at his headquarters compound in the city, but lived in a splendid villa in the hills across the Yangtze. Although Chungking was beyond the reach of the Japanese army, it had been repeatedly bombed during the past two and a half years. Incendiaries had reduced much of the central district to ash.

All but two of the thirty or so ambassadors accredited to the Chinese government eventually evacuated the city as a consequence, fleeing south of the Yangtze to escape the attacks. Only the British and Russians saved face by staying put. The British Embassy had been damaged by the bombing, but the Union Jack still flew on the lawn, symbolically close to Chiang's headquarters compound.

After his early meeting with his own people, and encouraged by a telegram from Churchill, Chiang held another conference later that day with the British, American, and Russian ambassadors to discuss the changed situation. His thinking was way ahead of everyone else's as he sat them down to outline his proposal for a grand military alliance against the Japanese in the Pacific.

The Americans should take the lead, in Chiang's view, but China, Britain, Canada, Australia, New Zealand, the Netherlands, and the Soviet Union should be in there too. If they all acted together, establishing a joint war council and agreeing not to conclude a separate peace with Japan that might leave China high and dry, they would surely prevail. That was the message that Chiang wanted the British, Americans, and Russians to take back to their respective governments.

Five hundred miles to the north, Mao Tse-tung of the Communist Party shared Chiang's optimism. The attack on Pearl Harbor had to be good news for China, if it meant that Japan was now fighting Britain and America as well.

Mao was in Yan'an (sometimes spelled Yenan). Like Chungking, it was an ancient city beyond the reach of the Japanese army. It had been the headquarters of China's Communist Party since 1936.

Yan'an was large enough to boast a theater and a university of sorts as well as schools and hospitals, but it was a backward place by Western standards. Medicines were in very short supply. Electricity was generated by foot pedal. Inhabitants grew their own food and were sometimes so ignorant of the outside world that they weren't entirely sure who the Japanese were.

Like Chungking, too, Yan'an had endured numerous air raids as the Japanese attempted to destroy Mao's guerrilla base. His thousands of followers had responded by burrowing into the hillsides, digging out the artificial caves that were traditional in that part of China. Some lived in army tents or peasant huts, combining military training with politics classes and hard work in the fields as they honed their skills and waited for the day when the warlords would all be gone and Marxism ruled in China.

Mao himself lived modestly in a sparsely furnished, three-room cave with his washing hanging outside. He read books of political theory by candlelight and grew his own vegetables, mostly tomatoes, and tobacco. His only real luxuries were a wooden bathtub and a four-poster bed with a mosquito net.

Mao was no friend of the imperialist British. He had little sympathy for them as they struggled to keep hold of Malaya and Hong Kong. He didn't like the Americans either, with their refusal to admit that their possessions in the Pacific and elsewhere amounted to a colonial empire in all but name.

But his enemy's enemies were his friends. If the Anglo-Americans were now in the war with the Japanese, Mao might be able to use the alliance to his advantage.

Soon after Pearl Harbor, he and his advisers began a charm offensive designed to woo British and American leaders. Their aim was to persuade them that the Communists in China were the right people to support against the Japanese. In theory, if not always in practice, the Communists weren't corrupt, like Chiang Kai-shek's forces. They were also more efficient in the field.

With backing from Britain and America now that they were in the war, Mao and his peasant army would surely win the battle against the Japanese. After that, they could all get back to the real problem and defeat Chiang Kai-shek as well.

The attack on Pearl Harbor had many implications for China, but it brought no immediate change for the ordinary people of the country. They were already at war with Japan, whether fighting in the fields or enduring the occupation of the larger cities. It was quite some time before the dramatic events elsewhere began to have any effect at home.

For foreign nationals, however, it was a different story, particularly the British and Americans in areas under Japanese occupation. From being wary neutrals in a faraway land, they suddenly discovered that they had become enemy aliens overnight, liable to be rounded up and interned as soon as the Japanese caught up with them.

Among the many expatriates dismayed to learn of Pearl Harbor was Michael Lindsay, a British lecturer at the University of Yenching. The American-run university stood on the outskirts of Beijing, a city firmly under Japanese control.

Lindsay was an active figure at Yenching. He had been hired from England to introduce Oxford's personal tutorial system to China. He was the son of Professor Alexander Lindsay, well known to the British as the Master of Balliol College, Oxford.

Lindsay senior had famously stood for Parliament in 1938, campaigning exclusively on an anti-Munich ticket. The professor hadn't won, but he had put a large dent in the majority of the governing party's candidate.

The by-election had been carefully orchestrated: the first test of British public opinion since the Munich agreement. Rival candidates had all withdrawn to ensure a straight two-way fight between Lindsay and Chamberlain's man. The electors of Oxford—and by extension the rest of the country—had duly made it clear what they thought of doing shabby deals with tinpot little dictators who looked like Charlie Chaplin.

Michael Lindsay shared his father's views. He was a mildly eccentric man, a bald, bespectacled academic who liked nothing better than to roar around Beijing on his motorbike, often with his Chinese wife, Hsiao Li, on the back.

Lindsay had used his protected status as a foreign national to obtain scarce medical supplies for the Chinese guerrillas opposing the Japanese. He had also provided them with radio sets that he had made himself, sometimes journeying to Hong Kong or Shanghai to buy spare parts. Suspecting that the Japanese knew about his clandestine activities, he had made plans for a swift escape from Beijing if ever they came to arrest him.

Pearl Harbor was the trigger. Lindsay was at home that morning when his wife tuned in to the BBC at Shanghai, expecting to hear the news, as usual. Instead she picked up a German broadcast announcing that Japan and the United States were at war.

Lindsay didn't waste a moment. Shoving a pistol into his pocket, he hurried over to the university president's house to borrow his car. Dr. John Stuart had arranged to lend it to Lindsay and a couple of other faculty members who wanted to join the guerrillas. They would need transportation if the Japanese came for them.

Lindsay returned after a while with his two colleagues in the car. His wife joined them with a pair of knapsacks, more guns, and bags full of food. Calculating that the Japanese would probably enter Yenching by the campus's main west gate, they drove to the east gate as fast as they could, ready to shoot their way out if they had to.

They learned later that Japanese secret police arrived at their house less than ten minutes after they had left. As it was, though, nobody tried to stop them as they fled, although there were plenty of Japanese soldiers about.

The Lindsays headed out of Beijing past the Summer Palace before parking the car near a temple. Nervous of the Japanese checkpoints on the road ahead, they had decided it would be safer to ditch the vehicle and proceed on foot. Shouldering their knapsacks, they set off through the fields as if going on a picnic.

Their plan was to link up with Mao's guerrillas in the countryside. It took them two days of discreet inquiry to make contact. After a long march through the night, looking back at the lights of Beijing, they arrived just before dawn at an isolated farmhouse on the slopes of a mountain.

Inside were thirty Chinese soldiers from the local guerrilla unit. The men hadn't heard about Pearl Harbor. Like Mao and Chiang, however, they were delighted when the Lindsays told them. They wanted to know all about it.

The Chinese were not alone. In French Indochina, millions of people were glad to learn that the Japanese invaders were now fighting the British and Americans as well. It must surely hasten the day when the Japanese were forced to withdraw from their countries for ever.

Indochina—modern Cambodia, Laos, and Vietnam—had been under the control of the Vichy French when the Japanese invaded in September 1940. Their initial aim had been to cut the railroad line from the port of Haiphong that supplied Chiang Kai-shek's army in China.

The French had grudgingly allowed the Japanese to occupy North Vietnam. The Japanese had been wary of occupying the south as well, for fear of alarming Britain and the United States. The Soviet Union's entry into the war had emboldened them, however. With the Russians no longer a threat in their rear, Japanese troops moved into South Vietnam in July 1941, preparing the ground for an invasion of the resource-rich Dutch East Indies.

Now they were in action all over the Pacific, fighting on many different fronts. There was no better time for the resistance in Vietnam to begin fighting back.

The resistance was organized by the man later known as Ho Chi Minh, the leader of Vietnam's independence movement. He had just returned to his native country after an absence of thirty years.

Ho had left home before the Great War and had traveled the world ever since. He had worked in America, Britain, France, China, and the Soviet

Union, picking up all sorts of revolutionary ideas on the way. It wasn't just the Japanese he wanted to kick out of his country now that he was back. It was the French as well.

Ho had been in hiding since his return in February. He and his fellow Communists were holed up in jungle caves near the Chinese border. They were ready to slip across at a moment's notice if either the Japanese police or the Vichy French came after them.

Meantime they were busy wooing local people and recruiting volunteers for the armed struggle. The plan was to rise against the Japanese when they were ready and then seize control of the country before the French could return.

Ho had prepared the ground with a proclamation to the Vietnamese people calling them to arms. His "Letter from Abroad" had been broadcast in June 1941 from a town in China, giving the authorities no clue as to his whereabouts. Ho had told his compatriots that the time was fast approaching when they should rise up and take the country's destiny into their own hands:

> *Men of wealth and position, soldiers, workers, peasants, intellectuals, civil servants, traders, young men, patriotic women! At this moment national liberation is our most pressing concern. We must all come together to overthrow the Japanese and French and their jackals . . .*
>
> *Revolutionary fighters, the hour has struck! Raise high the banner of insurrection.*
>
> *Help people all over the country to overthrow the Japanese and French. The sacred call of the Fatherland resounds in your ears.*[7]

Ho Chi Minh was looking to the United States for support, when the time arrived. The Americans would be delighted to see the back of the Japanese in Vietnam, and they were no friends of French colonialism. Ho considered the American Declaration of Independence to be the model for Vietnam to follow: free people taking command of their own destiny, without any interference from abroad. The United States of all nations would surely support them in that.

In India, Jawaharlal Nehru was just out of prison. The British had released him from Dehra Dun jail on December 4 after a year's incarceration for making a public speech against supporting Britain in the war.

Nehru was no stranger to prison. He had served several sentences during his campaign for Indian independence. Nor did prison hold any fears for him. He had been educated at Harrow, the same tough English boarding school as Winston Churchill, and was well able to cope.

Surprised at the length of his four-year sentence, Churchill had asked that his fellow alumnus should be treated leniently, rather than as a common criminal. His request had been ignored. Perhaps exasperated with Nehru's continuous troublemaking, the authorities had done little to ease the harshness of his life in jail. His privileges had been restricted and his books, newspapers, letters, and interviews had all been strictly rationed or delayed for weeks.

The one advantage of Nehru's time behind bars was that it had given him a chance to think seriously about the war. He had initially regarded it as a quarrel between two imperialist powers—Britain and Germany—each as bad as the other. Germany's invasion of the Soviet Union and the Japanese occupation of Indochina had persuaded him otherwise.

Nehru didn't think much of the British administration in India, but he bore the British little personal ill will. His daughter, Indira, was recently back from Oxford. He would much rather that victory in the war went to the British, Russians, and Chinese than to the Germans and now the Japanese.

All it needed, in fact, for millions of Indians to give their wholehearted support to the war, bringing in all their manpower on the Allied side, was a simple statement of intent from the British. An admission that the days of empire were over, that the Indians would be masters of their own destiny once the war was won.

The British were prevaricating, offering to appoint a few "representative Indians" to the executive council and making other grudging concessions that stopped well short of any promise of future independence. There had been discussions about independence before the war, but the talks had been put firmly on hold while the British concentrated on the far more important task of defeating the Germans first.

The British needed Indian manpower nevertheless, especially now that the Japanese were coming in India's direction. As a conciliatory gesture, therefore, the viceroy had announced on December 3 that all the political prisoners who had deliberately courted a jail sentence as part of Gandhi's campaign of civil disobedience should be released forthwith. Nehru was among them.

He was pleased to be out. Unlike Ho Chi Minh, who saw in Pearl Harbor the opportunity for an armed war of liberation, Nehru had no desire to fight the British. As a responsible member of India's National Congress Party, he was reluctant to weaken the British in their struggle against Hitler:

> *Pearl Harbor and what followed it suddenly created a new tension and gave a new perspective. . . . The war ceased to be a distant spectacle and began to approach India and affect her intimately. Among Congressmen the desire to play an effective part in these perilous developments became strong, and the jail-going business seemed pointless in this new situation. . . .*
>
> *We were eager to offer our co-operation in the war and especially for the defense of India, subject necessarily to a national government which would enable us to function in co-operation with other elements in the country and to make the people feel that it was really a national effort and not an imposed one by outsiders who had enslaved us.*[8]

While Nehru enjoyed his new freedom on the day of Pearl Harbor, his friend Mohandas Gandhi—known to some as the Mahatma, or " Great Soul"— was at home at Sevagram. He was just about to go to Bardoli in Gujarat for a month's retreat at an ashram.

Like Nehru, the Mahatma had conflicting views about the British. He had been awarded the Boer War medal after serving in the Indian Ambulance Corps at the Battle of Spion Kop (Winston Churchill had been there too). He had supported the British against the Boers and Zulus and had exhausted himself recruiting Indian troops for the Great War, arguing that they must do their share of fighting if they wanted to be equal partners in the British Empire.

Gandhi had also enjoyed the welcome he had received when he visited Britain. He had stayed with Michael Lindsay's father, the Master of Balliol, on a trip to Oxford. Lindsay had called him a saint, although others thought him a crackpot.

Nevertheless, Gandhi knew it was time for the British to leave India. In the light of the viceroy's release of civil-disobedience prisoners, he had arranged to meet Congress's working committee in Bardoli to discuss how the independence campaign should proceed. Opinion among Indians was deeply divided, but for want of any better idea, Gandhi thought they ought to carry on much as before.

He had said as much in a press release issued on December 7. "Civil disobedience has to go on. I must admit, however, that the conduct of the campaign has been rendered difficult by the Government action in discharging civil disobedience prisoners, but if we are to reach our goal, we have to cut our way through every difficulty."[9]

Unfortunately for Gandhi, Pearl Harbor and the attacks on Malaya and Thailand had radically changed the game. As Nehru had pointed out, it was all very well for Indians to sit on their hands when the war was comfortably far away. It would be a different matter entirely if the Japanese rampaged across Indochina into Burma. Whether they wanted to or not, millions of Indians would surely have to take up arms if it was their own homeland that was in danger of invasion.

EIGHTEEN

THE BRITISH EMPIRE DECLARES WAR

B ack in the United States, Roosevelt spent the rest of the afternoon at
his desk, working on his speech to Congress next day. Cordell Hull had
recommended a long explanation to the American people of how relations with Japan had sunk so low. Roosevelt was opting for something much
shorter and snappier.

His eldest son was with him as he worked. Like so many others, James
Roosevelt had been having an afternoon nap when he got the Pearl Harbor
call. His father wanted him to come over at once and stand by in case he
needed any personal help.

The speech was all Roosevelt's own work, according to his son. The president completed it just before 5:00 p.m. and called in Grace Tully, his
private secretary, to take dictation while he dragged on a cigarette.

She couldn't help worrying about Roosevelt the family man as she scribbled. Jimmy Roosevelt was a captain in the Marine Corps reserve. The
president's other three sons were also of military age. He could easily lose
all four of them in the war that was about to start.

So much was happening that Roosevelt didn't have time to join his wife
and the guests they had invited for dinner. He ate in his study instead. Harry

Hopkins, Grace, and his son ate with him, saying nothing about Pearl Harbor, giving him a much-needed break during the meal.

The Cabinet members arrived later for an 8:30 meeting. Most of them had been out of town when they were summoned. Labor Secretary Frances Perkins had been at her New York club, immersed in a report she was writing. She had had no idea that anything was amiss until the White House switchboard called her:

> *I hastily telephoned for a plane reservation. No one at the offices of the club had heard any unusual news. The taxicab driver, taking me to the plane, said, "They said on the radio there was shooting somewhere." By the time I got to the airport there were others hurrying to get to Washington. The company was putting on extra planes.*

The crowd outside the White House was singing "God Bless America" and "My Country, 'Tis of Thee" as Perkins arrived. She was shown upstairs to the president's study and found him leafing through the latest reports as the information continued to flood in:

> *The President nodded as we came in, but there was none of the usual cordial, personal greeting. This was one of the few occasions he couldn't muster a smile. However, he was calm, not agitated. He was concentrated; all of his mind and all of his faculties were on the one task of trying to find out what had really happened. His voice, as he told naval aides what to reply to dispatches, was low. He wasn't wasting any energy.*[1]

Roosevelt had changed in the two days since Perkins had last seen him. She wasn't the only one to notice that he looked much calmer now, relieved that a great weight had been removed from his shoulders. There was no longer any moral dilemma in his mind about whether or not the United States should enter the war.

The Cabinet meeting was brief and to the point, scheduled for only half an hour. In Roosevelt's view it was the most important such meeting since the Civil War days of 1861. Abraham Lincoln had been president then, looking out of the White House windows at the army campfires along the Potomac.

Frank Knox quickly summarized the latest information about Pearl Harbor for those who still weren't clear about what had happened. Roosevelt then read them the draft of his proposed address to Congress. Henry Stimson agreed with Cordell Hull that it should have been longer, saying much more about Japan's repeated aggression and contempt for international law. Everyone else was happy with the draft as it stood.

Congressional leaders arrived just before 9:00 p.m. for the president's next meeting. They were drawn from both Houses and political parties. Among them was a tight-lipped Senator Hiram Johnson, one of the leaders of the isolationist faction.

The Cabinet remained in the room as Roosevelt briefed the newcomers and arranged with them to address Congress at half past noon next day. The politicians were too stunned by the day's events to say much after he had finished. It was only Thomas Connally, chairman of the Senate Foreign Relations Committee, who felt the need to hear the sound of his own voice.

Connally had grandstanded to newspaper reporters as he waited to see the president. He had assured them that the United States would respond to Japan's dastardly treachery with steel-throated cannon and a sharp sword of retribution.

He was similarly florid as he lambasted Knox for being asleep on the job at Pearl Harbor. Wonderfully wise after the event, he vented his anger on the navy secretary, making all the obvious points as he waded into the defensive Knox:

> What did we do? Didn't you say last month that we could lick the Japs in two weeks? Didn't you say that our Navy was so well prepared and located that the Japanese couldn't hope to hurt us at all. . . . Why did you have all the ships at Pearl Harbor crowded in the way you did?[2]

There were no answers. Knox didn't know what had gone wrong either. He was flying to Pearl Harbor at the first opportunity to find out.

Through all of this Ed Murrow sat waiting on a bench in the hall, quietly chain-smoking as important officials came and went. He had not been surprised to learn that the president would not be joining them for dinner. Mrs. Roosevelt had left the table several times to find out what was happening. She had returned each time with a message from the president asking Murrow to wait.

Janet Murrow went back to their hotel at 11:00 p.m. Murrow stayed on, chatting briefly with Knox, Hull, Stimson, and Hopkins as they passed. He had almost given up when he got the nod around midnight and was ushered into the president's study at last.

He was accompanied by Bill Donovan, recently appointed by Roosevelt to set up a centralized U.S. intelligence agency modeled on the British secret service. Donovan had been in New York that afternoon, watching a football game at the Polo Grounds, when his name had been announced over the loudspeaker. He was to call Washington at once.

Donovan had learned of Pearl Harbor from Jimmy Roosevelt, who worked for his organization. He caught an army plane and was in Washington by 7:00 p.m.

He had been hoping to present the president with a precise analysis of the situation when they met. Unfortunately his new agency, set up to coordinate all intelligence about national security under one roof, was not yet trusted by the army and navy, the main suppliers of information. Jealous of other organizations, they often withheld what they knew.

Roosevelt was sitting in semidarkness as Murrow and Donovan entered. Lit only by the lamp on his desk, he looked very calm but dreadfully tired. Beer and sandwiches appeared as he quizzed Murrow about British morale during the Blitz and asked after various English friends. Roosevelt wondered if the Japanese attacks were part of a joint strategy by the Axis powers. It certainly seemed possible. He asked Murrow and Donovan if the American people would now support a declaration of war. Murrow and Donovan were pretty sure they would.

Quietly, apparently speaking on the record, Roosevelt told them what he knew about Pearl Harbor, giving details about the extent of the damage that had not yet been released to the press. He banged his fist angrily on the table as he complained about the number of aircraft destroyed on the ground.

His anger was genuine. Some observers thought that Roosevelt had been less surprised by the attack than the scale of the losses. He seemed shocked enough by both to Murrow and Donovan.

The two men spent just over half an hour with the president. Murrow had the feeling as the interview came to a close that the day's events were not wholly unwelcome to Roosevelt, despite all the calamities. The war had come at last, and it was the Japanese who had started it. They could be thankful for that much, at least.

For his part, Roosevelt wondered if Murrow the experienced war reporter had been as shaken by the Japanese attack as he had. He asked him as the reporter left:

"Did this surprise you?"
"Yes, Mr. President."
"Maybe you think it didn't surprise us!"[3]

Murrow was sure that it had. He had surreptitiously studied Hull, Stimson, and Knox as he waited in the corridor, eavesdropping on their conversation. Their surprise at Pearl Harbor wasn't faked. Murrow never had any time for the conspiracy theorists of later years who argued that Roosevelt and his advisers had known about it all along.

Donovan went back to his office after leaving the White House. Murrow headed straight for CBS's Washington bureau. Where else would a reporter go? Thirty minutes of face time with the president of the United States on the day of Pearl Harbor! Murrow had pulled off an astonishing scoop with what he had been told about the attack.

Yet how much could he say on the air? Roosevelt hadn't mentioned anything about their discussion being off the record, but he might just have forgotten at the end of an exhausting day. Murrow was as hungry for a scoop as any reporter, but he didn't want to reveal the extent of the damage at

Pearl Harbor if the information would be useful to the enemy. He certainly hadn't in the Blitz.

Murrow decided to say nothing. Going back to his hotel instead, he spent the rest of the night pacing up and down his bedroom, unable to decide whether he had been an idiot or not in passing up the biggest story of his career.

In Ottawa, Prime Minister Mackenzie King had spent the morning completing the formalities for Canada's declaration of war on Hungary, Finland, and Romania. All three countries had been supporting Germany with varying degrees of reluctance. The dominions of the British Empire were presenting a united front against them.

King went home after lunch, back to his summer estate at Kingsmere, just outside the capital. He lay down for a nap at three thirty, but had hardly closed his eyes when his adviser Norman Robertson phoned. There was a rumor that the Japanese had attacked Manila and Hawaii, but it was only a rumor.

King decided to take no action. He asked Robertson to call again when he had confirmation, and went back to sleep.

Robertson called at 4:30 to say that the rumor was true. Roosevelt had confirmed the attacks to Lord Halifax, Britain's ambassador to the United States. King told Robertson to get the Cabinet War Committee together for an evening meeting and then lay in bed for a while, mulling over the situation before getting dressed.

He changed his mind as he returned to Ottawa, summoning the entire Cabinet for a seven thirty meeting instead. He knew by then that Roosevelt's Cabinet was meeting at eight thirty. He wondered if he should recall the Canadian Parliament—which would take some time—or whether he had the authority to act without further consultation.

King and his advisers decided that they didn't need Parliament. They were already authorized to take appropriate action if anything British was threatened. The Canadians had troops in Hong Kong, the first of their soldiers to see action in the war.

Just before going into the Cabinet meeting, King told Robertson to prepare a formal declaration of war for submission to King George later that night, if necessary. He still didn't know whether the Japanese had declared war on Britain, or whether their German and Italian allies had declared war on the United States. All he knew for sure was that events were moving very fast. "This is the most crucial moment of all the world's history, but I believe the result will be, in the end, to shorten the war."[4]

Canada's war cabinet agreed with King. The British got in touch after the meeting to say that they would not declare war on Japan until the following day. They wanted Roosevelt to address Congress first and secure his country's agreement for military action.

King signed the order for submission to King George at 9:50 p.m. At 11:00 he heard on the radio that Canada, ahead of everyone else, had announced that a state of war was in existence. Half an hour later, he went back to Laurier House, his Ottawa home, and was in bed again by midnight.

In South Africa, Prime Minister Jan Smuts was preparing to follow Britain and Canada as soon as he had his Cabinet's agreement. He had scheduled a meeting for Monday morning to go through the necessary formalities for a declaration of war on Japan.

Smuts was solidly behind the British in the war. He had fought them in the Boer War, but had backed the Union ever since, much as Southerners in the United States had settled their differences with the North after the Civil War. The British wanted him for their own prime minister if anything ever happened to Churchill.

Smuts did not have everyone in South Africa with him, however. White opinion in the country was bitterly divided over the war. South Africans of British origin had freely volunteered for service and were fighting in the Western Desert. Quite a few Boers had joined them.

Other Boers backed Hitler, either because they liked his style or more often because they just wanted to see the British defeated. They viewed the war as an opportunity to break away from the empire and establish a Boer republic while the British were preoccupied elsewhere.

The attack on Pearl Harbor had introduced a new dimension. It had brought the war a lot closer to home with the Japanese just across the Indian Ocean. The South Africans lacked the military hardware to defend themselves properly if an invasion fleet suddenly appeared off their coast.

Smuts was acutely aware of the problem as he pondered his options. "Destiny is writing a new chapter in our tangled human story," he wrote on December 7.[5] A statement went out after Pearl Harbor assuring the South African public that the coastal defenses were manned at all times and aircraft patrols were operating around the clock.

Cape Town was blacked out, too, for the first time in the war. As on America's Pacific coast, the lights were swiftly dimmed the night after Pearl Harbor and the city lost its after-dark glow. If there were any Japanese out there, peering at Table Mountain through their periscopes, they wouldn't be allowed to carry out another Pearl Harbor on the southernmost tip of Africa.

In Australia, Prime Minister John Curtin learned of Pearl Harbor early in the morning, about the same time as the people of Japan. The War Cabinet met at once, and the service chiefs gathered to consider their response.

They had much to think about. Australia was no farther from Japan than was Hawaii. If the Japanese were coming down through the Philippines, there would be little to stop them advancing from one stepping-stone to the next until they arrived at Australia's vast and undefended northern coastline.

The Australian army couldn't stop them. Three of its four divisions were already fighting in the Middle East and North Africa. Brigades from the remaining division were scattered across Malaya and various Pacific islands. Defense of the homeland itself had not hitherto been a priority in the war.

Yet the Australians were ready. They hadn't been caught napping. The full Cabinet met that afternoon to agree on a whole range of emergency measures that had already been worked out in detail. They had known that the Japanese would strike somewhere, sooner or later.

Curtin went on the radio that evening to address the nation. "Advance

Australia Fair" was playing as he prepared to speak. He told the people what most of them already knew, that their country had a new enemy in the war:

> *The Australian Government this afternoon took the necessary steps which will mean that a state of war exists between Australia and Japan. To-morrow, in common with the United Kingdom, the United States of America and the Netherlands East Indies Governments, the Australian Government will formally and solemnly declare the state of war it has striven so sincerely and strenuously to avoid . . .*
>
> *As the dawn broke this morning, at places as far apart as Hono-lulu, Nauru, Ocean Island, Guam, Singapore and British Malaya, guns from Japanese warships, bombs from Japanese aircraft, shots from Japa-nese military forces, struck death to United States citizens and members of its defence forces; to the peaceful subjects of Great Britain and to her men on ships and on the land. The Pacific Ocean was reddened with the blood of Japanese victims.*[6]

Curtin didn't say so on the air, but he was glad of one thing at least. It was the Japanese who had started the war. Like Roosevelt in the White House, he was very relieved that the enemy had put themselves in the wrong by being the ones to strike the first blow.

As in Australia, the New Zealand government put its emergency plans into operation as soon as it learned of the attacks. Prime Minister Peter Fraser's little country was threatened with invasion for the first and only time in its history.

The front line for New Zealand lay in the Fiji Islands, a thousand miles to the north. The Japanese would have to take Fiji before they came any closer. The New Zealanders had already anticipated the move by building an airstrip on the islands and garrisoning it with their troops.

They went further after Pearl Harbor, extending the runway to accom-modate the largest American bombers flying in from California. They also shipped in every antiaircraft gun in New Zealand, reasoning that Fiji was where the guns would actually be needed.

At home Fraser recalled Parliament on the day of the attack and made plans for New Zealand to declare war the next day, at the same time as everyone else. Military reservists were called up, blackout restrictions were increased, and the use of gasoline for recreational purposes was banned.

New Zealand was ready for the Japanese. If there was a weakness in the country's armor, it was the lack of battleships to tackle an invasion fleet. New Zealand had always relied on the mother country for naval defense, the mighty dreadnoughts of the Royal Navy circling the globe to protect the king's imperial possessions.

It was a relief, therefore, that *Repulse* and *Prince of Wales* were still afloat. After all the bad news from Hawaii, at least the Royal Navy was still in business, ready to blast the Japanese out of the water if they ever ventured anywhere near New Zealand.

Back at Pearl Harbor itself, the sun was going down on an awful day, the single most awful day in American history. A sense of shock, outrage, and bewilderment hung over the place like a cloud as servicemen and civilians alike struggled to cope with the fallout from the attack.

The Japanese air force had vanished long ago, but that didn't mean the shooting had stopped. Martial law had been declared, and lives were still being lost as stray shots continued to ring out. Nervous sentries fired at each other. Antiaircraft gunners blasted away at low-flying warplanes attempting to land. The warplanes had that sinister Japanese word "USA" painted on the fuselage. Hitherto sentient Americans took it for granted that the Japs were using American aircraft now.

They assumed too that the air raids had been merely the prelude to an invasion. Japanese troops might already have landed, for all they knew. If not, they would surely come ashore that night under cover of darkness. Oahu was an island under siege as darkness fell.

It was dark in every sense of the word. A London-style blackout was in effect, the lights extinguished all along the coast. The rescue parties at work in Pearl Harbor, the soldiers digging trenches on the beaches, the nurses in the hospitals, the civilians in their own homes—all were being very careful not to show any illumination as they kept their heads down and wondered nervously what the night would bring.

At Admiral Kimmel's headquarters, the windows were being painted black so that his staff could work on without showing any lights. The painting was being done in a hurry, from the inside. It was having unfortunate effects on the admiral's staff as their eyes smarted from the fumes.

Elsewhere everyone not otherwise engaged remained awake, fully dressed, throughout the night. People of all kinds were ready to move at a moment's notice, if necessary. The shooting continued spasmodically all through the small hours, which did nothing for anyone's nerves. It did not need much imagination for a housewife to see herself raped by Japanese paratroops before the night was out.

The shooting sometimes developed into fierce firefights as whole units blazed away at one another. Tracer rounds lit up the sky, going in all directions, in one case for as long as ten minutes before someone called a halt. There was little order, even less fire discipline, as the troops manned their posts. The Americans on Oahu were horribly unprepared for war.

The good news, though, was that they had woken up at last. Their whole country had. As dawn came up next day on the destruction of Pearl Harbor, millions of people in Britain and Nazi-occupied Europe heard what had happened in the Pacific and quietly thanked God for it. So did countless other free-minded people across the world.

NINETEEN

AMERICANS GATHER AROUND THE RADIO

Roosevelt was up before dawn next morning, reading the latest dispatches over cups of black coffee. He worked on his speech later, updating it to include the attack on Midway that had happened overnight and adding a minor sentence suggested by Harry Hopkins. Roosevelt wasn't in Churchill's league for rousing oratory, but he was good enough for the occasion.

He was due to address a joint session of Congress at 12:30 p.m. His motorcade delivered him to the Capitol's south entrance at 12:20. The president was accompanied by his wife and escorted by his son James in marine uniform. He wore formal morning dress and the dark-blue sailor's cape that he had had since his days as assistant secretary of the navy.

The crowd applauded as he got out of the car, but there was none of the delirious cheering for war that capital cities all over Europe had seen in 1914. The Japanese were not regarded as a formidable enemy. The crowd understood nevertheless that they could not be defeated without considerable loss of life. People were sober, apprehensive even, as they gathered around their portable radios to hear what the president was going to say in Congress.

He was applauded again as he went in. The Republicans joined in the clapping. Plenty of them hated Roosevelt, but they hated the Japanese more. This was a time for forgetting political differences and standing shoulder to shoulder behind the leader of their country.

Even the isolationists were eager to get behind the president. Some remained obdurate, but others entered the chamber of the House arm in arm with old opponents to show their solidarity. The senators were followed by the justices of the Supreme Court in their black robes, members of the Cabinet, and various military leaders, including General Marshall and Admiral Stark.

The president entered at 12:29 on the arm of his son. Eleanor Roosevelt watched from a bad seat in the gallery as he went to the podium. Woodrow Wilson's widow was watching, too, as well as Ed Murrow and Lord Halifax, the British ambassador. All of them were conscious that they were witnessing a defining moment in American history.

Mrs. Roosevelt had a distinct feeling of déjà-vu as she waited for her husband to speak:

> *I was living through again, it seemed to me, the day when President Wilson addressed the Congress to announce our entry into World War 1. Now the President of the United States was my husband, and for the second time in my life I heard a president tell the Congress that this nation was engaged in a war. I was deeply unhappy. I remembered my anxieties about my husband and brother when World War 1 began; now I had four sons of military age.*[1]

The First Lady couldn't restrain her bitterness at the isolationists, the ones who had prevented her husband from building up American defenses in the Pacific. Pandering to popular opinion, congressmen and senators alike had insisted that Japan had no intention of fighting the United States. They had refused to allocate scarce resources to building up a military presence in the Pacific if it would be interpreted by the Japanese as evidence of hostile intent.

But this wasn't the moment for recrimination. Both houses put aside the follies of the past as the Speaker announced the president. They all listened intently as Roosevelt began to speak:

Yesterday, December 7, 1941—a date which will live in infamy—the United States of America was suddenly and deliberately attacked by naval and air forces of the Empire of Japan.

The United States was at peace with that nation and, at the solicitation of Japan, was still in conversation with its government and its Emperor looking toward the maintenance of peace in the Pacific.[2]

Roosevelt spoke for only six minutes, outlining the details, telling the people that hostilities existed and there was no blinking at the fact. The United States, its territory, and its interests were all in grave danger. He ended with a plea to both houses:

I ask that the Congress declare that since the unprovoked and dastardly attack by Japan on Sunday, December 7th, a state of war has existed between the United States and the Japanese empire.[3]

Roosevelt was greeted with a standing ovation when he finished. He returned to the White House while both houses discussed his proposal. Congress took just over half an hour to vote 388 to 1 in favor of war. The only opposing vote came from Jeannette Rankin, a Republican from Montana. She had also voted against war with Germany in 1917.

The Senate did not share her qualms. All 82 votes were unanimous. Roosevelt signed the declaration of war that afternoon.

The president's speech was heard across the nation as people gathered around their radios, listening to it live. It was also broadcast on television, thanks to a strenuous effort by CBS's sound engineers in New York.

CBS had never run a live radio broadcast on television before. The technology wasn't in place for the link-up. CBS's engineers worked for hours before the broadcast to bring the radio signal into the studio and connect it to the television. Several of the staff had slept the night in the studio rather than waste any time going home.

They managed to establish the radio link in time, but they were still without visuals. The studio was not yet equipped with outside broadcast cameras. If they had had an advance copy of the speech, they would have been able to use their wall map of the Pacific, showing Guam, Wake Island, and Midway as the president mentioned them. But events were moving too fast for advance copies of speeches.

In the end a single American flag solved the problem of what to show on screen while Roosevelt was talking. It was mounted on a table in the studio. Off camera, an electric fan did the rest.

Only a few people in New York were watching, though. The vast majority of Americans heard the speech on the radio.

Charles Lindbergh was among them. At home on Martha's Vineyard, he had spent the morning canceling America First meetings and writing a press release. He listened to Roosevelt's call to arms and agreed with every word, now that a conflict was unavoidable. He confided as much to his journal. "We have been attacked, and attacked in home waters. We have brought it on our own shoulders; but I can see nothing to do under these circumstances except to fight. If I had been in Congress, I certainly would have voted for a declaration of war."[4]

Joseph Kennedy concurred. The former ambassador to Britain was at his winter home in Palm Beach when he heard about Pearl Harbor. Kennedy had misjudged the British at every turn during his time in London, first supporting Chamberlain's appeasement policy, then announcing that the British wouldn't last more than a few weeks before surrendering to the Germans.

He himself had fled to the safety of the English countryside to avoid the Blitz. The king, the prime minister, the government, and the many other ambassadors who had remained in London had not been impressed. Nor had Kennedy's fellow Americans.

Recalled to the United States in disgrace, but still nursing presidential ambitions, Kennedy hurried to reestablish his credibility after Pearl Harbor. Like Lindbergh, he wrote to President Roosevelt offering the nation his services in some important capacity. Like Lindbergh, he was surprised to learn that Roosevelt preferred to manage without him.

In Texas that day seventeen-year-old Audie Murphy was rather more modest in his ambitions as the United States went to war. Small, underweight, barely literate, he would have been happy to serve his country in any capacity whatsoever.

Murphy had been out with friends in Greenville when he learned of Pearl Harbor. The baby-faced orphan had dreamed of being a soldier since he was twelve years old. Like so many young men, he was bursting to enlist as soon as he heard the president's call to arms. "I was half-wild with frustration. Here was a war itself; and I was too young to enlist. I was sure that it would all be over in a few months and I would be robbed of the great adventure that had haunted my imagination."[5]

Unfortunately for Murphy, it wasn't just that he was too young to join the army. He was too short as well, too skinny, a distinctly unimpressive physical specimen. He didn't have what it took to become a soldier.

Yet Murphy was determined to do his bit. He could stuff himself full of milk and bananas to reach the minimum weight requirement. His birth certificate had apparently been lost in a county courthouse fire, which meant that he could lie about his age if he had to. Audie Murphy was sure that he could manage to find a way into the war somehow. He wouldn't stop until he had.

In New York, at his parents' apartment on Park Avenue, wannabe author J. D. Salinger shared Murphy's anguish. He had already tried to join the army earlier in the year. He had been rejected because of a very minor heart defect.

Salinger was twenty-two, struggling to make a career as a writer. *The New Yorker* had rejected seven of his short stories that year, including one titled "I Went to School with Adolph Hitler." The magazine had finally accepted "Slight Rebellion Off Madison," an autobiographical tale about a character named Holden Caulfield.

With a Christmas theme, the story was due for imminent publication. Unfortunately for Salinger, *The New Yorker* was reassessing the story in the light of Pearl Harbor. He didn't know it yet, but the magazine was planning to defer publication indefinitely. A story about a rich New York teenager who hated everyone and everything wasn't what the public needed, now that there was a war on.

Salinger had been surprised at the depth of his own feeling when he learned of Pearl Harbor. For a young man who hated everything, he had found that he actually had a deep love of country and wanted to serve as best he could. It was frustrating to watch other young men hurrying to enlist while he had already tried and failed. His only hope now was that the rules might be relaxed if there was a pressing need for boots on the ground.

The actor Issur Danielovich shared Salinger's patriotism. He, too, was determined to get into the fight, although not by joining the army. The son of Jewish immigrants, he wanted to serve in the air force instead, so that he could hit back at the Germans by dropping bombs on them.

Danielovich had just graduated from New York City's American Academy of Dramatic Arts. Under the stage name Kirk Douglas, he was working as a waiter in New York until he could find something on Broadway. He occasionally served his equally broke friend Lauren Bacall, who nursed a single coffee for an hour without even leaving a tip. She wouldn't sleep with him, either.

Douglas worked at a branch of the popular Schrafft's chain. It was a favorite hangout for Jewish refugees from Germany, the rich ones who had been able to buy their way out while they still could. Although Jewish himself, Douglas couldn't warm to them, with their furs and their expensive jewelry. He thought they shouldn't be flaunting their wealth at a time when so many Jews in Europe were fearing for their lives.

Between shifts at the restaurant, Douglas had managed to find a theater job as an understudy-cum-assistant-stage-manager. He had even appeared onstage as a singing messenger boy. But he was still waiting for his big break—or even a decent part—when the Japanese hit Pearl Harbor.

Like everyone else, Douglas was horrified as the war that had been so distant and remote suddenly appeared on America's doorstep:

Pearl Harbor. The shock that the Japanese had come all the way across the Pacific and dropped bombs on Pearl Harbor, blown our men to bits,

*destroyed our Navy. All the other attacks had been far away, against
other countries, other people. Now they were attacking us. There was fear
of more attacks. People fled their homes along the beach. California was
blacked out.*[6]

The first reaction of Douglas's theatrical friends was to look for a way of
harnessing their acting skills for the war effort. There was an immediate
need for service training films and dramas with a military theme. They asked
Douglas to join them, but he decided that he wanted to do something more
active than that:

> *I was young and strong and healthy. I didn't want to become a member
> of some acting group. I felt a wave of patriotism, and a wave of Jewish-
> ness about what was happening in Europe with Hitler.*
>
> *We had no exact picture of the atrocities. But we knew enough.
> Hitler wanted to take over the world, eradicate the Jews—Deutschland
> über Alles. I wanted to fight, to drop bombs on them.*[7]

The air force seemed the right place for Douglas. He decided to become
a pilot if he could pass the necessary tests.

At Warner Bros. studio in Hollywood, the cast and crew of *Yankee Doodle
Dandy* were on set as Roosevelt's words came over the air. Actress Rose-
mary DeCamp, playing the mother of James Cagney's character, listened
quietly with the others:

> *The camera and the crew were standing still with grave faces. Jeanne
> Cagney, Walter Huston and I, made up and elaborately costumed,
> were standing at a little radio emitting the sound of President Roosevelt's
> voice along with a lot of static. Mike Curtiz, the director, and Jimmy
> Cagney came in through the freight dock and walked toward us.*
>
> *When they reached the set, Mike started to speak, but Walter held
> up his hands. The President finished with the grave news that we were*

*now at war with Japan and Germany. Then the national anthem
blared forth. Some of us got to our feet and sang the words hesitantly.*

*At the end, Jimmy said, clearing his throat, "I think a prayer goes in
here . . . turn that thing off." Someone did. We stood in silence for a full
minute, and Jeanne and I dabbed our makeup eyes.*[8]

Bob Dole was a freshman at Kansas University. Like most of his friends,
he had been vaguely following the war in Europe, but was far more interested in girls and basketball than events on the other side of the globe. It
had taken Pearl Harbor to shake him out of his stupor.

Dole had been in his fraternity house when the attack was announced
on the radio. He could hardly believe what he was hearing. By his own later
admission, his ignorance and indifference vanished in an afternoon.

He was listening again when President Roosevelt spoke to Congress at
lunchtime on Monday:

*I certainly didn't want to go to war—nobody in his right mind would—
but as my frat brothers and I crowded around radios listening to the
President's words, a sense of patriotism we'd never fully experienced before began to well in all of us.*

*We could sense the resolve in Roosevelt's voice as he concluded, "No
matter how long it may take us to overcome this premeditated invasion, the American people in their righteous might will win through to
absolute victory."*[9]

Dole immediately began to think about enlisting. The only question was
when. He couldn't decide whether to go at once, as others were doing, or
complete his semester first. He wrote to his parents next day to discuss it:

Dear Folks,

*I suppose you, like everyone else, are huddled around the radio listening
to war developments in the battle with Japan. All day yesterday, boys in
the house sat around their rooms, waiting for news bulletins to come
in. There are three or four boys who are considering enlisting this week*

in the Army Air Corps. It might be a good thing for me to do; at least it
would be better than spending your money at school![10]

In the end Dole elected to remain in school until his options became
clearer. He wanted to become a doctor in due course. Faced with a choice of
enlisting or waiting to be drafted, he eventually decided to enlist because
that offered a better chance of being assigned to the Army Medical Corps.

While young men all over the country held similar discussions after the
president's speech, Eleanor Roosevelt was preparing to fly to the West Coast.
After listening to her husband's speech, she spent the rest of the afternoon
at the Office of Civilian Defense in Washington before catching an evening flight from the airport. With her was New York's feisty mayor, Fio-
rello H. La Guardia. He had heard the president on the radio before flying
down to Washington to join her.

La Guardia was in charge of the nation's civilian defense effort. The First
Lady was his unpaid aide. They were responsible for the management of all
the blackout preparations, air-raid warning systems, and bomb-proof shel-
ters across the country.

The defenses were aimed at Germany, not Japan. Nobody seriously expected that they would be needed. The real purpose of the Office of Civilian Defense was psychological: to give people something to do and bring it
home to millions of Americans that war was coming and they needed to
get ready.

La Guardia and Mrs. Roosevelt were on their way to Los Angeles to see
how the work was progressing. Their presence would boost morale on the
West Coast, if nothing else. There was no chance of the president himself
coming in the immediate future.

It turned out to be a disturbing flight. The president's wife was working
in a forward compartment when she received a message from the pilots. A
newspaper in San Francisco had reported that the city was being bombed
by the Japanese.

They landed to refuel soon afterward. Mrs Roosevelt went straight to a telephone to find out if the rumor was true. La Guardia wanted to change the flight plan and go immediately to the stricken city if it was.

The rumor was false. They were aloft again when the pilots received orders to divert to Palm Springs, just in case. The orders were countermanded, and they proceeded to Los Angeles as planned. With most flights canceled until further notice, they found the airport almost deserted when they arrived.

La Guardia got busy at once, inspecting Los Angeles's firefighting equipment and the contingency plan for a Pearl Harbor–style emergency. Eleanor Roosevelt left him to it and went on to San Diego. With flights banned after dark, she traveled by overnight train for the rest of her tour. She found it most disconcerting, sitting on a darkened train amid a blacked-out countryside. It was a bit like being in a war zone.

For Gwen Terasaki, the Tennessee-born wife of a diplomat at the Japanese Embassy, December 8 in Washington went from bad to worse as she struggled to absorb what had happened. She was as outraged as any American at what the Japanese had done in Hawaii. The awkward part was that she also loved her husband, a right-hand man to Ambassador Nomura.

Gwen had taken their daughter to the movies on the Sunday afternoon. She hadn't learned about Pearl Harbor until returning to their apartment. Sudden silence and curious stares had told her that something was wrong.

Her husband called later, appalled at the Japanese attack. He was in no doubt that his country was doomed as a result of its own stupidity. He told his wife that he wouldn't be able to call again because the embassy telephones were about to be disconnected.

The FBI arrived on Monday morning. A polite but distant agent took down names and addresses and told Gwen not to leave the apartment without an FBI escort. The men were there for the family's protection, to make sure that Gwen and her half-Japanese daughter weren't assaulted in the street.

As the president prepared to make his momentous address to Congress,

Gwen was far more worried about what was going to happen to her mother, who was visiting from Tennessee. In the eyes of the FBI, her mother had been found at the home of an enemy alien and could not therefore return to Tennessee without official permission. The old lady wasn't at all happy about that.

Gwen herself knew that she would have to go wherever her husband went. He gave her the option of remaining in the United States, but she preferred to stay with him. That meant packing up the apartment while the rest of America was preparing for war, and moving with the embassy staff to a hotel in Virginia. They would stay there until they could be exchanged for Ambassador Grew and the other American diplomats in Tokyo.

Gwen Terasaki didn't want to go. Quitting the United States for Japan was the last thing she wanted to do at this particular juncture, not least because her husband faced possible execution at home for his secret attempts to avert a war. But there was little alternative that she could see:

> *I packed everything, paid all the bills, and closed the book, so to speak, but I held off as long as I could. I wanted to breathe the clean, sweet air of my native land, to walk its streets; and, as the leaves were being raked, smell the odor of burning leaves, a nostalgic reminder of my childhood. The aroma of burning leaves is not half so pleasant in other lands as it is in America.*[11]

The Terasakis were not the only ones to come under FBI surveillance that day. Albert Einstein, an American citizen since 1940, had also come onto the radar as a potentially subversive element now that the country was at war.

Einstein had lost his university job in Germany after Jews were banned from teaching in 1933. His books had been ceremonially burned as the Nazis celebrated their triumph. After a spell in England, Einstein had immigrated to the United States and accepted a post at the Institute for Advanced Study in Princeton.

His arrival in the United States had not been universally welcomed. Most Ivy League universities operated a quota system to keep the number of Jews down. Among ordinary Americans, there had been loud objections to an odd-looking Jew of crypto-Communist sympathies being allowed into the country at all.

Einstein worked at the institute's imposing new building on the outskirts of Princeton. He was popular with his students but distrusted by the powers that be because of his political leanings. J. Edgar Hoover had had his phone tapped and kept a file on him at the FBI's headquarters in Washington.

Einstein was a theoretical physicist. He was also a deeply committed pacifist who had never considered the military implications of his work until they had been pointed out to him. He had then grasped at once that a single atomic bomb built from his equations could destroy a whole city with one enormous explosion.

The knowledge weighed heavily on him. Left to himself, Einstein would never have allowed it to happen. But the Germans had the knowledge too. They were known to be working on designs for an atomic bomb, hurrying to get there first so that Hitler could have the weapon at his disposal to use wherever he wished.

Along with the Hungarian nuclear physicist Leo Szilard, Einstein had been one of a small group of scientists who had written to Roosevelt in 1939 to point out the danger. Their warning had been discounted at the time, but it was now being taken much more seriously. The day before Pearl Harbor, the government had decided to step up the research program and proceed at once to the construction of an atomic bomb before anyone else.

It was very exciting news for the scientists involved, doubly so now that the United States was in the war as well. The project was top secret, but Einstein was an obvious candidate for a leading role in the proceedings.

Unfortunately his political sympathies ruled him out of any involvement. Einstein didn't have the security clearance to work on his own equations.

At the British Embassy in Washington, there was quiet jubilation that afternoon as they heard Roosevelt calling for war against Japan and Congress backing his request. It was the best possible news, from Britain's point of view.

Nobody was happier about the developments than the Earl of Halifax, Britain's ambassador to the United States. He had been sent to the United States to explain the war to Americans and persuade them of the need to join in. He had found it a very uphill task.

Halifax had been amazed at the virulence of the anti-British feeling across the country. He had been physically assaulted only a few weeks before Pearl Harbor. Convinced that the British simply wanted to fight to the last American to defend their empire, a gang of America Firsters in Detroit had pelted him with eggs and tomatoes and told him to go home.

Halifax in turn had wondered which part of stopping Hitler in his tracks Americans didn't understand. It wasn't hard to grasp. But millions of Americans had failed to get the point until now.

Lady Halifax called for champagne on the day of Pearl Harbor. Mindful of the host country's sensibilities, she diplomatically told the American butler at the embassy that she and her husband wanted to drink a toast to celebrate a birth in the family.

Halifax's case for American entry into the war had not been made any easier by the behavior of some of his high-profile compatriots in the United States. A number of Britons had preferred to remain safe where they were rather than go home and fight. Americans had wondered how serious the situation could be if British men of military age felt no obligation to return to England to defend their homeland from invasion.

There was some excuse among the British community in Hollywood. The film stars had been advised to stay put and make patriotic movies as their contribution to the war effort. David Niven was among those who had ignored the advice, breaking his contract to go home and rejoin the army.

Niven had met Churchill four weeks before Pearl Harbor. He had asked the prime minister if the United States would ever join in the war. Churchill had been in no doubt that they would. "Mark my words. Something cataclysmic will occur!"[12]

Gone With the Wind's Leslie Howard had returned to England too. He was at Denham Studios at the time of Pearl Harbor, filming the interior scenes for *The First of the Few*. Released as *Spitfire* in the United States, and co-starring David Niven on loan from the army, the film was Howard's personal contribution to the British war effort.

Others had remained in Hollywood. Forty-seven-year-old Aldous Huxley was picnicking in the Mojave Desert on the day of the attack. He was visiting a ranch at Llano del Rio, fifty miles north of Los Angeles. He was preparing to move there to get away from the smog in the city and his script-writing job in Hollywood.

Huxley was a sick man with poor eyesight, so inept that he had yet to pass his driving test. He had convinced himself that he could be no earthly use to the war effort and was probably right. Nevertheless, his unwillingness to leave the comforts of California for the rigors of wartime Britain had won him few friends at home, even if he did send food parcels and contribute to British charity auctions in Hollywood.

Most unpopular of all were the writers W. H. Auden and Christopher Isherwood. Both of military age, they had accompanied each other to the United States in January 1939 and had since made no effort to return. Questions had been asked in the House of Commons about whether they should be served with call-up papers and forced to come back.

The literary press had been caustic. *The Spectator* had made rude remarks about "Certain intellectuals safe in America." *Horizon* had described the two of them as "far-sighted and ambitious young men with a strong instinct of self-preservation and an eye to the main chance."[13] British opinion didn't come much more contemptuous than that.

The criticism was fair, although there were mitigating circumstances. Isherwood detested mindless patriotism and held genuine pacifist sympathies. Heinz, his boyfriend from his time in Germany, had been conscripted into the Wehrmacht before the war (Isherwood's memoir of 1930s Berlin, *Goodbye to Berlin*, was later adapted as the musical *Cabaret*). Isherwood knew that he didn't have it in him to kill anyone German.

He had lived on the same Hollywood road as Aldous Huxley for a while, but had since moved to a Quaker school in Pennsylvania. His job was to teach English to German and Austrian refugees in an environment where nonviolence was part of the code.

Isherwood's conscience troubled him nevertheless. He did think about going back to England, but reasoned that a committed pacifist was the last thing they needed at a difficult time. Now that the United States was in the war, he would be perfectly happy to drive an ambulance somewhere in the Pacific. Freedom of conscience was one of the principles they would all be fighting for.

W. H. Auden was teaching English at the University of Michigan at Ann Arbor. He had gone to a theater in a German part of New York soon after Hitler's invasion of Poland. The feature had been *Sieg im Poland*, the Nazis' account of the attack.

Auden had been disconcerted to hear Germans in the audience screaming, "Kill them!" every time a Pole appeared on screen. Just before the fall of France, he had offered his services to the British Embassy, only to be told that only people with technical skills were needed at home. He had written to his friend and fellow poet Stephen Spender in March 1941:

> *If I thought I should be a competent soldier or air-warden I should come back tomorrow. It is impossible for me to know whether it is reason or just cowardice that makes me think I shouldn't be of much military effectiveness. All I can do, therefore, is to be willing to do anything when and if the government ask me (which I told the embassy here).*[14]

By December 1941 Auden had made up his mind to remain in the United States, despite all the derision at home. Like Aldous Huxley, he had convinced himself that he could be no use to the war effort, rather forgetting that millions of equally unmilitary British men had enlisted anyway and were quietly doing their bit. His real reason for staying in America was that he had fallen in love with a twenty-year-old New Yorker named Chester Kallman.

Kallman was in Los Angeles on the day of Pearl Harbor. He wrote to Auden on December 7 saying that he was having lots of casual sex and had just met a lovely soldier and his friend. Unfortunately Kallman was short of money and couldn't afford to take them anywhere.

Pearl Harbor barely impinged on Kallman's consciousness as he complained to Auden about his chronic lack of cash, with its inhibiting effect on his sex life. "It's all very depressing—and now war. . . . I feel bitter, vindictive, half-immersed in 'circular madness,' and up to my scalp in roaring hatred, and then to have these days of sheer sexual frustration."[15]

Kallman's self-absorption was less important to Auden on December 8 than the president's address to the nation. Although he wasn't yet an American citizen, Auden was eligible for the draft. His big worry after Pearl Harbor was that he might fail the psychiatrist's examination when the time came. The last thing he wanted now was to be humiliatingly rejected for active service because of his sexual orientation.

TWENTY

HMS *REPULSE* AND *PRINCE OF WALES* BEGIN THE FIGHT BACK

While Auden worried and the rest of America listened to Roosevelt on the radio, Britain's members of Parliament were hurrying back to Westminster for the debate on the war with Japan.

The MPs had been scattered all over the country on the Sunday night, attending to their constituencies while Malaya and Hong Kong were attacked. It wasn't until Monday morning that most of them found out. Summoned back to Parliament, they quickly dropped whatever they were doing and returned to London to attend the afternoon debate in the House of Commons.

The debate was not actually held in the Commons. The debating chamber had been bombed by the Luftwaffe earlier in the year and lay open to the sky. The members were meeting in the House of Lords chamber instead until it was safe to repair their own.

The air raid on the night of May 10 had been spectacular. While anti-aircraft guns thundered and searchlights probed the darkness, German incendiary bombs had rained down on the House of Commons and Westminster Hall next door. The roofs of both had quickly burst into flames.

First built in the 1090s and rebuilt three centuries later, Westminster Hall was and is one of the most historic buildings in England. It was the seat of English justice for many hundreds of years. Legal disputes were settled there and the common law dispensed, the beginnings of a judicial system that has taken root in Anglophone countries all over the globe.

Sir William Wallace, the Scottish leader played by Mel Gibson in *Braveheart*, was tried and sentenced to death in Westminster Hall in 1305. So were Sir Thomas More in 1535 and King Charles I in 1649. After the restoration of the monarchy, Oliver Cromwell's body was exhumed and his head placed on a spike on the roof of the hall for everyone to see. It remained there for many years before blowing down in a storm.

The hall was also the venue for coronation feasts, the lavish medieval banquets held to honor new sovereigns after they had been crowned in nearby Westminster Abbey. By ancient tradition, the king's champion, a knight in armor, rode into the hall on horseback during the meal, challenging all comers to mortal combat if they questioned the new monarch's right to the throne. By equally long tradition, the post of king's champion was always held by a member of the Dymoke family (and still is).

History like that was very important to the British, an integral part of their identity. An enormous chunk of it would have been lost if Westminster Hall had burned down. The House of Commons, on the other hand, dated only from the nineteenth century.

The fire chiefs had come to a swift decision as they surveyed the two burning roofs. They could save one building, but not both. They had opted for Westminster Hall and allowed the Commons to go up in smoke.

The displaced members of Parliament had reconvened in Church House (the Church of England's London conference center) for a few weeks before moving to the House of Lords. The Japan debate was set for three that afternoon, which didn't allow enough time for all of them to get back from their constituencies. The House was full nevertheless as Churchill arrived to make a formal statement about the declaration of war.

He had been very busy since his return from Chequers that morning. The Cabinet had met at noon. Churchill had written to the king afterward, asking his permission to leave the country for three weeks to see Roosevelt in Washington. With Anthony Eden in Moscow at the same time, the Lord Privy Seal would have to deputize in their absence.

Churchill did not need the House of Commons' agreement to declare war on Japan. Under the constitutional rules at the time, the decision was the king's, on the advice of his ministers. The decision had already been made. The war was declared ahead of Roosevelt's address to Congress, despite earlier plans to let the Americans go first.

The diarist Harold Nicolson was there to hear Churchill's statement. He had been as shocked as anyone at the BBC's announcement of Pearl Harbor. It seemed as insane to him as Hitler's invasion of Russia. Nicolson was hoping for another of Churchill's great wartime orations as the prime minister arrived to address the Commons:

> *The House has been specially summoned. Winston enters the Chamber with bowed shoulders and an expression of grim determination on his face. The House had expected jubilation at the entry of America into the war and are a trifle disconcerted. He makes a dull matter-of-fact speech.*[1]

Chips Channon was in the chamber too. True to his transatlantic roots, he listened attentively as the war was announced:

> *After Prayers the Prime Minister rose and made a brief and well-balanced announcement that the Cabinet had declared a state of war to exist at one o'clock with Japan. Nobody seems to know whether this recent and dramatic development is helpful to the Allied cause or not. It means immense complications, but will probably bring about America's immediate entry into the war . . .*
>
> *Geoffrey Lloyd whispered to me how lucky Winston was. Now Libya will be forgotten. Russia saved the Government in July; now Japan will do likewise.*[2]

Both Houses voted unanimously to endorse the war. Across the world, Cuba, Haiti, Panama, Honduras, Guatemala, Nicaragua, Costa Rica, El

Salvador, and the Dominican Republic were doing the same, all of them declaring war on Japan in solidarity with their aggrieved American neighbor.

Channon tuned in to Roosevelt later that afternoon. He picked up the president's address to Congress loud and clear across the Atlantic. The next day he and Averell Harriman discussed the new situation over dinner. Harriman was very forthright in his assessment. "Much talk of a possible Japanese invasion of California. Averell hopes that the American cities will be blitzed, so as to wake the people up. He attacked the American isolationists bitterly."[3]

Gil Winant, the American ambassador, returned to the U.S. Embassy after leaving Chequers that morning. He hadn't been back in Grosvenor Square for long when four pilots from the RAF arrived to see him.

They told him that they were Americans, volunteers from 71 and 121 Squadrons, the two Eagle squadrons based in England. They had been sent to offer their squadrons' services in the fight against the Japanese.

President Roosevelt telephoned while they were talking. Winant was summoned to the phone. The pilots were close enough to hear Roosevelt's voice at the other end as Winant mentioned the Eagles to him during their conversation.

The ambassador returned after hanging up to tell them that their offer was much appreciated by the president. They would be reassigned to the U.S. Army Air Force as soon as possible.

It was like that all day at the U.S. Embassy. The place was under siege as the American community in Britain rallied to the cause. They all wanted to touch base and find out how they could be of help, now that the two countries were allies in the same fight.

American newspapermen were among the most enthusiastic. After months of reporting the war as impartial observers, they had a raucous party at the Savoy that evening. Cheerfully forgetting "The Star-Spangled Banner"'s anti-British origins, they sang the American national anthem to their British friends, toasting an end to neutrality and the beginning of the United States' serious participation in the war.

Ordinary Londoners were more restrained in their reactions. They had gone happily to bed on Sunday with the news of Pearl Harbor. They had awoken on Monday to hear that Hong Kong and Malaya were being attacked too.

Thousands of Londoners had family in one place or the other, hitherto safe from the war. Euphoria at America's entry into the conflict had rapidly been tempered by fears for their own kith and kin, suddenly confronted by a brutal new enemy in the East.

The Japanese army had behaved appallingly in China. As well as the mass rapes and women bayoneted to death through the vagina, they had buried Chinese men alive and taken snapshots of heads flying through the air after beheadings. The Chinese who developed the photographs of the atrocities had smuggled out extra copies for the rest of the world to see. Japanese diplomats insisted that the pictures had been faked, but few believed them.

Mollie Panter-Downes, an English journalist writing for *The New Yorker*, detected a somber mood as the implications of a war with Japan sank in:

London felt as it did at the beginning of the war. Newsdealers stood on the corners handing out papers as steadily and automatically as if they were husking corn; people bought copies on the way out to lunch and again on the way back, just in case a late edition might have sneaked up on them with some fresher news.

Suddenly and soberly, this little island was remembering its vast and sprawling possessions of Empire. It seemed as though every person one met had a son in Singapore or a daughter in Rangoon; every post office was jammed with anxious crowds finding out about cable rates to Hong Kong, Kuala Lumpur, or Penang.

The initial shock and anger resulting from the Sunday evening radio announcement of the Japanese attack on the United States were terrific, but comfort was taken in the assumption that these early blows would be returned with interest at the earliest opportunity.[4]

Across the other side of the world, HMS *Repulse* and *Prince of Wales* were on their way to do exactly that. The U.S. Navy was still picking itself up the day after Pearl Harbor, but the Royal Navy had long been on a war footing and was ready to go. The two great ships were about to clear the Anambas Islands off Malaya before turning northwest toward the Gulf of Thailand. They were expecting to find the Japanese troop transports somewhere up ahead.

The crews of both vessels had gone to action stations at dawn. Thereafter they had remained at a second degree of readiness. Half of the ship's company was closed up at any one time as the task force zigzagged through mist and rain at a steady seventeen knots.

Cecil Brown's action station was on the exposed flag deck of *Repulse*, just below the bridge. Carrying his gas mask, helmet, antiflash hood, and life jacket, the CBS reporter had presented himself at five fifteen, only to be told by a cheerful sailor that the flag deck was the least protected part of the ship. People were always killed there in action.

It grew light at about 6:00. Brown saw that they were about four miles off the coast of the Anambas Islands. *Prince of Wales* was leading the way, flanked by the four destroyers a mile away. All *Repulse*'s guns were manned as their crews scoured the horizon for a sign of the enemy.

Breakfast was in the wardroom at seven thirty. Over the radio, the officers listened to Roosevelt's speech to Congress. Brown was surprised at their restrained reaction to the news:

> *I had never felt what I felt at that moment. I wanted to get up and give a toast with my water glass or jump on the table and shout. It was strange. None of the officers in the wardroom said anything, and since they showed no reaction I decided against being ostentatious.*[5]

The radio also gave further details of the raid on Pearl Harbor. *Repulse*'s officers were amazed at the extent of the losses, but broadly sympathetic to the U.S. Navy. They took the view that the Japanese would never have the advantage of surprise again.

The British all seemed very nonchalant to Brown. He concluded that their laid-back attitude to everything was just a way of coping with the war. Most of *Repulse*'s crew came from London or Plymouth, two of the most-bombed cities in the United Kingdom. With letters few and far between, they worried for their families at home as much as their families worried for them at sea.

It rained for most of the day. Visibility was reduced to less than two miles at one point, which was excellent news from the ships' point of view. There was less chance of the Japanese spotting them as they advanced to the attack.

The sailors were in a good mood at lunch, happy and singing. Apart from a few German bombs off the coast of Norway, *Repulse* had yet to see any action in the war. The men were looking forward to a real fight at last.

As their predecessors had done before Trafalgar, they were busy clearing away unnecessary furniture and preparing to change into clean clothes before going into action to reduce the risk of infection from wounds. Despite the heat, they had been ordered to wear long pants and long-sleeved shirts the next morning to protect themselves from fire or burning fuel.

Brown only had a bush jacket and shorts, but managed to borrow a pair of overalls from an engineer officer. He thought of writing a last letter to his wife, but decided there would be little point if the letter went down with the ship. He was finding the whole experience of sailing into action rather disconcerting.

They listened to the radio again later. A BBC reporter in London was interviewing people in Leicester Square, asking them if they had any friends in the Far East. Later still, the BBC reported that the fighting in Malaya was heavy and Bangkok had fallen to the Japanese.

It was getting toward evening before the weather began to improve. The clouds broke at around five twenty for the first time that day. The clear sky revealed a tiny speck in the distance, about four or five miles away.

A spotter in the defense control tower was the first to see it. A bugle call over the loudspeaker system immediately alerted the crew. At the words "Enemy aircraft" they all dropped whatever they were doing and raced to action stations.

Brown's colleague Gallagher from the *Daily Express* joined the rush. "We ran to the flag-deck. Everybody was running somewhere. Everyone seemed to carry tin hats. Passing us on the flag-deck as he made his way to the bridge, a lieutenant-commander said, 'Afraid they've spotted us. Only one of them, but . . .' and he was gone."[6]

The aircraft was a catapult plane from a Japanese cruiser. It was quickly joined by two others. They shadowed the squadron until nightfall while the British cursed their luck and railed at the ill-timed break in the clouds.

So that was that. The Japanese knew they were coming. The squadron increased speed to twenty-six knots in order to engage the enemy as fast as possible next morning now that they had been spotted.

Brown changed his mind about writing to his wife. He sat down after supper to pen her a last letter, just in case. He was in the wardroom later when Captain Tennant's voice came over the loudspeaker. He had a message from Admiral Phillips aboard *Prince of Wales*:

> *A signal has just been received from the Commander-in-Chief who very much regrets to announce having to abandon the operation. We were shadowed by three planes. We were spotted after dodging them all day. Their troop convoy will now have dispersed. It would be very obvious that if we continued, enemy air concentration would be awaiting us and it would be unwise to continue.*
>
> *I know that you all share with us the disappointment in not engaging the enemy at this time, but I am sure that you will agree with the C-in-C's judgment. We are, therefore, going back to Singapore.*[7]

Repulse obediently turned about. There were gloomy faces all around as they began the dispiriting voyage back to port. No one was more disappointed than reporter Cecil Brown. He had made the wrong call, choosing to go to sea for a few days when the real story was on land.

TWENTY-ONE

FIRST MASS GASSING OF JEWS
IN NAZI-OCCUPIED EUROPE

While HMS *Repulse* and *Prince of Wales* turned about and headed back to Singapore, Adolf Hitler was preparing to return to Germany. He was taking the train overnight from his eastern HQ near Rastenburg. He was due to arrive back in Berlin early on Tuesday morning.

Like Churchill, Hitler had been very busy since the announcement of Pearl Harbor. After recovering from his initial surprise, he had quickly telephoned Goebbels in Berlin, telling him to summon the Reichstag for a meeting on Wednesday, December 10. He wanted to brief Germany's rubber-stamp parliament on his response to the attack.

Hitler had every reason to fear American entry into the war, but he didn't appear to be concerned as he discussed Pearl Harbor with his advisers at the Wolf's Lair. Heinrich Himmler was one of them as they debated how to put the most positive spin on the news for the German people.

Hitler's enthusiasm for the Japanese attack seems to have been based on the idea that the Americans would be fully occupied in the Far East from now on. The British too would be even more thinly stretched than they were already as they struggled to keep hold of Malaya and Burma.

Most important of all, American supplies and munitions bound for the

British and Russian armed forces would now be withheld for a while as the Americans took care of their own requirements first. There was a window of opportunity here, a chance for Germany to finish the Russians off and then the British while their American backers were preoccupied elsewhere. That was apparently the reason for Hitler's optimism.

If his generals raised any objections to taking on a powerful new enemy, they were quickly overruled. Hitler had already made up his mind to declare war on the United States, if only to retain the initiative by anticipating the inevitable and getting in first. He gave orders that night for German U-boats to begin sinking American ships at once, even though their two countries were not yet formally at war.

He also signed Directive No. 39, officially abandoning the Wehrmacht's offensive against the Red Army and ordering his troops to hunker down for the winter. Like Napoleon before him, Hitler blamed the cold and ice for his army's failure in Russia after such an encouraging start. "The severe winter weather which has come surprisingly early in the east, and the consequent difficulties in bringing up supplies, compel us to abandon immediately all major offensive operations and go over to the defensive."[1]

Having bitten the bullet, Hitler returned to Berlin to address the Reichstag. He set off on the evening of Monday, December 8, taking General Jodl, Field-Marshal Keitel, and a host of others with him.

Details of Hitler's personal train are vague, but it was heavily armored and well protected. The railroad station lay right in the middle of the compound, a few hundred yards from Hitler's bunker.

Once his entourage had entrained and he was safely aboard, the gates in the barbed wire opened and the train set off through the forest. The journey across Poland was due to take all night. All being well, the Führer would arrive back in Berlin sometime around midmorning on Tuesday, December 9.

In the Latvian capital of Riga, snow was falling that Monday morning as Jews from the ghetto were herded outside and lined up for the march to Rumbula railroad station. Many thousands of them were being compulsorily "resettled" to make room for Jews arriving from Austria and Germany.

Rumbula was just over six miles from the ghetto. A previous batch of Jews had been allowed to take a single suitcase with them. That had proved too heavy for many of them to carry, so this time their successors were told to dump their luggage. It would follow later by truck.

More than eleven thousand people set off for the station that day, shuffling along in columns one thousand strong. They were all apprehensive as they started off, knowing that many Jews were being murdered in Latvia, but hoping for the best. Nothing much could happen to them if they all stuck together. They believed there was safety in numbers.

Their Latvian countrymen watched them go with indifference. The German army had been welcomed with open arms when it arrived on July 1. Delighted to be rid of their Soviet oppressors, ordinary Latvians dressed in their Sunday best had hung out the flags and thrown flowers at German soldiers as they marched into Riga.

As well as hating the Russians, many Latvians shared the German distaste for Jews. The exodus to Rumbula was German-organized and -led, but the guards shepherding the Jews along the road were all in Latvian uniform. They had no hesitation in beating stragglers or shooting them if they dropped out. They were no better than the Germans in that respect.

Max Kaufmann had already lost his wife to the Germans, but he was not one of the Jews ordered to report that morning. Instead, bribing one of the drivers at work, he set off in a truck, ostensibly to gather firewood. In reality he followed the displaced Jews to see where they were being taken:

From afar I also saw two other columns, which were drawing closer to the Rumbula railway station. There they halted. In this way, the organizers wanted to create the impression that from there they would be transported to points further on. But in reality they were herded in groups into the forest and slaughtered . . .

At the edge of the road, hidden by a small wood, stood two trucks and between sixty and eighty soldiers. They were soldiers of the German Wehrmacht. Only a short distance past the wood we saw machine guns set close together in the snow. As far as I could judge, they reached from Rumbula to the banks of the Daugava River, about three kilometers away.[2]

Kaufmann's driver tried to persuade him that the machine guns were just there to discourage escape. The Jews were being taken to a small rise about 250 yards from the station. Russian prisoners of war had dug huge burial pits for them in the high ground above the water table.

Frida Michelson, one of only three people known to have survived the massacre, never forgot what happened next:

> Our column started pouring into the forest. At the entrance stood a large wooden box. An SS man armed with a club stood next to it and shouted over and over: "Drop all your valuables and money in this box. . . ."
>
> We were driven on. A bit further, a Latvian policeman ordered: "Take off your coat and throw it on top of the rest." There was already a mountain of overcoats. . . . The shooting, the uninterrupted shooting, was becoming louder. We were nearing the end.[3]

Another policeman was ordering Michelson to strip to her underwear when his attention was distracted for a moment. She seized the opportunity to feign death in the snow and survived by lying motionless as piles of discarded shoes were thrown on top of her until she had completely disappeared from view. Eleven thousand other people were not so lucky.

The killing was done by just a dozen Germans. They were equipped with Russian submachine guns carrying a fifty-round magazine. The guns could be set to fire a single shot. This meant that each magazine could account for fifty Jews if each was dispatched with a single bullet in the head.

The executioners were not volunteers. They were members of Gruppenführer Friedrich Jeckeln's personal bodyguard, ordered to do the job. With previous experience at Babi Yar in Ukraine, where 33,000 Jews had been murdered over two days in September, Jeckeln was in command of the operation to liquidate Riga's Jews.

He had tried to find more soldiers to share the workload, but no one had been prepared to volunteer, not even under pressure. After witnessing a similar massacre on November 30, some had flatly refused to have anything more to do with the operation.

Others—quite a few others—were fortified by liquor as they went to work. Copious amounts of spirits were available for anyone who needed a drink. Ella Medale, another of the three survivors, saw one Latvian guard crying, another ashen-faced, a third swaying back and forth, horribly drunk as he insisted that Jewish blood must flow that day.

The victims went meekly to their deaths. Families clung together as they either stepped down into the grave pits or stood on the edge, waiting to be shot in the back of the head. It was all very brisk and clinical. The Germans needed to get through it quickly to complete the work by dusk.

Yet it wasn't satisfactory. A few coldhearted SS officers took photographs, quite indifferent to the murder of eleven thousand human beings. Other German soldiers were privately appalled, not only in Riga but all over the occupied territories.

The old officer class didn't like it, for a start. Shooting women and children was unworthy of the German army, unworthy of the country that had produced Goethe and Beethoven. It wasn't what their troops should be doing.

Many of the troops didn't like it either. As Himmler later sarcastically remarked to SS leaders, eighty million good Germans knew at least one "decent Jew," even if they shared his opinion that the rest were swine. The men didn't like to see perfectly decent people being led away and murdered for no good reason at all.

In response to the troops' increasing disquiet, a solution to that and other problems was being tried out in Poland that same morning. An experiment was being conducted in the little village of Chelmno. If it went well, Nazi methods of liquidating the Jews in the occupied territories would change forever.

Chelmno lay beside a river just under forty miles northwest of Lódz, close to the Rzuchów forest. Not to be confused with the larger town of the same name, it had had a population of only 250 before German settlers displaced the previous inhabitants. Besides the church, the only building of any significance in the place was the manor house. It stood in seven acres of grounds on the outskirts of the village.

Himmler's men had just spent a month turning the manor house into a temporary holding camp for the Jews and Gypsies in the neighborhood. They had bricked up the basement windows and built a wooden fence around the main part of the property, too high for anyone to see over. They had staffed the camp with SS guards and brought in Polish prisoners to do the dirty work that would shortly be needed.

The manor house had been selected for the new camp because of its geographical location. Chelmno was some distance from the nearest town, yet easily accessible by road and rail. It was central to the district's Jewish population, with buildings readily adaptable for the purpose that the Nazis had in mind.

Chelmno went into operation on December 8. It was the first camp of its kind to do so under the Nazis. It wasn't a work camp or a concentration camp for keeping people captive. It was an extermination camp pure and simple: a place where human beings were sent to be murdered.

The first seven hundred of them were Jews from Kolo, a little town to the north. While the Japanese were attacking Pearl Harbor on December 7, the Jews had been rounded up and told that they were being sent to work in Germany.

The next morning, at the same time as the Jews of Riga were starting out for Rumbula, the Jews of Kolo had been paraded at the manor house at Chelmno, from where the journey to Germany was supposed to begin. They had been ordered to strip naked and hand over their clothes for disinfection. They had also been required to surrender their valuables in return for an official receipt.

After the Jews had stripped and handed over their money, they were taken in groups to the basement, where they were told they would have a bath before setting out for Germany. Instead they found themselves hustled outside and pushed straight through the open rear doors of a large van. Polish prisoners with whips were there to make sure they kept moving and did what they were told.

The doors were bolted shut as soon as the Jews had been crammed in. A driver in a gas mask took his seat in a separate compartment at the front and started the engine. Walter Burmeister, an SS underofficer, explained how the system worked, once it was up and running:

When they had undressed they were sent to the cellar of the manor house and then along a passageway onto the ramp and from there into the gas van. In the manor house there were signs marked "to the baths." The gas vans were large vans, about 4–5 meters long, 2.2 meters wide and 2 meters high . . . The floor of the van had an opening which could be connected to the exhaust by means of a removable metal pipe. When the lorries were full of people, the double doors at the back were closed and the exhaust connected to the interior of the van.

The Kommando member detailed as driver would start the engine right away so that the people inside the lorry were suffocated by the exhaust gases. Once this had taken place, the join between the exhaust and the inside of the lorry was disconnected and the van was driven to the camp in the woods where the bodies were unloaded.[4]

It wasn't the first time the Nazis had killed people that way. They had carried out similar experiments on old people and mental defectives to see if it would work. What they wanted to know now was whether gassing was feasible on a much larger, industrial scale.

Secrecy was paramount as they began their experiment. The SS guards at Chelmno were sworn to silence on pain of execution by firing squad, or at the very least service on the Russian front, if they told anyone about their work. They received extra pay for the job and an additional ration of alcohol and cigarettes.

The Polish prisoners who assisted them got no pay but quickly learned to rob the new arrivals as they handed over their valuables. The Poles also had access to the women. They enjoyed all the sex they wanted from Jewish girls reluctantly complying with their demands for fear of something worse happening if they didn't. The SS guards raped them, too. A room in the basement had been set aside for the purpose.

The experiment was a big success. A grand total of seven hundred Jews was "processed" on that first day at Chelmno. The figure was the same for the next four days before rising thereafter. The Nazis were establishing an extraordinarily efficient method of committing mass murder without their troops having to see or hear anything about it.

December 8 was the "day of infamy" for the Jews at Chelmno. None of them knew about Pearl Harbor as they undressed that morning. They went to their deaths unaware that the mighty United States was about to enter the war on their side, that the tide would soon turn in their favor, that the brutal Germans and their accomplices would not remain in the ascendant for ever.

The Jews knew only that something had gone terribly wrong somewhere. The leaking exhaust in the van would kill them all if somebody didn't get the doors open soon.

The gassing was being done at the behest of Reinhard Heydrich. From his base in Prague, he was in charge of the Einsatzgruppen, the death squads rounding up the Jews of Eastern Europe for deportation and murder. His job was to coordinate the work and ensure that it was carried out as efficiently as possible.

The operation was running into problems, which was why Heydrich had convened a conference to discuss it at the Wannsee on December 9. Some people were arguing that it would be stupid to kill all the Jews, now that the war was likely to be a long one. They should be used as skilled labor instead.

Others agreed that there was a labor shortage, but argued that Jews could not be trusted to fill the gap. Sent to work in German factories, they would seize every opportunity to sabotage the war effort. Better just to get rid of them instead, no matter how large the numbers and the associated logistical problems.

Pearl Harbor had complicated matters still further. As a member of the Reichstag, Heydrich was due to attend on December 10 to hear Hitler's speech. Between that and the recent unexpected reverses on the Russian front, this was no longer the right time to decide how to dispose of the Jews in the occupied territories.

Heydrich responded accordingly. His staff set to work on December 8 and contacted everyone who had been invited to the Wannsee Conference next day. The gathering was postponed in the light of current developments. It would be reconvened later, sometime in the New Year.

The Jews of Eastern Europe were getting the worst of it from the Nazis, but they hadn't all been rounded up yet. Some were in hiding, or else living in plain sight as gentiles. Others had disappeared into the forests to join the partisans. Still others were in uniform, either fighting for the Red Army or the Free Polish Army under General Władysław Anders.

Menachem Begin had been in Warsaw when the Germans invaded Poland. A law graduate and political activist, he had fled to Wilno (now Vilnius, in Lithuania), only to see the town occupied by the Russians soon after his arrival. As a prominent Zionist and alleged agent of British imperialism, he had been arrested in September 1940 and sentenced to eight years in prison.

Begin had had a bad time in prison. The conditions were dreadful. The guards had confiscated his dictionary and an English-language biography of Disraeli on his arrival. As a punishment, he had been forced to sit facing a blank wall for sixty hours, his knees touching the wall, his eyes focused on a single spot.

After nine months Begin had been one of two thousand prisoners removed from Wilno and sent deep into Russia to work in a gulag labor camp just south of the Arctic Circle. He had been en route to the Pechora River when Germany invaded the Soviet Union.

It was wonderful news for a Polish Jew. The two despicable regimes were now at war with each other. As a Polish national, Begin had been set free a few weeks later. He had been removed from a crowded freighter on the river and taken to a transit camp, from where the released prisoners were expected to make their own way south to join the fight against Germany.

After the lice, diarrhea, and cramped conditions of the freighter, Begin was glad to be ashore again. The Russians gave him a little money before he set out, but it didn't last long. He found his way to the nearest outpost of the Polish army, only for them to take one look at his feeble body and say that they didn't need him. Jews were regarded as poor fighters.

Instead Begin decided to look for his sister and her husband, who had been deported before his arrest. He spent the next few months traveling through Soviet Central Asia, jumping trains, sleeping rough, eating whenever he could.

Begin caught up with his sister eventually. By December 1941 he was sufficiently restored to think about applying to join the Polish army again. The catalyst for this had been the Russian arrest of two Polish Jewish leaders on December 4.

The two men were Zionists, like himself. Begin might well be next if he didn't join the Polish army instead. He learned later that the men had been executed, in his view because the Russians no longer needed them alive after Pearl Harbor and the United States' entry into the war.

Knowing that Begin faced rearrest by the Russians, the Free Polish Army accepted him when he reapplied. As he began his military career, though, Private Begin's real ambition was not to fight the Germans, vile though they were. It was to get an exit permit to Palestine as soon as he possibly could.

Palestine was the ultimate goal. It was administered by the British under a mandate from the League of Nations, but that didn't stop Begin from seeing the British as the occupying power. It seemed to him that they had reneged on the 1917 Balfour Declaration, which had supported the idea of a Jewish homeland in Palestine, and could only be removed by armed resistance. If he was going to fight anyone in this war, he wanted to fight the British in Palestine and win the land back for the Jewish people.

In Dresden, Victor Klemperer was bemused when he learned of Pearl Harbor that Monday morning. Like so many other people, he wondered what on earth the Japanese thought they were up to. Making war on the United States seemed inexplicable to him.

The son of a rabbi, Klemperer had converted to Christianity before World War I. He had fought for Germany in the war and had the medals to prove it. Thereafter he had returned to work as a university professor until the Nazis had made it impossible for him to continue in his job. They had also forced him to leave his house and move into accommodation that was restricted to Jews.

Klemperer was in dire straits now. His wife was Aryan, but that was little protection against the Nazis. His telephone had been confiscated long ago. He had been forced to give up his typewriter as well, despite claiming that it belonged to his wife.

Klemperer was also wearing the new Star of David, the yellow symbol of Jewishness that the Nazis had recently introduced as a badge to be shown at all times. Jews were forbidden to cover up the star or hide it in any way. They were heavily punished if they did.

Klemperer had been too scared to go out for the first few days of wearing the star. His life as a Jew was difficult enough without any added complications. It meant, for instance, that he could no longer go to the barber's to get his hair cut, because he would be turned away. He couldn't buy cigarettes either.

He had also run into anti-Semitism on the street. A gang of Hitler Youths had mobbed him on Chemnitzer Platz, snickering at a Yid with a yellow star. They wouldn't have known the former professor was Jewish if he hadn't been wearing it.

Quite a few Germans behaved like the Hitler Youths, pushing Jews off the pavement, kicking them out of the shops if they tried to go shopping outside the hours permitted for their kind. There were plenty of little Hitlers strutting about the streets of Dresden, making life hell for the wearers of the yellow star.

Paradoxically, however, there were other Germans too, people who didn't like the idea of the star any more than the Jews did. Shopping for vegetables, Klemperer had gazed longingly at some tomatoes in short supply—forbidden goods, unavailable to Jews. The stallholder had sold him some anyway, and some even rarer onions, telling him quietly that she knew how things were for Jews.

A porter had confided to him that they were all human beings. He personally knew some very good Jews. An acquaintance had taken a risk by chatting with Klemperer on the streetcar, defying a recent order from Goebbels to have nothing to do with Jews. Other Germans pointedly gave up their seats to Jewish women or went out of their way to raise their hats to complete strangers wearing the yellow star.

One way and another, Klemperer was unsure what to make of his former fellow citizens in Germany. There were two radically different aspects to the national character. On balance, though, he was in no doubt that plenty of Germans disliked the persecution of the Jews. That was little consolation when they were doing nothing to stop it.

Klemperer's biggest fear now was deportation. He had heard shocking accounts of the German Jews who had already been deported to Poland. They had left penniless and almost naked, with only the clothes on their backs. Friends abroad had heard similar stories and were urging him to get out while he still could, immigrate to the United States without delay. What they didn't understand was that it was far too late for anything like that now.

Would Pearl Harbor change things? Most of the people Klemperer had spoken to so far thought it would probably make the war last longer, if anything. That was hardly good news for the Jews still trapped in Germany.

In Berlin the radio propagandist William Joyce agreed that Pearl Harbor was bound to prolong the war, rather than anything else. He had always thought it would be a disaster for Germany if the United States entered the war on the Allied side. Now it looked as if his worst nightmare was about to come true.

Joyce was American-born himself, although Irish in origin. Virulently anti-Semitic, he had traded his British passport for German citizenship after the outbreak of war. He worked now for German radio, broadcasting Nazi propaganda to the British in their own language. His listeners called him Lord Haw-Haw because of his fake upper-class accent.

Joyce was consumed by a hatred of Jews, but even he had been shocked by the recent appearance of the yellow star on Berlin's streets. He had first seen it on the overcoat of a harmless old man in a Homburg hat—a far cry from the Communist agitators and capitalist fat cats whom he habitually associated with Jewishness. Joyce had felt pity for the old man, rather than loathing.

He was scheduled to make a radio broadcast on December 8. He decided to play down Pearl Harbor when he got to the studio, concentrating instead on the dangers of Bolshevism for the occupied people of Finland. But he did mention the Japanese attack in passing, putting an optimistic spin on the implications for the wider war. "Well, England has got her allies now. She has got her losing Bolsheviks and she has got the unprepared Yanks, who can no longer help her as they once did. The Yankees' hands will in future be very full indeed, and so, we think, will England's."[5]

In Amsterdam, Otto Frank shared Victor Klemperer's uneasiness about the deportation of Jews to Poland. Like Klemperer, he had fought for Germany in World War I. Unlike Klemperer, though, he had seen the light in 1933, emigrating from Frankfurt as soon as Hitler came to power.

Frank had taken his family to Holland, in the belief that they would be safe from Nazi persecution there. He had set up a company in Amsterdam selling spices and pectins for jam. His family had been happy and prosperous in their new life until the German invasion of May 1940.

The anti-Jewish laws introduced since then were making their lives increasingly miserable. Worst of all for Frank's daughters, Anne and Margot, had been their exclusion from school. The girls had been forced to attend a Jews-only school instead. They had been forbidden by law from visiting their Christian friends anymore.

Frank's business had suffered too. As a Jew he wasn't allowed to own his own company under the new rules. He had therefore transferred the ownership to gentile colleagues while quietly remaining in control as an employed "adviser." But the Germans were wise to it. They had put the wheels in motion for the company to be liquidated forthwith.

In desperation, Frank had applied for exit visas to the United States without success. He had applied to Cuba, too, and was still waiting to hear. His mother was safe in Switzerland, but he couldn't go there either.

The Franks had been stripped of their German citizenship in November. They had also been required to submit a full list of their possessions to the authorities. To cap it all, on December 5 every non-Dutch Jew in Holland had been ordered to register for something that the Germans termed "voluntary emigration."

Frank disliked the sound of that. If his family was to emigrate, he wanted it to be a destination of his own choosing, not somewhere the Germans had selected for them. He would much rather remain in Amsterdam and go into hiding than do what the Germans told him to.

He had already chosen somewhere for his family to hide, if it became necessary. The upstairs annex of his office building on the Prinsengracht was as good a place as any. Working only after office hours and at weekends, Frank had had the back rooms furnished and made habitable without anybody outside his trusted circle knowing anything about it.

He had also had the windows at the front of the building painted blue, and the ones in the connecting corridor pasted over with semitransparent paper so that no one could see in. After that, he had stocked the annex with canned food, clothes, bed linen, and cooking utensils, everything the Franks would need for a prolonged stay out of sight of the Germans.

All Otto Frank could do now was wait and hope. Perhaps Pearl Harbor would change things, bring the Germans to their senses at last. If not, then it would only take one hostile knock on the door for Frank, his wife, and children to disappear from public view at a moment's notice.

TWENTY-TWO

HMS *REPULSE* AND *PRINCE OF WALES* GO DOWN FIGHTING

After his train journey from Poland, Hitler arrived back in Berlin around eleven o'clock on the morning of Tuesday, December 9. He had a busy day ahead. He had to assess the overnight reports from the Russian front, where the Red Army was continuing to regain ground. He also needed to think about Pearl Harbor and work on his speech to the Reichstag next day.

On top of all that, Hitler was scheduled to meet Said Amin al-Husseini, the Grand Mufti of Jerusalem, later in the day. The man was pushing for a public declaration about the Jews in Palestine that Hitler wasn't yet ready to give.

According to the Luftwaffe adjutant who met him at the station, it was the undesirability of war with the United States that dominated Hitler's thoughts as he drove to the Chancellery. Japan's ambassador was pressing for an immediate opening of hostilities with America, but the Germans were under no obligation to comply if Japan hadn't been attacked. There was wiggle room for Germany to remain neutral under the terms of the Tripartite Pact.

The Wehrmacht certainly didn't want war. Most generals shared the view of ordinary Germans that fighting the United States would be a calamitous mistake. There were all sorts of good reasons for staying out of it if they could.

The Americans didn't want war either, according to Germany's man in Washington. The chargé d'affaires at the German Embassy had just reported to Berlin that Roosevelt would be most reluctant to fight on two fronts, even if Congress would allow him to. In the chargé's opinion, the president would declare war on Germany and Italy only if he deemed it necessary to beat them to the punch.

That being so, Hitler might have done better to bide his time that day, waiting to see how the situation developed. It would be possible to portray the Americans in the same light as the Japanese if they were the ones to declare war first, when Germany hadn't attacked them and only wanted peace.

Yet the chance to kick Roosevelt while he was down was too good to miss. Hitler wasn't the man to ignore it. His was an all-or-nothing nature: the taking of enormous gambles combined with a maniacal desire to see everything go up in flames. He had already made up his mind for war, without seriously consulting anyone else.

He was so busy when he got back to the Chancellery that morning that he didn't have time to complete his speech for the Reichstag next day. He therefore postponed the gathering for twenty-four hours, rescheduling it for Thursday, December 11.

At the other end of the street from the Chancellery, the remaining diplomats at the American Embassy on Pariser Platz faced an acute dilemma as Hitler deliberated with his advisers. The diplomats couldn't decide whether to burn the embassy's codebooks in preparation for a severance of relations with Germany. It was the right thing to do if there was going to be a war between their two countries, but they would look pretty stupid if there wasn't.

The signs for war were all there. The embassy's channels of communication were being cut off one by one. The telegraph office was refusing to accept their telegrams anymore, even ones to the American government. By late Tuesday, the embassy's telephones had mysteriously ceased to function as well. The Americans in Berlin were on their own, unable to communicate with Washington or anyone else.

They decided to burn the codes. Their classified correspondence went into the furnace as well. The work began on Tuesday evening and wasn't completed until the early hours of Wednesday morning.

Across the Atlantic, President Roosevelt was waiting for Germany to make the first move. He had deliberately avoided any reference to Germany or Italy during his speech to Congress the previous day. Against advice, he had mentioned only Japan when calling for war.

Roosevelt had kept quiet about the other two Axis powers because he knew from decoded intercepts that Germany had promised to join Japan if it came to war with the United States. Even allowing for the worthlessness of German pledges, he was pretty sure that Hitler would be forced to declare war soon enough. It would be only a matter of a day or two at most.

Roosevelt gave a talk to the nation that Tuesday night, one of his "fireside chats" on the radio. Millions of Americans tuned in to hear him. A far larger number than usual listened soberly as he filled them in on what was happening and quietly called on them to prepare for the ordeal that lay ahead:

> We are now in this war. We are all in it—all the way. Every single man, woman and child is a partner in the most tremendous undertaking of our American history. We must share together the bad news and the good news, the defeats and the victories—the changing fortunes of war.
>
> So far, the news has all been bad. We have suffered a serious setback in Hawaii. Our forces in the Philippines, which include the brave people of that Commonwealth, are taking punishment, but are defending themselves vigorously. The reports from Guam and Wake and Midway Islands are still confused, but we must be prepared for the announcement that all these three outposts have been seized.[1]

Roosevelt gave it to the people straight, openly admitting that he didn't yet know how bad the damage was at Pearl Harbor, although it was pretty bad. He had words of comfort, too, assuring his listeners that American industry had been quietly gearing up for war ever since the fall of France in 1940. There was plenty of food as well, enough for the Americans to supply their military allies as well as themselves.

It wasn't until the end of his talk that he came to Germany:

Your Government knows that for weeks Germany has been telling Japan that if Japan did not attack the United States, Japan would not share in dividing the spoils with Germany when peace came. She was promised by Germany that if she came in she would receive the complete and perpetual control of the whole of the Pacific area—and that means not only the Far East, not only all of the islands in the Pacific, but also a stranglehold on the west coast of North, Central and South America.

We also know that Germany and Japan are conducting their military and naval operations in accordance with a joint plan. That plan considers all peoples and nations which are not helping the Axis powers as common enemies of each and every one of the Axis powers.[2]

Roosevelt's message was clear enough. Without actually calling for war on Germany and Italy, he was in no doubt that war was inevitable. "We expect to eliminate the danger from Japan, but it would serve us ill if we accomplished that and found that the rest of the world was dominated by Hitler and Mussolini."[3]

Roosevelt concluded by telling his audience that all right-thinking people were on America's side. The United States was fighting for decent people everywhere, for universal human values, and, as he put it, liberty under God.

Out in the Pacific the shooting had just about stopped at Pearl Harbor, but the place was still in deep shock. The enormity of what had happened was only just beginning to sink in.

Admiral Kimmel was still in command of the navy, although not for much longer. A massive cleanup operation was under way as the sailors hurried to repair their defenses in case of further attack. The wounded men had all been taken to hospital, but there were still sailors alive on the sunken battleships, trapped in underwater air pockets and desperately banging on the hull to attract attention.

The air force was clearing the runways of wrecked aircraft, looking to defend Oahu with the few serviceable fighter planes that remained. They weren't going to be caught out twice, if the Japanese struck again.

The army was on the alert too. Many of the troops had been dispersed from their barracks and were living in tents around the island. They were busy preparing beach defenses to repel a Japanese invasion. A follow-up attack would surely come by sea, if it was going to come at all.

After the rude interruption of his breakfast on December 7, James Jones had spent the rest of the morning running messages for the officers at Schofield. Later that day, his company had been sent to defend a beach near Makapuu Point, as he afterward recorded:

> I shall never forget the sight as we passed over the lip of the central plateau and began the long drop down to Pearl City. Down toward the towering smoke columns as far as the eye could see, the long line of army trucks . . . wound serpentlike up and down the drawers of red dirt through the green of cane and pineapple. Machine guns were mounted on the cab roofs of every truck possible.
>
> I remember thinking with a sense of the profoundest awe that none of our lives would ever be the same, that a social, even a cultural watershed had been crossed which we could never go back over, and I wondered how many of us would survive to see the end results.[4]

Jones had been fully occupied since then digging trenches and laying out coils of barbed wire along the beach. Machine guns and heavier artillery were pointing out to sea, ready to blast the Japanese out of the water before they got anywhere near land. The stable door was being firmly bolted, even if the horse had already gone.

In Honolulu, reporter Betty McIntosh was busy collecting people's memories of the attack for the *Star-Bulletin*:

In the nightmare of Monday and Tuesday, there was the struggle to keep normal when planes zoomed overhead and guns cracked out at an unseen enemy. There was blackout and suspicion riding the back of wild rumors: Parachutists in the hills! Poison in your food! Starvation and death were all that was left in a tourist bureau paradise.

I talked with evacuees. From Hickam, a nurse who had dropped to the floor in the hospital kitchen as machine gun bullets dotted a neat row of holes directly above her; from Schofield, a woman who wanted me to send word to her sweetheart "somewhere in Honolulu" that she was still alive; from Pearl Harbor, a nurse who wanted scraps of paper and pencil stubs to give to the boys in the hospital who had last messages they wanted to send home; a little girl named Theda who had a big doll named Nancy and who told me in a quiet voice that "Daddy was killed at Hickam."[5]

At the Japanese consulate, the diplomats were confined to their compound, guarded around the clock until arrangements could be made for their repatriation. Protected by diplomatic immunity, they were to be taken to San Diego as soon as transport was available. They would be exchanged later with their American counterparts in Japan. The spy Yoshikawa was among them, having succeeded at his work beyond his wildest dreams.

Bernard Kühn, his intended German successor, was under arrest. Instead of keeping his head down on the day of the Japanese attack, Kühn had gone straight up to the roof of his house overlooking the harbor to signal the Japanese consulate. The authorities had quickly picked him up and taken him into custody. Without diplomatic immunity, he was facing the death penalty for espionage.

On the heights above the city, families with young children were sheltering in the navy's storage tunnels at Red Hill. Intended to protect fuel from aerial attack, the tunnels had been under construction for months. Along with the natural tunnels formed by lava caves, they were being hurriedly adapted for human occupation before the Japanese returned for another raid.

The two English boys Noel and Michael Cunningham-Reid were among the children evacuated to the caves. Already familiar with war, they took it all in their stride, as Noel recalled:

> *After the Japs had gone, we were shuffled into the caves under the volcanic rock. The authorities had prepared miles and miles of huge caves. A lot of the population were put in there. We stayed there for many days. I thought it was very stupid. If the Japs had invaded, they would have blown up all the exits and left us all to die.*
>
> *Lots of things were laid on for the children. We didn't have the imagination of grown-ups, so we weren't that frightened. The preparations were quite good. We had a reasonable time.*[6]

Even in the bordellos they were helping out. The brothels around River Street had been temporarily closed under martial law, but several of them were giving shelter to evacuees instead. The girls were doing the cooking and cleaning, taking care of people who needed looking after.

It was a new beginning for many of the prostitutes, a chance to escape their profession at last and look for war work instead. Everybody was rallying around, doing whatever they could to help, now that their country was in the fight.

Farther west, across the international date line, it was already the morning of Wednesday, December 10, as HMS *Repulse* and *Prince of Wales* headed at full speed toward the coast of Malaya. A report had just come in of a Japanese landing at Kuantan, about 180 miles north of Singapore. The warships had changed course to investigate.

It was a boiling-hot day as the sun rose. The rain of the day before had given way to clear blue skies and beautiful green water. The ships looked magnificent as they powered ahead, flashing signals back and forth. Their crews were standing by the guns, ready for action at a moment's notice.

The ships were about ten miles off the Malayan coast when they turned south, steaming parallel to the shore to see what they could find. After a fruitless search, they headed out to sea again, turning north and then east, still looking for the Japanese. It was a few minutes after eleven when the Japanese found them instead.

The first the crew of *Repulse* knew of it was a call to action stations over the loudspeaker. Enemy aircraft had been spotted. There were nine of them, flying in line astern.

CBS's Cecil Brown was on the flag deck as the aircraft approached. He estimated their height at twelve thousand feet, although others thought ten thousand. Whichever figure was correct, Brown couldn't help noticing that they were heading straight for *Repulse*.

He watched, fascinated, as the aircraft approached. Whatever thoughts ran through his mind as the Japanese came out of the sky to kill him, fear of missing out on a big story was no longer among them:

> *I gape open-mouthed at those aircraft coming directly over us, flying so that they will pass from bow to stern over the Repulse. The sky is filled with black puffs from our ack-ack. They seem a discordant profanation of that beautiful sky. But the formation of Japanese planes, coming over one behind the other, is undisturbed.*
>
> *Now they are directly overhead. For the first time I see the bombs coming down, materializing suddenly out of nothingness and streaming toward us like ever-enlarging tear drops. There's a magnetic, hypnotic, limb-freezing fascination in that sight.*
>
> *It never occurs to me to try to duck or run. Open-mouthed and rooted, I watch the bombs getting larger and larger. Suddenly, ten yards from me, out in the water, a huge geyser springs out of the sea, and over the side, showering water over me and my camera.*[7]

The bombing was remarkably accurate. One bomb scored a direct hit on the catapult deck, exploding in the hangar below. It killed perhaps fifty people as bits of the ship cartwheeled through the air.

"Bloody good bombing for those blokes," remarked a gunner.[8]

Repulse in turn had shot down one of the Japanese aircraft. It burst into flames before crashing into the sea. Brown was intrigued to see no fear in the British sailors' faces as they fought back, nor any loathing of the enemy. They appeared to view the fight simply as a contest, a sort of sporting fixture with guns.

There were loudspeakers on every deck in *Repulse*, positioned at every action station. They had been drowned out by the noise of antiaircraft fire as the bombs rained down, but became audible again after the aircraft had departed. A dry-mouthed bugler struggled to hit the right notes as he blew the call that nobody ever wanted to hear at sea. *Fire*.

Prince of Wales was in trouble too. The battleship had reduced speed and was signaling that there was a man overboard. One of the destroyers was going alongside to help.

A few minutes' lull followed before a second wave of aircraft appeared. They carried torpedoes this time, far more dangerous than bombs at sea. They were flying at a much lower altitude, heading mostly for *Prince of Wales* as the larger, more important target of the two.

The aircraft broke formation as they came in to attack. Wheeling around, they closed in from all angles and directions, and from both sides of the two ships. They were a few hundred yards away, low over the water, when they dropped their torpedoes. Their gunners raked the ships with machine-gun fire as the planes turned away.

The torpedoes ran straight and true. Both ships were zigzagging frantically to escape, but there were too many torpedoes to avoid them all. *Prince of Wales* was hit in the stern. Two torpedoes destroyed the steering gear and propellers, effectively crippling the vessel for any further action.

The great battleship began to list soon afterward, hoisting the two black balls signal indicating that it was not under control. *Repulse* was luckier. Captain Tennant signaled Admiral Phillips aboard *Prince of Wales* to say that the cruiser had managed to dodge nineteen torpedoes so far, without once being hit.

It was about twelve twenty when a third wave of aircraft arrived. O. D. Gallagher of the *Daily Express* watched helplessly as they homed in on the stricken battleship:

All the aircraft made for her. I do not know how many there were in this last attack, but it was afterwards estimated that there were between fifty and eighty Japanese torpedo-bombers in operation during the entire action. Prince of Wales *fought desperately to beat off the determined killers who attacked her like a pack of dogs on a wounded buck. . . .*

I saw one plane drop a torpedo. It fell nose-heavy into the sea and churned up a thin wake as it drove straight at the immobile Prince of Wales. *It exploded against her bows. A couple of seconds later another hit her—and another.*

I gazed at her turning slowly over on her port side, her stern going under, and dots of men jumping into the sea, and was thrown against the bulkhead by a tremendous shock as Repulse *was hit by a torpedo on her port side.*[9]

Two more struck *Repulse* in quick succession, only seconds apart. The ship seemed to stagger as it lost speed and then began to list to port. A great cheer went up from the crew as the gunners downed another aircraft, but it was the last they gave on board. The ship was going down fast.

Five minutes after the attack began, Captain Tennant's voice came over the loudspeaker. "All hands on deck! Prepare to abandon ship. God be with you."[10]

Gallagher couldn't swim. He was glad of his life belt as he joined an orderly queue and followed it down the ladder to a lower deck, closer to the water. *Repulse* was already listing so far to port that it was possible to walk down the starboard side of the ship into the sea.

Taking a deep breath, Gallagher plunged into the water. He thought he was going to sink forever until his life belt buoyed him up. Knowing that he would be sucked down again when *Repulse* went under, he kicked away from the ship as soon as he surfaced, only to find himself in pools of fuel oil that felt as thick as velvet.

Brown found himself in the oil too, after taking a twenty-foot jump from the side of the hull. On the bridge, Captain Tennant was determined to go down with his ship, as Admiral Phillips was about to do aboard *Prince of Wales*. The other officers grabbed Tennant against his will and threw him into the sea instead to save his life.

Midshipman Christopher Bros wasn't so lucky. He was trapped with twenty-five men in the tiny transmitting station at the bottom of the ship. Water was pouring in faster than the men could escape.

Bros quelled the panic before ordering them out one by one, remaining until last himself. The others all managed to slip through the tiny hatch before the water rose too high. He was too late and drowned.

A dozen Royal Marines weren't so lucky either. They ran back toward the stern as *Repulse* went down, because it was less of a jump into the sea from there. The men misjudged it and were sucked into the still-turning propellers before they could escape, as Able Seaman Reg Wood recalled. "Men who hadn't got clear were caught in the turbulence from the propellers and catapulted into the air to a tremendous height. A lot of them landed near to me. All of them were dead."[11]

In the water, Lieutenant Richard Pool followed Gallagher in swimming away from the ship before turning back for a last look. The memory stayed with him for the rest of his life:

> I was just in time to see the last of her. About sixty feet of *Repulse's* bow was sticking out of the water, the sun glittering on her light grey topside and on her red anti-fouling bottom. The ship seemed to hang poised for a few seconds and then, to the accompaniment of subterranean rumblings, *Repulse* slid under the surface.[12]

The survivors gave three cheers for the "old girl" as she went down. They cheered Captain Tennant as well. He had handled the ship with remarkable skill to avoid nineteen torpedoes, even if the odds had been too great in the end. One of his officers paid tribute later:

> I shall be proud all my life to have served under such a Captain and with such men. The Captain was terrific. I was on the same Carley float as he and I can only say that he was so wonderful that I nearly burst into tears. And what a cheer the ship's company gave when they knew he was safe.[13]

Cecil Brown in the water nearby foolishly opened his mouth as *Repulse* sank. He took in a stomachful of oil as the wave swept over him. Fortunately the oil was a problem for the sharks and sea snakes as well. Between that and all the explosions, they posed little threat to the sailors as they grappled with the same difficulties and struggled to survive.

Somewhere in the distance, *Prince of Wales* was also about to go down, but Brown had no eyes for that anymore. Fifty miles out to sea, his head barely above the waves, all he could think about now was where they all went from here.

Next to him, two teenage sailors laughed and joked as they considered the same problem. Brown could hardly believe his ears as they decided that there was nothing for it but to swim back to Singapore, 150 miles away to the south.

"Race you," one of them said to the other.[14]

In fact the destroyers picked up a lot of the survivors, as many as they were able to find. It was simply a case of remaining afloat, clinging to the wreckage, and signaling frantically as the ships searched among the debris.

The Japanese left one aircraft behind to keep the two capital ships under observation until they sank. Some fighters arrived after a while, too late to join in the attack. The newcomers made no attempt to hinder the destroyers picking up survivors. A rumor circulated that they had actually signaled the destroyers to the contrary. "We have completed our task. You may carry on."[15]

Whatever the truth, the Japanese had certainly completed their task. In just over an hour, they had humbled the Royal Navy as it had never been humbled before. Only once since the Battle of Trafalgar in 1805 had British naval supremacy seriously been threatened by anybody: the Germans at Jutland in 1916. That battle had been a draw at worst.

The sinking of *Repulse* and *Prince of Wales* was an unmitigated disaster by comparison. A no-account navy from the Far East had taken on the British and won. Tinny little aircraft had done for the pride of the British fleet, despite the experts' assessment that such an attack against the latest anti-aircraft defenses could never hope to succeed.

The British were quick to learn the lessons. There were all sorts of conclusions to be drawn from the disaster off the Malayan coast, but one lesson stood out among all the rest. It was obvious to the survivors even as they waited in the water to be rescued. The age of the battleship was over.

TWENTY-THREE

HITLER AND MUSSOLINI DECLARE WAR ON THE UNITED STATES

Carrying just over two thousand survivors from *Repulse* and *Prince of Wales*, the three rescuing destroyers arrived back in Singapore toward midnight on December 10. One by one, HMS *Electra* and *Express*, and the Australian destroyer *Vampire*, tied up at the dockside and began to unload their cargoes of dead and wounded while stunned islanders waited to help.

Lines of ambulances stood ready in the darkness to receive the injured. Those who could still walk were helped ashore by medical orderlies and volunteers from other ships. There were cigarettes, sandwiches, and tots of rum for those who wanted them—unlimited amounts of rum, perhaps to make the men vomit up all the oil they had swallowed during the sinking.

Officers sat at dockside tables, recording each man's name, rank, and number before he was taken away. Some of the rescued men had died on the way back to port. Their bodies were covered in blankets as they came ashore on stretchers.

The able-bodied were driven away in buses, taken to the Fleet Shore Accommodation for a proper meal and a hot shower before being put to bed. *Repulse*'s officers were escorted to HMS *Exeter*, a few yards away along the dock, where a buffet supper had been set out in the wardroom.

With a bandage around his head, Captain Tennant was waiting to greet each officer individually as he entered. Despite the loss of his ship, Tennant's reputation was riding high after his adroit handling of *Repulse* during the action. His swift decision to order the abandoning of the ship at the end had saved countless lives.

After a few stiff whiskeys, *Repulse*'s officers were taken ashore to the Fleet Shore Accommodation, where they were issued with shirts, shorts, and washing gear. Then they headed to the officers' club for a long scrub in the shower before another lavish meal. It was almost dawn before they were able to collapse at last and fall asleep on the mattresses that had been laid out for them on the floor of the club.

Cecil Brown badly needed sleep, too, but his most urgent priority was to file his story. He had inquired with concern after his friend Gallagher as soon as he came ashore. Gallagher was alive and well, which was good news. He was already on his way to Singapore to tell the story, which was bad.

Brown had to get there too. With Captain Tennant's aid, he managed to procure a car with a Malay driver to take him the eighteen miles to Singapore in the middle of the night. Brown just had time to note the deep pain in Tennant's eyes as he shook hands with him in *Exeter*'s wardroom before hurrying ashore. In pouring rain he drove straight to the press office to give the world a personal account of the calamity he had just witnessed in the South China Sea. It was the biggest scoop of his career.

In fact the world already knew about the sinkings, if not the full details. Japanese naval headquarters in Tokyo had issued a statement within a few minutes of *Prince of Wales* going down. The news was immediately broadcast on Tokyo radio. By 3:53 p.m., Singapore time, Japan's Domei news agency was also broadcasting the story in English.

British warships on the same wavelength as the two ships had followed the disaster as it unfolded. At the naval base in Singapore, news of the sinkings was flashed to the Admiralty in London at 1:45 p.m., just over twenty minutes after *Prince of Wales* had gone down. There was no chance of keeping it secret from the local population, so Duff Cooper went on Singapore radio that evening to say what had happened.

He invoked the Dunkirk spirit as he spoke. "This is not the first time in our long history of glory that we have met with disaster and have surmounted it. Indeed there is something in our nature and of our fathers before us, that only disaster can produce."[1]

In London, Winston Churchill had only just woken up when he heard. He was still in bed, going through the paperwork in his dispatch box, when Sir Dudley Pound, the First Sea Lord, telephoned:

> *His voice sounded odd. He gave a sort of cough and gulp, and at first I could not hear quite clearly. "Prime Minister, I have to report to you that the* Prince of Wales *and the* Repulse *have both been sunk by the Japanese—we think by aircraft. Tom Phillips is drowned."*
>
> *"Are you sure it's true?"*
>
> *"There is no doubt at all."*
>
> *So I put the telephone down. I was thankful to be alone. In all the war I never received a more direct shock. . . . As I turned over and twisted in bed the full horror of the news sank in upon me. There were no British or American capital ships in the Indian Ocean or the Pacific except the American survivors of Pearl Harbor, who were hastening back to California. Over all this vast expanse of waters Japan was supreme, and we everywhere were weak and naked.*[2]

The House of Commons met at 11:00 a.m. After standing up and sitting down twice, Churchill made a short statement about the sinking at 11:32. He had been assuring people since Pearl Harbor that all wasn't lost in the Pacific because at least *Repulse* and *Prince of Wales* were still afloat. Now he had to admit that they were gone too.

The news was released to the press and radio at the same time as Churchill spoke. It was the lead story in all the evening newspapers. By early evening almost everyone in Britain had heard what had happened. A shocked nation could scarcely believe it. The Royal Navy had been trounced by the

Japanese, suffering a blow to its prestige from which it would never fully recover.

Harold Nicolson summed up the people's mood in his diary:

The sinking of the Prince of Wales *has made an impression out of all proportion. They ignore the Russian victories, the Libyan advance and the entry of America. They are faced with the fact that two of our greatest battleships have been sunk within a few minutes by the monkey men, and that we and the Americans have between us lost command of the Pacific.*[3]

What would happen now? Nicolson had offered to bet Charles de Gaulle, leader of the Free French in London, that Germany would certainly declare war on the United States. *"Jamais de la vie,"* de Gaulle had adamantly replied.[4] He had refused to take the bet, though, in case events proved Nicolson right. In a world growing crazier by the minute, anything seemed possible.

A few hours after the sinking, four American destroyers arrived in the area to search for any remaining survivors. The ships had been in Singapore when the call for help went out. They found oil and debris on the surface, and a few floating bodies, but nobody still alive.

Repulse and *Prince of Wales* lay on the seabed by then, several miles apart. Both had sunk to about two hundred feet. They were clearly visible from the air when the weather was good and the sea was calm, but less easily spotted from water level.

A week after the attack, one of the men who had sunk *Repulse* returned to view his handiwork. Lieutenant Haruki Iki had been in the last wave of torpedo bombers to attack the cruiser. He had dropped his torpedo from a hundred feet before shouting "Banzai!" and heading triumphantly back to base.

Iki was in the area again on December 18, reconnoitering the Anambas Islands. After completing his mission, he took a short detour to see the sunken ships, circling both at about six hundred feet.

Iki had two bouquets of flowers with him. One was to honor the men of his squadron who hadn't returned from the raid. The other was to salute the British sailors who had gone down with their ships.

Despite their jubilation and the cries of "Banzai!," the Japanese had taken no pleasure in the sinking of the two vessels, beyond a job well done. They weren't the "monkey men" of Harold Nicolson's imagination. They had modeled their own service on the Royal Navy and had always had good relations with the British in times of peace.

It was part of Buddhist culture that there were no enemies in death. It was in Japan's ancient Bushido code, too, that men who had died bravely in battle, as the sailors and airmen all had, should be honored after death.

Iki's bouquets were composed of mixed flowers, with a lot of hibiscus. He dropped the first over *Repulse* to commemorate the two aircraft from his flight shot down by the cruiser. Then he flew on to *Prince of Wales* and dropped the second in memory of the 840 British sailors who had lost their lives as the two ships went down. In Japanese eyes they were all good men in death.

Back in England, the disaster was still fresh in Winston Churchill's mind as he rose to address the House of Commons at midday on December 11. He had undertaken to give the members a fuller briefing about the disasters in the Far East:

> No one must underrate the gravity of the loss which has been inflicted in Malaya and Hawaii, or the power of the new antagonist who has fallen upon us, or the length of time it will take to create, marshal, and mount the great force in the Far East which will be necessary to achieve absolute victory . . .
>
> Not only the British Empire now but the United States are fighting for life; Russia is fighting for life, and China is fighting for life. Behind these four great combatant communities are ranged all the spirit and hopes of all the conquered countries in Europe, prostrate under the cruel domination of the foe.[5]

Churchill concluded by reminding the House that about four-fifths of the human race would be on the Allies' side in the long struggle that lay ahead. In his view that number was an underestimate, if anything.

Even as Churchill was sitting down after his speech, Hitler and Mussolini were preparing to stand up and declare war on the United States. They had arranged to begin their speeches at the same time, 3:00 p.m., and make the announcement soon afterward. Given the chance thus to sign their own death warrants, both men had seized it with alacrity.

The American Embassy in Rome was surrounded by policemen as the diplomats burned their codebooks that morning. The Italians on the staff were in tears as chargé d'affaires George Wadsworth was summoned to the Foreign Office to hear the declaration of war. He duly presented himself to Count Ciano at 2:30 p.m., as requested:

> Count Ciano received me most brusquely, so unlike his usual, promiscuously friendly manner. When I walked into his office he halted me halfway to his desk by rising, making it quite clear that I was not to sit down.
>
> With a scowl on his face he recited his piece as though he had learned it by heart, saying in one sentence that he must inform me that Italy considered herself at war with the United States. I bowed my head and said, "I'm very sorry to hear it."[6]

Wadsworth notified the State Department as soon as the interview was over. There was no need to encode the message. The Italians allowed him to send it direct from their Foreign Office without making him go back to his own embassy.

Mussolini announced the war a few minutes later, as agreed with Hitler. He addressed a large crowd from the balcony of the Palazzo Venezia, his usual platform for such announcements. It was from that same balcony that he had declared war on France and Britain in June 1940.

With France defeated and the British about to surrender, Mussolini had been cheered by a crowd of thousands when he took Italy into the war on the Axis side. Without the matériel or natural resources for a long struggle, he had expected to seize parts of France and large tracts of Britain's East African possessions in return for minimal Italian participation.

Instead the British had sunk Italian battleships and shot down the Italian bombers sent to join the Luftwaffe in the Blitz. Far from surrendering East Africa, they had kicked the Italians out of Abyssinia and Somaliland and made so much trouble for them in Libya that Mussolini had been forced to call on the Germans for help.

The crowd in the square was accordingly less than ecstatic when Mussolini told them that Italy was now at war with the United States as well. Some of them had been hoping to hear that the war would be over soon, not that it was about to escalate:

> *The powers of the steel pact, Fascist Italy and National Socialist Germany, ever closely linked, participate from today on the side of heroic Japan against the United States of America. . . .*
>
> *Italians! Once more arise and be worthy of this historical hour! Victory will be ours.*[7]

Mussolini's fine words were received by a largely skeptical audience. Sunny June had given way to cold December in the Piazza Venezia. Count Ciano was there to hear his father-in-law speak:

> *Mussolini gave a speech from the balcony—a brief and cutting speech, which fell on a great crowd. A very pro-Japanese setting. News of the naval victories has excited the Italian imagination.*
>
> *The demonstration, however, was not very enthusiastic. We must not forget that it was three o'clock in the afternoon, the people were hungry, and the day was quite cold. These are all elements which do not create enthusiasm.*[8]

Mussolini's speech was suitably brief for a cold winter's day. Hitler's was much longer. Indoors at the Kroll Opera House (the Reichstag was still in ruins after the fire of 1933), he harangued the Reischstag deputies for almost an hour and a half before reaching the purpose of his address at last and winding up his tirade.

Dwarfed by the enormous German eagle on stage behind him, Hitler began by denouncing Churchill's refusal to make peace in 1940, so necessitating a war against all reason and common sense. He talked about Rome, Carthage, and ancient Greece, deploring all the burning, looting, and murder by barbarous people from the East that only civilized countries like Germany could forestall.

Hitler thanked God for giving him the vision to see that the Soviet Union was about to launch an invasion of Europe. He was grateful that he had had the foresight to attack first, doing what had to be done. He complained of the Jews and Roosevelt, listing at interminable length all the help the United States had so far given Britain in the war, in breach of all the rules of neutrality.

He had been speaking for well over an hour when he came finally to the point of his oration:

> In the whole history of the German nation, of nearly 2,000 years, it has never been so united as today and, thanks to National Socialism, it will remain united in the future. Probably it has never seen so clearly, and rarely been so conscious of its honor.
>
> I have therefore arranged for his passports to be handed to the American chargé d'affaires today. . . .⁹

The rest was lost in applause as the members of the Reichstag rose to their feet as one and cheered loudly for their own destruction.

Hitler's speech was relayed by loudspeaker to the crowds in Pariser Platz. A mob had earlier appeared out of nowhere and was standing menacingly outside the American Embassy while the Führer spoke. The diplomats inside closed the metal blinds on the windows and waited uneasily for the attack to come.

A telephone rang instead. The diplomats were informed that an official car was on its way to collect Leland Morris, the chargé d'affaires. He was to be taken to the Foreign Office on Wilhelmstrasse. Foreign Minister Ribbentrop had something to say to him.

Morris complied. He was ushered into Ribbentrop's presence. Paul Schmidt, the interpreter, liked Morris and felt sorry for him as Ribbentrop curtly read out a statement without inviting Morris to sit down:

> *The Government of the United States having violated in the most flagrant manner and in ever increasing measure all rules of neutrality in favor of the adversaries of Germany and having continually been guilty of the most severe provocations toward Germany ever since the outbreak of the European war, provoked by the British declaration of war against Germany on September 3, 1939, has finally resorted to open military acts of aggression . . .*
>
> *The German Government, consequently, discontinues diplomatic relations with the United States of America and declares that under these circumstances brought about by President Roosevelt Germany too, as from today, considers herself as being in a state of war with the United States of America.*[10]

With a theatrical flourish, Ribbentrop handed the document to Morris when he had finished. He gave the American a stiff bow to indicate that the audience was terminated.

"Your President has wanted this war. Now he has it," Ribbentrop added contemptuously as he spun on his heel and turned away.[11]

The Americans hanged him five years later.

EPILOGUE: REFLECTIONS FROM LATER LIFE

A dmiral Kimmel lost his job a few days after Pearl Harbor, as did General Short. Both men were demoted and recalled to the United States. At the subsequent inquiry into the attack, they pointed out that all sorts of things beyond their control had gone wrong on that awful day. Nevertheless they were censured for serious errors of judgment and dereliction of duty.

It was certainly true that plenty of others deserved to share the blame. Arguing that Kimmel and Short had been made scapegoats for failings in Washington, the U.S. Senate passed a nonbinding resolution in 1999. By 52 votes to 47, the Senate declared that Kimmel and Short had performed their duties competently and professionally and were not guilty of dereliction of duty.

The resolution repeated earlier calls for the two men to be posthumously restored to their full wartime rank. No president has ever complied.

Private James Jones later saw action on Guadalcanal, but was discharged from the army in 1944 after injuring his ankle. His first novel, *From Here to Eternity*, was published to great acclaim in 1951. Closely based on his Pearl

Harbor experiences, it was followed in 1962 by *The Thin Red Line*, a similar account of the fierce fighting on Guadalcanal. Both novels later became award-winning movies.

Edgar Rice Burroughs resumed his writing career after Pearl Harbor and sent Tarzan into battle. After fighting the Germans in North Africa, Tarzan joined the RAF and took a crack at the Japanese in *Tarzan and the Foreign Legion*.

As Burroughs told it, Tarzan was hitching a ride on a U.S. Liberator when it was shot down by the Japanese in Sumatra. Struggling to survive in the jungle, the American crew thought the English lord was a typical stuffed shirt until they saw him kill a tiger with his knife—standard operating procedure for British peers in the RAF.

Noel and Michael Cunningham-Reid were removed from Oahu after the Japanese attack and later went to live on Doris Duke's estate in New Jersey. After a visit to the dentist in Princeton, Noel fell into conversation with an agreeable old gent in a bus shelter who turned out to be Albert Einstein.

The boys returned to the United Kingdom after Germany's surrender and were in time to celebrate V-J Day at school in England. Noel later became a racing driver before taking over the running of the family estate. Michael joined their stepfather, Lord Delamere, in Kenya, remaining there for the rest of his life.

After his Pearl Harbor scoop, Frank Tremaine directed United Press's coverage of the Pacific theater for the remainder of the war. He was rewarded with a ringside seat aboard USS *Missouri* when the Japanese surrendered to General MacArthur in 1945.

The ceremony took place in Tokyo Bay, only a few miles from where Cdre. Perry had humiliated the Japanese in 1853. Tremaine watched from a 16-inch gun turret above the deck. He then became UP's first postwar bureau chief in Tokyo and remained with the news agency for the rest of his working life.

Without the benefit of diplomatic protection, the hapless German spy Bernard Kühn was found guilty of espionage in February 1942 and sentenced to execution "by musketry." The sentence was commuted to fifty years' hard labor after he agreed to tell the authorities everything he knew about the German and Japanese spy networks in Hawaii.

Kühn's wife and daughter also went to prison. All three were deported to Germany after the war.

Takeo Yoshikawa managed to destroy all evidence of his spying activities on the morning of Pearl Harbor. With no grounds for detaining him, the Americans allowed him to be repatriated to Japan with the other diplomats from the Honolulu consulate.

Yoshikawa didn't prosper at home. He remained in naval intelligence for the rest of the war, but went into hiding during the American occupation of Japan, fearing prosecution for his part in the attack.

Disguised as a Buddhist monk, Yoshikawa didn't surface again until after the Americans had left. He then opened a candy store, only to find himself shunned by ordinary Japanese as word of his spying activities spread. He was blamed for starting the war and was sometimes even held responsible for the dropping of the atomic bomb.

Abandoned by the Japanese government, unpopular with ordinary people, Yoshikawa had great trouble finding work. He was eventually forced to live off his wife for the rest of his life. She sold insurance.

Kazuo Sakamaki didn't prosper either. As the only survivor of the ten midget submariners who attacked Pearl Harbor, he suffered great ignominy at home after becoming the first Japanese to be taken prisoner by the Americans during the war.

Sakamaki's name was officially expunged from Japanese records when it was learned that he had failed to commit suicide rather than fall into enemy hands. His minisub had been captured too, instead of being scuttled, as it should have been.

The vessel was later taken on a tour of the United States to encourage the purchase of war bonds. Reunited with it at a fiftieth-anniversary conference in Texas in 1991, Sakamaki apparently burst into tears at the sight.

Admiral Yamamoto fared far worse than either Yoshikawa or Sakamaki. Although he disapproved of the attack on Pearl Harbor, he had planned it with great efficiency. The Americans marked his card accordingly.

After the Japanese defeat on Guadalcanal, Yamamoto set off on a morale-boosting tour of the South Pacific. The U.S. Navy decrypted the schedule in advance, including the timing of his flights and the type of aircraft that he would be using.

President Roosevelt gave the go-ahead for Yamamoto to be shot down. On April 18, 1943, a squadron of long-range P-38 Lightnings did just that. They intercepted Yamamoto's aircraft over Bougainville in the Solomon Islands and sent it crashing into the jungle with its port engine in flames. A Japanese search party found Yamamoto's body the next day with an American bullet through his head.

After leading the attack on Pearl Harbor, Mitsuo Fuchida was granted an audience with Emperor Hirohito and became a national hero. He was outraged after the war when the United States put Japanese soldiers on trial for war crimes. The men were accused of torturing and maltreating American prisoners of war.

In Japanese culture, suicide was preferable to surrender. Soldiers who put their hands up had disgraced themselves and deserved no respect. They had forfeited the right to considerate treatment.

Convinced that the American handling of Japanese captives would have been no better, Fuchida sought evidence from returning prisoners of war early in 1947. He was surprised to hear that, far from being tortured by the Americans, the prisoners had been treated very well, with Christian forgiveness.

The idea of turning the other cheek instead of seeking the revenge that Bushido demanded was new to Fuchida. Intrigued, he decided to learn more about Christianity. He soon became a convert, touring the United States in 1952 as a member of the Worldwide Christian Missionary Army of Sky Pilots.

The cruiser USS *Phoenix* was one of the few large warships to escape the attention of Fuchida's pilots at Pearl Harbor. Anchored off Ford Island, the ship escaped without a scratch and quickly put to sea in a fruitless search for the Japanese aircraft carriers.

After continuous war service, *Phoenix* was sold to the Argentinian navy in 1951. Renamed *General Belgrano*, the cruiser was sunk by a British submarine during the Falklands War of 1982.

Greer Garson and the cast of *Mrs. Miniver* returned to work after Pearl Harbor, shooting a revised script that left no doubt where the movie's sympathies lay. Henry Wilcoxon, the actor playing the vicar, had lost a brother at Dunkirk. The last scene of the movie, when he explained to a grieving congregation exactly what it was the British were fighting for, had a massive impact around the world.

Winston Churchill reckoned *Mrs. Miniver* was worth several battleships to the Allied cause. Even Germany's propaganda minister Goebbels was impressed. The England portrayed in the film was unrecognizable to the British, but it was a smash hit on both sides of the Atlantic, the biggest success of Greer Garson's career.

The script of the Humphrey Bogart vehicle *Aloha Means Goodbye* also had to be reworked after Pearl Harbor. Instead of a Japanese attack on Hawaii, it became an assault on the Panama Canal under the new title *Across the Pacific*. Bogart, Mary Astor, and Sidney Greenstreet did their best with it, but failed to recapture the magic of *The Maltese Falcon*.

Bogart then starred in another movie, originally entitled *Everybody Comes to Rick's*. The anti-Nazi script, set in Vichy-controlled North Africa, had not found a buyer in the strictly neutral isolationist days before Pearl Harbor. A few days after the attack, it was snapped up by Warner Bros. for twenty thousand dollars and retitled *Casablanca*.

Kirk Douglas tried to join the U.S. Air Force to drop bombs on the Nazis, but failed the aptitude tests. Lacking the necessary quick reflexes for aircrew training, he joined the U.S. Navy instead and dropped depth charges on Japanese submarines.

One of the charges exploded prematurely in shallow water, putting Douglas in hospital for five months with serious internal injuries. He was honorably discharged from the navy in 1944.

Lance-Corporal Dirk Bogarde became an infantry officer in 1943 and served in northwest Europe, India, and Java. The experience lent authority to the many officer roles that he later played on stage and screen.

Despite his small size, Audie Murphy managed to join the U.S. Army in 1942 and had an outstanding war. He saw action in Sicily, Italy, and France, won the Medal of Honor at nineteen and became an American hero, one of the country's most decorated combat soldiers.

Murphy took to acting after the war, playing himself in the 1955 biopic *To Hell and Back* and variations of himself in several Westerns. He suffered intermittently from the condition now known as post-traumatic stress disorder and is buried in Arlington National Cemetery.

Like Murphy, J. D. Salinger managed to join the army in 1942, despite his minor heart defect. He landed on Utah Beach on D-day and later fought in the Battle of the Bulge. He married a German woman immediately after the war, but the marriage broke up upon his return to the United States. *The Catcher in the Rye*, Salinger's seminal novel of teenage alienation, was published in 1951.

Norman Mailer had an undistinguished war. He did everything he could to defer being drafted, claiming that he was involved in important literary work relevant to the war effort. Unimpressed, the army drafted him anyway and sent him to the Philippines as a cook.

Mailer saw no action, although he did once go out on a patrol. Like James Jones, he used his military experience in his first novel, *The Naked and the Dead*. Published in 1948, the book was a huge success at the time, although much less admired now.

Kurt Vonnegut volunteered for the army rather than wait to be called up. He was taken prisoner at the Battle of the Bulge and sent to Dresden, the first beautiful city he had ever seen. Vonnegut was sheltering in an underground slaughterhouse during the Allied bombing raids of February 13 and 14, 1945, which reduced the city to rubble.

He helped recover the bodies afterward, an experience that stayed with him for the rest of his life. Like Jones and Mailer, Vonnegut made good use of his wartime experience in his literary work, most notably *Slaughterhouse Five*, a masterly indictment of the futility of war.

Paradoxically, the raids on Dresden that disgusted Kurt Vonnegut probably saved Victor Klemperer's life. With an Aryan wife and a good military record from World War I, he was one of the last Jews in the city awaiting a summons for "resettlement" in the East. The summons was imminent when Allied bombs destroyed the list of Jews at Gestapo headquarters.

Tearing off the hated yellow star, Klemperer wasted no time reinventing himself as a displaced German who had lost his identity card in the raids. He was issued with temporary papers and set off at once for Bavaria, where no one could recognize and unmask him. Klemperer and his wife were in a little village near Dachau when the Americans arrived. He later had a distinguished career as a university professor in East Germany.

Otto Frank and his family went into hiding in July 1942. After being betrayed to the Germans, they were sent to Auschwitz, where Otto's wife died. His daughters, Anne and Margot, died in Belsen, leaving behind only Anne's diary of her time in hiding, which had been kept safe by a family friend.

Menachem Begin reached Palestine in May 1942 and joined the Irgun in December. There was strong disagreement among Zionists about whether to attack the British in Palestine when they were the ones fighting the Nazis. Begin was in no doubt that force was necessary. He thought it was the only way to secure Palestine for the Jews.

Under Begin's leadership the Irgun began a hit-and-run guerrilla campaign against the British in February 1944. In July 1946 Begin ordered the bombing of the King David Hotel in Jerusalem and the hanging of two British sergeants whose booby-trapped bodies were then strung up in a eucalyptus grove. He was awarded the Nobel Peace Prize in 1978.

Chaim Herzog never shared Begin's dislike of the British. As a Haganah-activist-turned-British-army-officer, he saw the concentration camps in Germany in 1945 and had a brief glimpse of Himmler after his capture by British troops. Herzog became president of Israel in 1983.

Reinhard Heydrich's infamous conference at the Wannsee was postponed until January 20, 1942. Plans for implementing the "final solution" to the Jewish problem went into operation soon afterward. Heydrich didn't live to see the full fruits of his work. He was attacked by Czech partisans at the end of May and died of his injuries a week later, the first leading Nazi to pay the price for his crimes.

Friedrich Jeckeln, the SS officer responsible for the murder of 25,000 Jews over two days at Rumbula, as well as 33,000 over two days at Babi Yar in Ukraine, was captured by Soviet troops in April 1945. He admitted his guilt and took full responsibility for what his subordinates had done.

Jeckeln was tried by a Soviet military court at the end of January 1946. Apparently repentant, he nevertheless acknowledged the justice of a death sentence for his crimes. He and several others were hanged on a communal outdoor gallows at Riga on February 3, 1946.

Four thousand people came to watch as flatbed trucks backed onto the gallows tree. The prisoners were held down as nooses were placed around their necks. Then the trucks drove away, leaving the Nazis to swing in the wind until they were dead.

Ezra Pound continued to make anti-Semitic broadcasts on Italian radio for much of the war. He was arrested by the U.S. Army in May 1945 and taken to the United States to stand trial for treason. Pound pleaded insanity and spent the next twelve years in St. Elizabeth's, a psychiatric hospital in Washington, D.C. He returned to Italy after his release in 1958.

Second Lieutenant Bob Dole of the U.S. Army was badly wounded in

Italy in April 1945. Paralyzed in both arms and legs, prey to all sorts of hospital infections, he wasn't expected to live for more than a few days. Dole recovered eventually, although he was never able to lift his right arm above his head again. He became a Republican senator for Kansas and ran for president in 1996 against Bill Clinton.

CBS reporter Cecil Brown had been expelled from Italy in 1941 for his hostility toward the regime. He was so critical of the British in Singapore after the sinking of HMS *Repulse* that his war correspondent credentials were revoked there too, and he was declared persona non grata.

Brown then fell out with CBS in 1943 after expressing a personal opinion about the war in a news broadcast. He spent the rest of the war reporting for the Mutual Broadcasting Company.

After escaping from Beijing, Michael Lindsay and his wife hid with guerrillas for two years before walking five hundred miles across Japanese-held territory to reach Mao Tse-tung's headquarters at Yan'an. Mao himself welcomed them at dinner.

The Lindsays' son, James, was born in a hospital cave at Yan'an in 1945. In due course James inherited the family title and became Baron Lindsay of Birker. Probably the only hereditary British peer to have been born in a cave in China, he is certainly the only one to have been born at Communist Party headquarters.

Emperor Hirohito retained his throne after the war. There has always been controversy about how much responsibility he should have borne for Pearl Harbor, as Japan's supreme ruler. Allied lawyers were firmly of the view that he should have been prosecuted with the other war criminals, instead of being granted immunity and allowed to get away with it.

Hirohito was nevertheless permitted to remain in place. If any guilt attached to him, it was quietly redistributed among Japan's other war leaders, leaving him free to preside as a figurehead over the postwar reconstruction of a modern, nonmilitarist Japan that posed no threat to its neighbors. Hirohito died in 1989.

By contrast, there was never any doubt about Tojo's guilt. The former prime minister tried to commit suicide when the Americans came for him in September 1945, but succeeded only in shooting himself in the chest without hitting the heart. Tojo underwent surgery in a U.S. Army hospital and was then taken to Sugamo Prison in Tokyo to await trial.

He was fitted with false teeth while he waited. U.S. Army dentures were engraved with the owner's name for identification purposes, but the navy's Jack Mallory decided to do something different for Tojo. He engraved the words "Remember Pearl Harbor" instead.

Mallory engraved them in Morse code, so that Tojo wouldn't notice, but the joke soon reached higher authority. The naval dentist was ordered to reclaim the teeth from a puzzled Tojo and grind the words away before returning them to their owner.

Once Tojo was restored to health, he and the other ringleaders faced an international military tribunal on multiple charges of waging aggressive war in violation of international law. Tojo was also accused of "ordering, authorizing and permitting inhumane treatment of prisoners of war and others." He disputed the charges, but took full responsibility for anything that Japan had done. He was sentenced to death in November 1948.

The sentence was carried out at Sugamo just after midnight on December 23. Tojo was summoned to the chaplain's office the day before to learn the exact time. He was weighed on a set of scales before leaving the room so that the hangman would know exactly how much rope to give him.

Twenty minutes before the appointed hour, American guards collected Tojo and three other condemned men from their cells and took them to the Buddhist chapel for a brief religious ceremony and a final sip of wine. After giving three "Banzais" for the emperor, the men surrendered their dentures and spectacles and handed over traditional parcels of hair and nail clippings for delivery to their families. They were then led across the courtyard to the execution block.

Tojo's request to die in his smartest uniform had been refused. Without teeth or spectacles, he cut a sorry figure in U.S. Army fatigues with a large P (for "prisoner") on the back. At the entrance to the execution chamber, he was formally identified in front of witnesses from Britain, China, the Soviet Union, and the United States.

He then climbed the thirteen steps to the gallows unaided. A hood went over his head and the noose was tightened. He was dispatched at once, just over a minute after entering the room. He was officially dead by ten and a half minutes past midnight.

Tojo's body was cremated later that morning. As with the Nazi leaders at Nuremberg, his ashes were scattered secretly so that no trace of him would remain to become a shrine, although rumors to the contrary persist.

Today Tojo is one of fourteen Class-A war criminals venerated at Tokyo's Yasukuni Shrine, a memorial to almost two and a half million men, women, and children who have died in the service of Japan. Class-A war criminals are those found guilty of waging aggressive war or committing crimes against peace.

The international tribunal's verdict against Tojo was not unanimous. There was no such thing as a Class-A war criminal until the victorious Allies invented the term after the war. Judges from India, France, and the Netherlands therefore voiced doubts about finding the Japanese guilty in retrospect.

In the end, only India's Radhabinod Pal was prepared to find all the defendants not guilty of Class-A war crimes. He was fully aware of Japanese atrocities—Class-B and -C crimes, in his opinion—but argued that the United States had deliberately provoked the Japanese into war. He saw the trial of Tojo and the other defendants as a "sham employment of legal process for the satisfaction of a thirst for revenge."

Many Japanese shared Pal's view. There is a memorial to him at Yasukuni. The shrine is a place of pilgrimage for Tokyo residents, a popular day out.

As the Japanese see it, they were the victims of a war against Britain and the United States that had to be fought to preserve their independence. The dropping of atomic bombs on Hiroshima and Nagasaki was the real crime. The Japanese visiting Yasukuni are in no doubt about that. Their own atrocities against tens of thousands of helpless people over a large swath of the Far East are never mentioned at Yasukuni. Nor is Pearl Harbor.

NOTES

CHAPTER 1. WHERE ARE JAPAN'S AIRCRAFT CARRIERS?

1. Heinrich Haape, *Moscow Tram Stop* (London: Collins, 1957), p. 203.
2. Ibid.
3. Ibid., p. 205.
4. Max Domarus, *Hitler: Reden und Proklamationen 1932–1945* (Munich: Süddeutscher Verlag, 1965), p. 1788.
5. Steven Lehrer, *Wannsee House and the Holocaust* (London: McFarland & Co., 2001), p. 143.
6. Ibid., p. 144.

CHAPTER 2. STILL A CHANCE TO CALL IT OFF

1. "Campaign Address at Boston, Massachusetts," October 30, 1940. Online by Gerhard Peters and John T. Woolley, The American Presidency Project.www.presidency.ucsb.edu/ws/?pid=15887.
2. *Public Papers of the Presidents of the United States* (Washington: U.S. Government Printing Office, various dates).
3. Scott Eyman, *Lion of Hollywood* (London: Robson, 2005), p. 345.
4. Axel Madsen, *William Wyler* (London: W. H. Allen, 1974), p. 216.
5. Ibid.
6. Stefan Kanfer, *Tough without a Gun* (London: Faber, 2011), p. 72.

7. Duff Cooper, *Old Men Forget* (London: Hart-Davis, 1953), p. 300.

8. Diana Cooper, *Trumpets from the Steep* (London: Hart-Davis, 1960), p. 127.

9. Edwin Hoyt, *Hirohito* (New York: Praeger, 1992), p. 125.

10. Gordon Prange, *At Dawn We Slept* (New York: Penguin, 1982), p. 11.

11. Leonard Mosley, *Hirohito* (London: Weidenfeld & Nicolson, 1966), p. 254.

12. *Meiji Japan through Contemporary Sources*, vol. 2 (Tokyo: Center for East Asian Cultural Studies, 1973), p. 16.

CHAPTER 3. ALL QUIET IN THE PACIFIC

1. Terry Crowdy, *The Enemy Within* (Oxford: Osprey, 2006), p. 281.

2. Takeo Yoshikawa and Norman Stanford, "Top Secret Assignment," *US Naval Institute Proceedings*, December 1960.

3. Franklin Odo, *No Sword to Bury* (Philadelphia: Temple University Press, 2004), p. 90.

4. Ibid., p. 93.

5. George Hendrick, *James Jones and the Handy Writers' Colony* (Carbondale: Southern Illinois University Press, 2001), p. 22.

6. James Jones, *To Reach Eternity* (New York: Random House, 1996), p. 11.

7. James Jones, *From Here to Eternity* (Bath, England: Chivers Press, 1980), p. 203.

8. Richard Greer, "Dousing Honolulu's Red Lights," *Hawaiian Journal of History* 34 (2000), p. 190.

CHAPTER 4. JAPANESE FORCES ON THE MOVE

1. Charles Beard, *President Roosevelt and the Coming of the War* (New Haven: Yale University Press, 1954), p. 532.

2. Elliott Roosevelt, *The Roosevelt Letters, vol. III* (London: Harrap, 1952), p. 403.

3. H. O. Thompson, "How Japan Planned War," *Nevada State Journal*, December 5, 1942, p. 1.

4. Gwen Terasaki, *Bridge to the Sun* (London: Michael Joseph, 1958), p. 76.

5. Siegfried Knappe, *Soldat* (Ramsbury, England: Airlife, 1993), p. 205.

6. Robert Kershaw, *War without Garlands* (Hersham, England: Ian Allan, 2008), p. 530.

7. Hans von Luck, *Panzer Commander* (New York: Praeger, 1989), p. 64.

8. Ibid.

CHAPTER 5. ADMIRAL NAGUMO HOISTS A SIGNAL

1. Donald Goldstein, *The Pearl Harbor Papers* (Washington: Brassey's, 1993), p. 191.

2. http://www.pearlharboronline.com/13parts.htm.

3. Ibid.

4. Ibid.

5. *Pearl Harbor Attack* (*PHA*), U.S. Congress, Joint Congressional Committee on the Investigation of the Pearl Harbor Attack (Washington: U.S. Government Printing Office, 1946) (hereafter cited as *PHA*), part 12, pp. 238–39.

6. Ibid., p. 245.

7. Ibid., part 20, p. 4528.

8. Ibid.

9. Ibid., pp. 4530–31.

10. Ibid., pp. 4534–35.

11. Joseph Grew, *Ten Years in Japan* (London: Hammond, 1944), p. 421.

12. Ibid., p. 422.

13. Ibid., p. 423.

14. Cordell Hull, *The Memoirs of Cordell Hull* (London: Hodder & Stoughton, 1949), p. 1094.

CHAPTER 6. WHERE ARE AMERICA'S AIRCRAFT CARRIERS?

1. Bonner Fellers, letter to Admiral Kimmel, March 6, 1967, Thomas Kimmel collection.

2. Ibid.

3. Edward Hudson, obituary, *New York Times*, October 28, 1987.

4. Cecil Brown, *Suez to Singapore* (New York: Random House, 1942), p. 286.

5. John Beck, *MacArthur and Wainwright* (Albuquerque: University of New Mexico Press, 1976), p. 9.

6. John Peck, *Honolulu Star-Bulletin*, December 7, 1941, p. 7.

7. Crowdy, *The Enemy Within*, p. 282.

8. *PHA*, part 12, p. 270.

9. Donald Goldstein, *The Pearl Harbor Papers* (Washington: Brassey's, 1994), p. 156.

CHAPTER 7. "THE JAPANESE WILL NOT GO TO WAR"

1. John Toland, *Infamy* (London: Methuen, 1982), p. 4.

2. Beard, *President Roosevelt and the Coming of the War*, p. 549.

3. Ibid., p. 550.

4. Joseph Grew, *Turbulent Era* (London: Hammond, 1953), p. 1250.

5. Gordon Prange, *December 7, 1941* (London: Harrap, 1989), p. 21.

CHAPTER 8. AN ENGLISHWOMAN DANCES ON DECK

1. Walter Lord, *Day of Infamy* (New York: Henry Holt, 1957), p. 19.

2. Prange, *December 7, 1941*, p. 48.
3. Lord, *Day of Infamy*, p. 22.
4. Gordon Prange, interview with Fuchida, December 10, 1963, quoted in *December 7, 1941*, p. 404, n. 82
5. Lord, *Day of Infamy*, p. 25.

CHAPTER 9. A STRANGE PERISCOPE AT SEA

1. *PHA*, part 12, p. 248.
2. Ibid., part 36, pp. 57, 59.
3. Ibid., part 37, p. 705.
4. Blaine Taylor, *Pearl Harbor's WWII Collector's Edition: The Official 50th Anniversary Magazine*, 1991.
5. *PHA*, part 32, p. 479.
6. Ibid., part 22, p. 221.

CHAPTER 10. "TORA! TORA! TORA!"

1. Prange, *December 7, 1941*, p. 67.
2. Ibid., p. 101.
3. Ibid., p. 103.
4. Ibid., p. 93.

CHAPTER 11. A JAPANESE PILOT GRINS AT JAMES JONES

1. James Jones, *To Reach Eternity* (New York: Random House, 1996), p. 16.
2. Prange, *December 7, 1941*, p. 140.
3. Ibid., p. 144.
4. Lord, *Day of Infamy*, p. 73
5. Prange, *December 7, 1941*, p. 158
6. Toland, *Infamy*, p. 11.
7. Prange, *December 7, 1941*, p. 151
8. John Deane Potter, *Admiral of the Pacific* (London: Heinemann, 1965), p. 107.

CHAPTER 12. LORD MOUNTBATTEN'S NEPHEW AND CBS-TV'S FIRST BREAKING NEWS STORY

1. Noel Cunningham-Reid, author interview, March 13, 2015.
2. Michael Cunningham-Reid, unpublished memoir, collection of Fiona Cunningham-Reid.
3. Frank Tremaine and Kay Tremaine, *The Attack on Pearl Harbor* (Fredericksburg, Tex: Admiral Nimitz Foundation, 1997), p. 10.

4. Ibid., p. 11.
5. Thomas DeLong, *Madame Chiang Kai-shek and Miss Emma Mills* (London: McFarland, 2007), p. 146.
6. Michael Conway, "The Visualizers: A Reassessment of Television's News Pioneers," Ph.D. diss., University of Texas at Austin, 2004, p. 125.
7. Hull, *The Memoirs of Cordell Hull*, p. 1095.
8. Ibid., p. 1096.
9. Robert Sherwood, *Roosevelt and Hopkins* (New York: Grosset & Dunlap, 1950), p. 431.
10. Grew, *Turbulent Era*, p. 1253.
11. Joseph Grew, *Ten Years in Japan* (London: Hammond, 1944), p. 427.

CHAPTER 13. EDGAR RICE BURROUGHS WATCHES THE WAR GAMES

1. Mitsuo Fuchida, interview with Gordon Prange, December 10, 1963.
2. Joan Fawcett, letter, December 15, 1941, collection of Soozi Stokes.
3. Tremaine and Tremaine, *The Attack on Pearl Harbor*, p. 133.
4. Fawcett, letter, December 15, 1941.
5. Jim Campbell, "Who Could Forget?," *College Football Historical Society Newsletter* (November 1998), p. 7.
6. Tom Wilson, "When Willamette Went to War," http://www.d3football.com, December 7, 2003. Other accounts suggest that the rifles and bayonets were distributed the next day, December 8.
7. Edgar Rice Burroughs, letter, December 9, 1941, Danton Burroughs and ERB, Inc. Collection, Tarzana, Calif.
8. AraBelle Fuller, Diary, December 7, 1941, collection of Danielle Oser.
9. Ibid.
10. Elizabeth McIntosh, *Washington Post*, December 6, 2012.
11. John Finn, CNN interview, September 15, 2009, www.cnn.com/2009/US/09/15/finn.medal.of.honor/index.html.

CHAPTER 14. FUTURE U.S. PRESIDENTS REMEMBER THE MOMENT

1. Harry Truman, letter to Ethel Noland, December 14, 1941, quoted in David McCullough, *Truman* (New York: Simon & Schuster, 1993), p. 269.
2. Nigel Hamilton, *JFK* (London: Century, 1992), p. 424.
3. Robert Caro, *The Path to Power* (London: Collins, 1983), p. 757.
4. Gerald Ford, *A Time to Heal* (London: W. H. Allen, 1979), p. 57.
5. Richard Nixon, *The Memoirs of Richard Nixon* (London: Sidgwick & Jackson, 1978), p. 25.

6. Ronald Reagan, *An American Life* (London: Hutchinson, 1990), p. 96.
7. Edmund Morris, *Dutch* (London: HarperCollins, 1999), p. 188.
8. Lawrence Grobel, *The Hustons* (London: Bloomsbury, 1990), p. 227.
9. Mark Harris, *Five Came Back* (Edinburgh: Canongate, 2014), p. 1
10. Ibid.
11. Maria Riva, *Marlene Dietrich* (London: Bloomsbury, 1993), p. 517.
12. Jay Parini, *John Steinbeck* (London: Heinemann, 1994), p. 316.
13. Michael Lennon, *Norman Mailer* (New York: Simon & Schuster, 2014), p. 43.
14. Charles Shields, *And So It Goes* (New York: Henry Holt, 2011), p. 44.
15. Ibid., p. 45.
16. Charles Lindbergh, *The Wartime Journals of Charles A. Lindbergh* (New York: Harcourt Brace Jovanovich, 1971), p. 560.
17. A. M. Sperber, *Murrow* (London: Michael Joseph, 1987), p. 202.
18. Alexander Kendrick, *Prime Time* (Boston: Little Brown, 1969), p. 239.
19. William Bullitt, *For the President* (London: André Deutsch, 1973), p. 531.
20. Ibid., p. 532

CHAPTER 15. BRITAIN CHEERS THE NEWS

1. Averell Harriman, *Special Envoy* (London: Hutchinson, 1976), p. 111.
2. John Winant, *A Letter from Grosvenor Square* (London: Hodder & Stoughton, 1947), p. 199.
3. Winston Churchill, *The Second World War* (London: Cassell, 1981), p. 538.
4. Ibid., p. 539.
5. Earl of Longford, *Eamon de Valera* (London: Hutchinson, 1971), p. 392.
6. Ibid., p. 393.
7. Ivan Maisky, *Memoirs of a Soviet Ambassador* (London: Hutchinson, 1967), p. 221.
8. Anthony Eden, *The Eden Memoirs* (London: Cassell, 1965), p. 285.
9. Ibid.
10. Dirk Bogarde, *Snakes and Ladders* (London: Penguin, 1988), p. 35.
11. Malcom Muggeridge, *Chronicles of Wasted Time* (London: Collins, 1973), p. 114.
12. Philip Caine, *American Pilots in the RAF* (London: Brassey's, 1993), p. 167.
13. Ibid., p. 196.
14. Robert Rhodes James, *Chips* (London: Weidenfeld & Nicolson, 1967), p. 313.
15. Kathleen Riley, *The Astaires* (Oxford, England: Oxford University Press), 2014, p. 183.
16. Chaim Herzog, *Living History* (London: Weidenfeld & Nicolson, 1997), p. 42.
17. Princess Wilhelmina, *Lonely But Not Alone* (London: Hutchinson, 1960), p. 176.

18. James Leasor, *Rudolf Hess* (London: George Allen & Unwin, 1963), p. 187.

19. Peter Padfield, *Hess* (London: Weidenfeld & Nicolson, 1991), p. 285.

CHAPTER 16. OPINION DIVIDED IN EUROPE

1. Otto Dietrich, *The Hitler I Knew* (London: Methuen, 1957), p. 70.

2. Wilhelm Keitel, *The Memoirs of Field-Marshal Keitel* (London: William Kimber, 1965), p. 162.

3. David Irving, *Hitler's War* (London: Hodder & Stoughton, 1977), p. 352.

4. Galeazzo Ciano, *Diary* (London: Phoenix, 2002), p. 472.

5. Noel Stock, *The Life of Ezra Pound* (San Francisco: North Point Press, 1982), p. 391.

6. Richard Dimbleby, *The Frontiers Are Green*, (London: Hodder & Stoughton, 1944), p. 231.

7. Ibid., p. 233.

CHAPTER 17. THE RESPONSE IN THE FAR EAST

1. Courtney Browne, *Tojo* (London: Angus & Robertson, 1969), p. 121.

2. Ibid.

3. Douglas MacArthur, *Reminiscence* (London: Heinemann, 1966), p. 117.

4. Cooper, *Trumpets from the Steep*, p. 128.

5. Cecil Brown, *Suez to Singapore* (New York: Random House, 1942), p. 297.

6. Ibid.

7. Khac Huyen, *Vision Accomplished?* (New York: Macmillan, 1976), p. 54; Jean Lacouture, *Ho Chi Minh* (London: Penguin, 1968), p. 59.

8. Jawaharlal Nehru, *Mahatma Gandhi* (Bombay: Asia Publishing House, 1967), p. 125.

9. D. G. Tendulkar, *Mahatma* (New Delhi: Ministry of Information and Broadcasting, 1962), p. 15.

CHAPTER 18. THE BRITISH EMPIRE DECLARES WAR

1. Frances Perkins, *The Roosevelt I Knew* (London: Hammond, 1948), p. 303.

2. Thomas Connally, *My Name Is Tom Connally* (New York: Crowell, 1954), p. 249.

3. Ed Murrow, CBS radio talk, September 23, 1945.

4. J. W. Pickersgill, *The Mackenzie King Record* (Toronto: Toronto University Press, 1962), p. 298.

5. W. K. Hancock, *Smuts* (Cambridge, England: Cambridge University Press, 1968), p. 363.

6. John Curtin, Australian radio broadcast, December 7, 1941.

CHAPTER 19. AMERICANS GATHER AROUND THE RADIO

1. Eleanor Roosevelt, *The Autobiography of Eleanor Roosevelt* (London: Hutchinson, 1962), p. 175.
2. Franklin Roosevelt, *Nothing to Fear* (London: Hodder & Stoughton, 1947), p. 302.
3. Ibid., p. 303.
4. Lindbergh, *The Wartime Journals*, p. 561.
5. Audie Murphy, *To Hell and Back* (New York: Henry Holt, 1949), p. 7.
6. Kirk Douglas, *The Ragman's Son* (New York: Simon & Schuster, 1988), p. 99.
7. Ibid., p. 100.
8. Doug Warren, *Cagney* (London: Robson Books, 1983), p. 142.
9. Bob Dole, *One Soldier's Story* (New York: HarperCollins, 2006), p. 75.
10. Ibid., p. 76.
11. Terasaki, *Bridge to the Sun*, p. 83.
12. David Niven, *The Moon's a Balloon* (London: Hamish Hamilton, 1971), p. 222.
13. Brian Finney, *Christopher Isherwood* (London: Faber, 1979), p. 179.
14. Humphrey Carpenter, *W. H. Auden* (London: George Allen & Unwin, 1981), p. 292.
15. Richard Davenport-Hines, *Auden* (London: Heinemann, 1995), p. 216.

CHAPTER 20. HMS *REPULSE* AND *PRINCE OF WALES* BEGIN THE FIGHT BACK

1. Harold Nicolson, *Diaries and Letters 1930–1964* (London: Collins, 1980), p. 220.
2. Henry Channon, *Chips* (London: Weidenfeld & Nicolson, 1967), p. 313.
3. Ibid., p. 314.
4. Mollie Panter-Downes, *London War Notes* (London: Longman, 1973), p. 185.
5. Brown, *Suez to Singapore*, p. 299.
6. O. D. Gallagher, *Retreat in the East* (London: Harrap, 1942), p. 41.
7. Brown, *Suez to Singapore*, p. 309.

CHAPTER 21. FIRST MASS GASSING OF JEWS IN NAZI-OCCUPIED EUROPE

1. Adolf Hitler, *Directive No. 39*, December 8, 1941 (first paragraph).
2. Max Kaufmann, *Churbn Lettland* (Konstanz, Germany: Hartung-Gorre, 2011), p. 68.
3. Andrew Ezergailis, *The Holocaust in Latvia* (Riga: Historical Institute of Latvia), 1996, p. 257.
4. E. Klee, *The Good Old Days* (New York: Free Press, 1988), p. 219.
5. William Joyce, radio broadcast, December 8, 1941, quoted in Mary Kenny, *Germany Calling* (Dublin: New Island, 2003), p. 180.

CHAPTER 22. HMS *REPULSE* AND *PRINCE OF WALES* GO DOWN FIGHTING

1. Roosevelt, radio address, December 9, 1941, quoted in *Peace and War: United States Foreign Policy, 1931–1941* (Washington: U.S. Government Printing Office, 1943).
2. Ibid.
3. Ibid.
4. Willie Morris, *James Jones* (New York: Doubleday, 1978), p. 35.
5. McIntosh, *Washington Post*, December 6, 2012.
6. Noel Cunningham-Reid, author interview, March 13, 2015.
7. Brown, *Suez to Singapore*, p. 315.
8. Ibid., p. 316.
9. Gallagher, *Retreat in the East*, p. 50.
10. Ibid., p. 51.
11. Alan Matthews, *Sailors' Tales* (London: Books for Dillons Only, 1997), online version at http://www.forcez-survivors.org.uk.
12. Richard Pool, *Course for Disaster* (London: Leo Cooper, 1989), p. 67.
13. *Repulse* officer's letter (from Singapore, undated, illegible signature) to Lieutenant Dennis Aldridge, Royal Marines, collection of Daphne Hughes.
14. Brown, *Suez to Singapore*, p. 330.
15. Frank Owen, *The Fall of Singapore* (London: Michael Joseph, 1960), p. 62.

CHAPTER 23. HITLER AND MUSSOLINI DECLARE WAR ON THE UNITED STATES

1. *Singapore Free Press*, December 11, 1941, quoted in Martin Middlebrook, *Battleship* (London: Allen Lane, 1977), p. 269.
2. Churchill, *The Second World War*, vol. 3, p. 551.
3. Nicolson, *Diaries and Letters 1930–1964*, p. 221.
4. Ibid.
5. Churchill, *The Second World War*, vol. 3, p. 552.
6. Reynolds Packard, *Balcony Empire* (London: Chatto & Windus, 1943), p. 241.
7. http//www.ibiblio.org.
8. Ciano, *Diary*, p. 473.
9. Hitler's speech to the Reichstag, December 11, 1941, monitoring service, British Broadcasting Corporation.
10. German Declaration of War with the United States: December 11, 1941, Avalon Project, Lillian Goldman Law Library, Yale University.
11. George F. Kennan, *Memoirs, 1926–1950* (London: Hutchinson, 1968), p. 135.

BIBLIOGRAPHY

Adams, Henry H. *Witness to Power*. Annapolis: Naval Institute Press, 1985.

Alexander, Paul. *Salinger*. London: Picador, 2013.

Ambrose, Stephen. *Eisenhower*. New York: Simon & Schuster, 1991.

———. *Nixon*. New York: Simon & Schuster, 1987.

Anderegg, Michael. *William Wyler*. Boston: Twayne, 1979.

Archer, Jules. *Ho Chi Minh*. Folkestone, England: Bailey Brothers & Swinfen, 1973.

Astley, Joan Bright. *The Inner Circle*. London: Hutchinson, 1971.

Avon, Earl of. *The Eden Memoirs*. London: Cassell, 1965.

Bach, Steven. *Marlene Dietrich*. London: HarperCollins, 1992.

Baker, Carlos. *Ernest Hemingway*. London: Collins, 1969.

Beasley, Maurine. *Eleanor Roosevelt*. Kansas: University Press, 2010.

Bedford, Sybille. *Aldous Huxley*. London: Chatto & Windus, 1974.

Begin, Menachem. *White Nights*. London: Futura, 1978.

Behr, Edward. *Hirohito*. London: Hamish Hamilton, 1989.

Benson, Jackson. *The True Adventures of John Steinbeck*. London: Heinemann, 1984.

Berg, Scott. *Lindbergh*. London: Macmillan, 1998.

Birdnow, Brian. *Gerald Ford*. New York: Nova Science, 2012.

Bix, Herbert. *Hirohito and the Making of Modern Japan*. London: HarperCollins, 2001.

Birkenhead, Earl of. *Halifax*. London: Hamish Hamilton, 1965.

Bourne, Peter. *Jimmy Carter*. New York: Scribner, 1997.

Boyd, Carl. *Hitler's Japanese Confidant*. Kansas City, Kans.: University Press, 1995.

Brendon, Piers. *Ike*. London: Secker & Warburg, 1987.

Brian, Denis. *Einstein*. New York: Wiley, 1996.

Brinkley, Douglas. *Gerald R. Ford*. New York: Henry Holt, 2007.

Brown, Cecil. *Suez to Singapore*. New York: Random House, 1942.

Browne, Courtney. *Tojo: The Last Banzai*. London: Angus & Robertson, 1969.

Bullitt, Orville. *For the President*. London: André Deutsch, 1973.

Bullock, Alan. *Hitler*. London: Odhams Press, 1964.

Bush, George. *All the Best*. New York: Scribner, 1999.

Butow, Robert. *Tojo and the Coming of the War*. Princeton: Princeton University Press, 1961.

Cagney, James, and Doug Warren. *Cagney*. London: Robson, 1983.

Caine, Philip. *American Pilots in the RAF*. London: Brassey's, 1993.

Calic, Edouard. *Reinhard Heydrich*. New York: William Morrow, 1986.

Callahan, Raymond. *The Worst Disaster*. Newark: University of Delaware Press, 1979.

Carey, Gary. *All the Stars in Heaven*. London: Robson Books, 1982.

Caro, Robert. *The Years of Lyndon Johnson*. London: Collins, 1983.

Carpenter, Humphrey. *W. H. Auden*. London: George Allen, 1981.

Carter, Jimmy. *An Hour Before Daylight*. New York: Simon & Schuster, 2002.

Cave Brown, Anthony. *The Last Hero*. London: Michael Joseph, 1982.

Channon, Sir Henry. *Chips*. London: Weidenfeld & Nicolson, 1967.

Chernin, Ted. "My Experiences in the Honolulu Chinatown Red-Light District." *Hawaiian Journal of History* 34, pp. 203–17 (2000).

Churchill, Winston. *The Second World War*, vol. III, pp. 537–40. London: Cassell, 1981.

Ciano, Galeazzo. *Diary 1937–1943*. London: Phoenix Press, 2002.

Clark, Alan. *Barbarossa*. London: Weidenfeld & Nicolson, 1995.

Clark, Ronald. *Einstein*. London: Hodder & Stoughton, 1979.

Collier, Richard. *The Road to Pearl Harbor*. New York: Atheneum, 1983.

Coogan, Tim Pat. *De Valera*. London: Arrow, 1995.

Cooper, Artemis. *Cairo in the War*. London: Hamish Hamilton, 1989.

Cooper, Diana. *Trumpets from the Steep*. London: Hart-Davis, 1960.

Cooper, Duff. *Old Men Forget*. London: Hart-Davis, 1953.

Crafford, F. S. *Jan Smuts*. London: George Allen, 1948.

Crowdy, Terry. *The Enemy Within*. Oxford, England: Osprey, 2006.

Crozier, Brian. *The Man Who Lost China*. London: Angus & Robertson, 1977.

Dallek, Robert. *John F. Kennedy*. London: Allen Lane, 2003.

Davenport-Hines, Richard. *Auden*. London: Heinemann, 1995.

Dederichs, Mario. *Heydrich*. London: Greenhill Books, 2006.

DeLong, Thomas. *Madame Chiang Kai-shek and Miss Emma Mills*. London: McFarland & Co., 2007.

Dietrich, Otto. *The Hitler I Knew*. London: Methuen, 1957.

Dimbleby, Jonathan. *Richard Dimbleby*. London: Hodder & Stoughton, 1975.

Dimbleby, Richard. *The Frontiers Are Green*. London: Hodder & Stoughton, 1943.

Domarus, Max. *Hitler: Reden und Proklamationen*. Munich: Süddeutscher Verlag, 1965.

Douglas, Kirk. *The Ragman's Son*. London: Simon & Schuster, 1988.

Duke, Pony. *Too Rich*. New York: HarperCollins, 1996.

Eyman, Scott. *Lion of Hollywood*. London: Robson Books, 2005.

Ezergailis, Andrew. *The Holocaust in Latvia*. Riga: Historical Institute of Latvia, 1996.

Farndale, Nigel. *Haw-Haw*. London: Macmillan, 2005.

Ferrell, Robert. *Dear Bess*. New York: W. W. Norton, 1985.

Fest, Joachim. *Hitler*. London: Weidenfeld & Nicolson, 1974.

Finney, Brian. *Christopher Isherwood*. London: Faber, 1979.

Fishgall, Gary. *Pieces of Time: The Life of James Stewart*. New York: Scribner, 1997.

Ford, Gerald. *A Time to Heal*. London: W. H. Allen, 1979.

Freedland, Michael. *The Warner Brothers*. London: Harrap, 1983.

Furuya, Keiji. *Chiang Kai-shek*. New York: St. John's University, 1981.

Gallagher, O. D. *Retreat in the East*. London: Harrap, 1942.

Gerwath, Robert. *Hitler's Hangman*. New Haven: Yale University Press, 2011.

Gilbert, Martin. *Winston S. Churchill*. London: Heinemann, 1985.

Giles, James. *The James Jones Reader*. Secaucus, N.J.: Carol Publishing, 1991.

Glad, Betty. *Jimmy Carter*. New York: W. W. Norton, 1981.

Glancy, Mark. *When Hollywood Loved Britain*. Manchester: University Press, 1999.

Goldstein, Donald. *The Pearl Harbor Papers*. Washington: Brassey's, 1993.

Gopal, Sarvepalli. *Jawaharlal Nehru*. Oxford, England: Oxford University Press, 1989.

Graber, G. S. *The Life and Times of Reinhard Heydrich*. London: Robert Hale, 1981.

Greer, Richard. "Dousing Honolulu's Red Lights." *Hawaiian Journal of History* 34, pp. 185–91 (2000).

Grew, Joseph. *Report from Tokyo*. London: Hammond, 1943.

———. *Ten Years in Japan*. London: Hammond, 1944.

———. *Turbulent Era*. London: Hammond, 1953.

Griffiths, Richard. *Marshal Pétain*. London: Constable, 1970.

Guderian, Heinz. *Panzer Leader*. London: Arrow, 1990.

Haape, Heinrich. *Moscow Tram Stop*. London: Collins, 1957.

Halifax, Earl of. *Fullness of Days*. London: Collins, 1957.

Hamilton, Ian. *In Search of J. D. Salinger*. London: Heinemann, 1988.

Hamilton, Nigel. *J.F.K.* London: Century, 1992.

Harriman, Averell. *Special Envoy*. London: Hutchinson, 1976.

Harris, Mark. *Five Came Back*. Edinburgh: Canongate, 2014.

Harris, Warren. *Clark Gable*. London: Aurum, 2003.

Haugland, Vern. *The Eagle Squadrons*. Newton Abbot, England: David & Charles, 1979.

Hauner, Milan. *Hitler*. Basingstoke: Palgrave, 2008.

Hendrick, George. *James Jones and the Handy Writers' Colony*. Carbondale: Southern Illinois University Press, 2001.

Herzog, Chaim. *Living History*. London: Weidenfeld & Nicolson, 1997.

Heston, Charlton. *In the Arena*. London: HarperCollins, 1995.

Higham, Charles. *Merchant of Dreams*. London: Sidgwick & Jackson, 1993.

Hills, George. *Franco*. London: Robert Hale, 1967.

Holmes, Richard. *Churchill's Bunker*. London: Profile Books, 2009.

Hough, Richard. *Mountbatten*. London: Weidenfeld & Nicolson, 1980.

———. *The Hunting of Force Z*. London: Collins, 1963.

Howard, Roger. *Mao Tse-tung and the Chinese People*. London: George Allen, 1978.

Hoyt, Edwin. *Hirohito*. New York: Praeger, 1992.

Hull, Cordell. *The Memoirs of Cordell Hull*. London: Hodder & Stoughton, 1948.

Hunt, Frazier. *The Untold Story of Douglas MacArthur*. London: Robert Hale, 1954.

Huston, John. *An Open Book*. London: Macmillan, 1980.

Huyen, Khac. *Vision Accomplished?* New York: Macmillan, 1976.

Irving, David. *Hess*. London: Macmillan, 1987.

———. *Hitler's War*. London: Hodder & Stoughton, 1977.

Jeffers, Paul. *The Napoleon of New York*. New York: John Wiley, 2002.

Jones, James. *From Here to Eternity*. Bath: Chivers Press, 1980.

———. *To Reach Eternity*. New York: Random House, 1998.

Kaminsky, Stuart. *John Huston*. London: Angus & Robertson, 1978.

Kanfer, Stefan. *Tough without a Gun*. London: Faber, 2011.

Kanroji, Osanaga. *Hirohito*. Los Angeles: Gateway, 1975.

Kaufmann, Max. *Churbn Lettland*. Konstanz, Germany: Hartung-Gorre, 2011.

Keitel, Wilhelm. *The Memoirs of Field-Marshal Keitel*. London: William Kimber, 1965.

Kendrick, Alexander. *Prime Time*. Boston: Little, Brown, 1969.

Kennan, George F. *Memoirs, 1926–1950*. London: Hutchinson, 1968.

Kenny, Mary. *Germany Calling*. Dublin: New Island, 2003.

Kido, Marquis. *The Diary of Marquis Kido*. Frederick, Md.: University Publications of America, 1984.

Kirkpatrick, Sir Ivone. *Mussolini*. London: Odhams, 1964.

Klemperer, Victor. *I Shall Bear Witness*. London: Weidenfeld & Nicolson, 1998.

Knappe, Siegfried. *Soldat*. Shrewsbury, England: Airlife, 1993.

Kraus, René. *Old Master*. New York: E. P. Dutton, 1944.

Lacouture, Jean. *Ho Chi Minh*. London: Allen Lane, 1968.

Lasky, Victor. *Jimmy Carter*. New York: Richard Marek, 2008.

Layton, Edwin. *And I Was There*. New York: William Morrow, 1986.

Leasor, James. *Rudolf Hess*. London: George Allen, 1963.

———. *Singapore*. London: Hodder & Stoughton, 1968.

Lee, Carol Ann. *The Hidden Life of Otto Frank*. London: Penguin, 2003.

Lennon, Michael. *Norman Mailer*. New York: Simon & Schuster, 2014.

Lindbergh, Charles. *Autobiography of Values*. New York: Harcourt Brace Jovanovich, 1978.

———. *The Wartime Journals of Charles A. Lindbergh*. New York: Harcourt Brace Jovanovich, 1970.

Lindsay, Hsiao Li. *Bold Plum*. Morrisville N.C.: Lulu Press. 2007.

Longford, Earl of. *Eamon de Valera*. London: Hutchinson, 1971.

Lord, Walter. *Day of Infamy*. New York: Henry Holt, 1957.

Luck, Hans von. *Panzer Commander*. New York: Praeger, 1989.

Lynn, Kenneth. *Hemingway*. London: Simon & Schuster, 1987.

MacArthur, Douglas. *Reminiscences*. London: Heinemann, 1966.

Madsen, Axel. *John Huston*. London: Robson Books, 1979.

———. *William Wyler*. London: W. H. Allen, 1974.

Maisky, Ivan. *Memoirs of a Soviet Ambassador*. London: Hutchinson, 1967.

Marder, Arthur. *Old Friends, New Enemies*. Oxford, England: Clarendon Press, 1981.

Martin, Sir John. *Downing Street*. London: Bloomsbury, 1991.

McCullough, David. *Truman*. New York: Simon & Schuster, 1993.

Middlebrook, Martin. *Battleship*. London: Allen Lane, 1977.

Montague, Patrick. *Chelmno and the Holocaust*. London: I. B. Taurus, 2011.

Moody, Joanna. *From Churchill's War Rooms*. Stroud, England: Tempus, 2007.

Morris, Edmund. *Dutch*. London: HarperCollins, 1999.

Morris, Willie. *James Jones*. New York: Doubleday, 1978.

Moseley, Ray. *Mussolini's Shadow*. New Haven: Yale University Press, 1999.

Mosley, Leonard. *Hirohito*. London: Weidenfeld & Nicolson, 1966.

———. *Lindbergh*. London: Hodder & Stoughton, 1976.

Muggeridge, Malcolm. *Chronicles of Wasted Time*. London: Collins, 1973.

Munn, Michael. *Charlton Heston*. London: Robson, 1986.

———. *Kirk Douglas*. New York: St. Martin's Press, 1985.

Murphy, Audie. *To Hell and Back.* New York: Henry Holt, 1949.

Murray, Nicholas. *Aldous Huxley.* London: Little, Brown, 2002.

Nanda, B. R. *Mahatma Gandhi.* London: Allen & Unwin, 1959.

Neffe, Jürgen. *Einstein.* Cambridge, England: Polity, 2008.

Nehru, Jawaharlal. *A Bunch of Old Letters.* London: Asia Publishing, 1960.

Nicolson, Harold. *Diaries and Letters, 1930–1964.* London: Collins, 1980.

Niven, David. *The Moon's a Balloon.* London: Hamish Hamilton, 1971.

Nixon, Richard. *The Memoirs of Richard Nixon.* London: Sidgwick & Jackson, 1978.

Norman, Charles. *Ezra Pound.* London: Macdonald, 1970.

Odo, Franklin. *No Sword to Bury.* Philadelphia: Temple University Press, 2004.

Owen, Frank. *The Fall of Singapore.* London: Michael Joseph, 1960.

Packard, Reynolds. *Balcony Empire.* London: Chatto & Windus, 1943.

Padfield, Peter. *Hess.* London: Weidenfeld & Nicolson, 1991.

Paloczi-Horvath, George. *Mao Tse-tung.* London: Secker & Warburg, 1962.

Panter-Downes, Mollie. *London War Notes.* London: Longman, 1973.

Parini, Jay. *John Steinbeck.* London: Heinemann, 1994.

Pemberton, William. *The Life and Presidency of Ronald Reagan.* New York: M. E. Sharpe, 1999.

Perkins, Frances. *The Roosevelt I Knew.* London: Hammond, 1948.

Pickersgill, J. W. *The Mackenzie King Record.* Toronto: University of Toronto Press, 1962.

Pool, Richard. *Course for Disaster.* London: Leo Cooper, 1989.

Potter, John Deane. *Admiral of the Pacific.* London: Heinemann, 1965.

Prange, Gordon. *At Dawn We Slept.* London: Michael Joseph, 1982.

———. *December 7, 1941.* London: Harrap, 1989.

———. *God's Samurai.* London: Brassey's, 1990.

Preston, Paul. *Franco.* London: HarperCollins, 1993.

Prüller, Wilhelm. *Diary of a German Soldier.* London: Faber, 1963.

Reagan, Ronald. *An American Life.* London: Hutchinson, 1990.

Rhodes James, Robert. *Anthony Eden.* London: Weidenfeld & Nicolson, 1986.

Ribbentrop, Joachim von. *The Ribbentrop Memoirs.* London: Weidenfeld & Nicolson, 1954.

Riley, Kathleen. *The Astaires.* Oxford, England: Oxford University Press, 2014.

Riva, Maria. *Marlene Dietrich.* London: Bloomsbury, 1993.

Roberts, Andrew. *The Holy Fox.* London: Weidenfeld & Nicolson, 1991.

Rollyson, Carl. *The Lives of Norman Mailer.* New York: Paragon House, 1991.

Roosevelt, Eleanor. *The Autobiography of Eleanor Roosevelt.* London: Hutchinson, 1962.

Roosevelt, Franklin. *Nothing to Fear.* London: Hodder & Stoughton, 1947.

———. *The Roosevelt Letters*. London: Harrap, 1952.

Roosevelt, James. *Affectionately, F.D.R.* London: Harrap, 1960.

Roseman, Mark. *The Villa, the Lake, the Meeting*. London: Allen Lane, 2002.

Russell, William. *Berlin Embassy*. London: Michael Joseph, 1942.

Sawyer, Dana. *Aldous Huxley*. New York: Crossroad, 2004.

Schloss, Eva. *After Auschwitz*. London: Hodder & Stoughton, 2013.

Schmidt, Paul. *Hitler's Interpreter*. London: William Heinemann, 1951.

Sherwood, Robert. *Roosevelt and Hopkins*. New York: Harper, 1950.

Shields, Charles. *And So It Goes*. New York: Henry Holt, 2011.

Shilon, Avi. *Menachem Begin*. New Haven: Yale University Press, 2012.

Silver, Eric. *Begin*. London: Weidenfeld & Nicolson, 1984.

Simmonds, Roy. *John Steinbeck: The War Years*. Lewisburg, Pa.: Bucknell University Press, 1998.

Smith, Howard K. *Last Train from Berlin*. London: Cresset, 1942.

Sperber, A. M. *Bogart*. London: Weidenfeld & Nicolson, 1997.

———. *Murrow*. London: Michael Joseph, 1987.

St. Pierre, Brian. *John Steinbeck*. San Francisco: Chronicle Books, 1983.

Stahlberg, Alexander. *Bounden Duty*. London: Brassey's, 1990.

Steely, Skipper. *Pearl Harbor Countdown*. London: Pelican, 2008.

Stinnet, Robert. *Day of Deceit*. London: Constable, 2000.

Stock, Noel. *The Life of Ezra Pound*. San Francisco: North Point Press, 1982.

Taliaferro, John. *Tarzan Forever*. New York: Scribner, 2001.

Tansill, Charles. *Back Door to War*. Chicago: Henry Regnery, 1952.

Tarpley, Webster. *George Bush*. Washington, DC: Executive Intelligence Review, 1992.

Terasaki, Gwen. *Bridge to the Sun*. London: Michael Joseph, 1958.

Thorn, James. *Peter Fraser*. London: Odhams, 1952.

Toland, John. *Infamy*. London: Methuen, 1982.

Tremaine, Frank, and Kay Tremaine. *The Attack on Pearl Harbor*. Fredericksburg, Tex.: Admiral Nimitz Foundation, 1997.

Tsuji, Masanobu. *Singapore: The Japanese Version*. London: Constable, 1960.

Ugaki, Matome. *Fading Victory*. Pittsburgh: University of Pennsylvania Press, 1991.

Weitz, John. *Hitler's Diplomat*. London: Weidenfeld & Nicolson, 1992.

Whalen, Richard. *The Founding Father*. London: Hutchinson, 1965.

Whiting, Charles. *American Hero*. York, England: Eskdale, 2000.

Wighton, Charles. *Heydrich*. London: Odhams Press, 1962.

Wilhelmina, Princess. *Lonely But Not Alone*. London: Hutchinson, 1960.

Winant, John. *A Letter from Grosvenor Square*. London: Hodder & Stoughton, 1947.

INDEX